7/26

ESSAYS IN CHRISTOLOGY FOR KARL BARTH

Photo Maria Netter, Basel

KARL BARTH

ESSAYS IN CHRISTOLOGY

For

KARL BARTH

Edited

by

T. H. L. PARKER

LUTTERWORTH PRESS

LONDON

232.04
P228

130384

ALL RIGHTS RESERVED

First published 1956

PRINTED IN GREAT BRITAIN BY
LATIMER, TREND AND CO. LTD., PLYMOUTH

Jesus Christ, as witnessed by the Scripture, is the one Word of God which we hear and obey and in which we trust in life and death. We condemn the false doctrine that the Church should recognize as God's revelation, beside this one Word, as source of its message, yet other facts or powers, forms or truths.

Declaration of the Synod of Barmen, May 29–31, 1934

CONTENTS

A LETTER TO KARL BARTH

Dear Dr. Barth,

We should like, in our own name and on behalf of many other British theologians, to send you our greetings on your seventieth birthday, on May 10, 1956, to wish you happiness and prosperity and to pray for God's blessing on you and your work.

Our greetings take the form of this collection of Christological essays. We did not think it proper to write, and I am sure you would not want to receive, a volume in praise of Karl Barth (though I assure you such a book would not have been difficult to write!). But we decided the best way we could record our appreciation for your work was by showing that we have grasped and approved its main and basic purpose. We are conscious that you have placed many questions before the Church since 1918; but what you have forced theologians to do above all else is to take more and more seriously the Biblical witness to Christ and to view Him consistently in His office as Mediator. It is this that we have tried to do in these essays. We have not set out to give a complete Christology, but have selected what seem to us the most important subjects. Our aim has been to consider them in the light of the revelation of God in Jesus Christ and to work them out under the guidance of the witness of the Bible. Apart from this, we have worked quite independently—no doubt an acute critic could discern not inconsiderable differences between us, even in our Christology. Yet I believe that our agreements will be found to be even more considerable.

And who is this "we"? That question is not very easy to answer. We began, three or four years ago, by being a group of "younger theologians". Whether we are still "younger" I should not like to decide. And, indeed, it would be hard to say just what "younger" means in this context, and when one ceases to be "younger"; whether it depends on the number of books one writes or the number of one's grey hairs remains, as Sir Thomas Browne would say, yet undiscovered. We are on safer ground, however, when we say that the contributors represent a good many shades of opinion in the British Churches, and that some of us are professional theologians and philosophers and some have charge of parishes big or little. And this last is as it ought to be, for it would be a sorry state of affairs if what you have to say to us had penetrated to the universities but not the parishes. I recall with pleasure the remark of an old clergyman from a remote country parish, a man who devoted his summers to the King of games—cricket—and served the Queen of the sciences in the winter. During a cricket match he said to me: "Do you ever read any Karl Barth, Parker? I like to read Karl Barth—him and the Fathers."

We constitute a group for the purposes of this book because we respect and admire your work as a theologian and churchman. This, I am sure, is the reason why all those who were approached gladly consented to contribute. It is not necessary to say to you that we would not wish to be called Barthians. But there may be some reading this letter who will jump to the conclusion that contributors to a "Barth Festschrift" are, in fact, *ex officio* Barthians—that is, rather queer fish who take every fly you cast, or should we rather put it, plankton who gamely try to swallow and digest the great white whale? Without being Barthians, we recognize the importance of your work for our own Churches, and are happy to take this opportunity of thanking you publicly.

H. R. Mackintosh concluded his study of you with these noble words: "At the moment he stands in the midst of his theological work, which cannot but take years to complete. Nothing more enriching for the whole Church could be thought of than that the time for completion should be given him, if God will, and that more and more his living influence should pass from land to land." This is how we feel, too.

Yours very sincerely,

T. H. L. PARKER

Little Ponton,
Lincolnshire.

Introduction

THE PLACE OF CHRISTOLOGY IN BIBLICAL AND DOGMATIC THEOLOGY

by T. F. TORRANCE

Professor of Dogmatics, University of Edinburgh

Introduction

THE PLACE OF CHRISTOLOGY IN BIBLICAL AND DOGMATIC THEOLOGY[1]

by

T. F. TORRANCE

CHRISTIAN knowledge of God arises out of the self-revelation of God in and through Jesus Christ, for in Him the Word of God has become man in the midst of man's estrangement from God, committing Himself to human understanding and creating communion between man and God. Biblical and dogmatic theology is the careful unfolding and orderly articulation of this knowledge within the sphere of communion with God, i.e. the sphere of reconciliation into which we are drawn by the activity of His Word, and of the obedience of faith in which all our thinking and speaking is brought into conformity to the self-communication of His Word. The way which God has taken in Jesus Christ to reveal Himself and to reconcile us to Himself is the way which we have to make our own in all true understanding and thinking and speaking of Him. Theology, therefore, involves a knowledge which is determined and controlled in its content by what is given in Jesus Christ, and operates with a mode of rational activity which corresponds to the nature of the object of this knowledge in Jesus Christ. It is the incarnation of the Word which prescribes to dogmatic theology both its matter and its method, so that whether in its activity as a whole or in the formulation of a doctrine in any part, it is the Christological pattern that will be made to appear. That does not mean that all theology can be reduced to Christology, but because there is only one Mediator between God and man, the Man Christ Jesus, in the orderly presentation of the doctrines of the Chris-

[1] In writing this article in honour of Karl Barth I wish to acknowledge my indebtedness throughout it to the second half-volume of his prolegomena to the *Kirchliche Dogmatik*, which I have been helping to see through the press in an English edition at the time of writing.

tian faith, every doctrine will be expressed in its inner coherence with Christology at the centre, and in its correspondence to the objective reality of God's revelation in Jesus Christ who is true God and true Man.

In the nature of the case, we are not concerned in dogmatic theology with working out into a logical system our understanding of God and creation, grace and human nature, in terms of the divine Being and creaturely effect after the fashion of scholastic theology in philosophical *Summae*. Nor are we concerned with the religious consciousness and with working it out into a systematic form according to its own immanent laws and the knowledge obtainable from our understanding of these laws, after the fashion of Schleiermacher, even if that is conditioned and determined by the historical consciousness of the Church as in so much post-Tridentine Roman theology. In contrast, dogmatic theology is concerned above all with the Word of God made flesh in Jesus Christ, with the revelation of the Word fulfilled in the apostolic testimony and tradition, and with the obedient conformity to the Word on the part of the Church in its listening to it and its teaching about it. The task of dogmatics is therefore to unfold and present in an integrated and ordered form the content of the Word of God in the sphere of its effective operation in the Church; not only to give consistent expression to the response of the Church in faith and understanding to the Word, but to bring the mind of the Church to ever renewed conformity to the work and activity of God in His Word, and so to serve the Church in its attainment unto the unity of the faith and of the knowledge of the Son of God, and in its growing up in all things into Christ who is the Head of the Church.

The significance of this should become clearer if it is presented in the three stages that correspond to the activity of the Word: in the incarnation of the Word, in the apostolic foundation of the Church, in the disciplined articulation of the Church's understanding of the Word.

1. *The Incarnation of the Word of God*

We begin with faith in Jesus Christ as truly God and truly Man and seek to unfold our understanding of the double fact

that in Jesus Christ the Word of God has become man, has
assumed a human form, in order as such to be God's language
to man, and that in Jesus Christ there is gathered up and embodied, in obedient response to God, man's true word to God
and his true speech about God. Jesus Christ is at once the complete revelation of God to man and the correspondence on
man's part to that revelation required by it for the fulfilment of
its own revealing movement. As the obedient answer to God's
revelation Jesus yields from the side of man the fulfilled reception and faithful embodiment which belong to the content of
God's complete revelation of Himself to man. In the Hebrew
idiom, revelation is not only the uncovering of God but the uncovering of the ear and eye of man for God. It is revelation
which achieves its end in man and does not return void to God.

Several facts require emphasis here.

(a) The incarnation shows us quite unmistakably that there
is an essential bi-polarity in God's revelation of Himself to man.
God is God and not man, and yet in the incarnation God has
become man, this particular Man, Jesus Christ, without ceasing
to be God. In Him divine nature and human nature are united,
really and eternally united, in one Person. In Him the eternal
Word of God has assumed human nature and existence into
oneness with Himself in order thus, as truly divine and truly
human, to become the final Word of God to man and the one
Mediator between God and man. In other words, the incarnation shows us that God reveals Himself (God) in terms of what
is not-God (man), that revelation is given to us only in terms
of what it is not, in the humanity of those to whom it is given,
so that from first to last we have to reckon with an essential bi-
polarity. In the nature of the case we cannot get behind the
"what He is not" to the "what He is in Himself", any more
than we can get behind the back of Jesus to the eternal Son of
God. We cannot divide between the so-called form and content, between the human word of revelation and revelation itself, any more than we can divide asunder the human and the
divine natures which are united in the one Person of Jesus
Christ. The *inconfuse, immutabiliter, indivise, inseparabiliter* of
Chalcedonian Christology apply equally to our understanding
of revelation. Revelation is not only act from the side of God

but also from the side of man, in the form of the humanity of Christ which is of the very substance of revelation. The divine form and the human form of revelation must neither be confounded nor be separated. The incarnation means that now revelation is determined and shaped by the Humanity of Christ, that we know of no revelation of the Word of God except that which is given through Christ and in the form of Christ. Jesus Christ is the Truth, Truth as God is Truth, and that same Truth in the form of Man, Truth answering itself, Truth assuming its own true form from the side of man and from within man. As such He is not only the Truth of God in man, but the Truth for man and in man, and therefore the Truth of man.

(b) The Incarnation shows us that revelation is not only act of God in man and from the side of man, but real act of man achieved through human obedience to the Word of God. The Incarnation was wholly act of God but it was no less true human life truly lived in our actual humanity. Jesus Christ is not only Word of God to man, but Believer. In His obedient life He yielded the perfect response of man to the divine revelation which is that revelation in human form. Here the doctrine of *anhypostasia* and *enhypostasia* applied to the incarnation applies equally to our understanding of revelation.[1] Revelation is entirely God's action but within it, it is the concrete action of Jesus Christ that mediates revelation and is revelation. Revelation is supremely God's act but that act is incarnated in our humanity, giving the human full place within the divine action issuing forth out of man's life. The human obedience of Jesus does not only play an instrumental but an integral and essential part in the divine revelation.

Revelation involves, then, the freedom of God to be present to man and to open up man for God and to realize from the

---

[1] "By *anhypostasia* classical Christology asserted that in the *assumptio carnis* the human nature of Christ had no independent *per se* subsistence apart from the event of the incarnation, apart from the hypostatic union. By *enhypostasia*, however, it asserted that in the *assumptio carnis* the human nature of Christ was given a real and concrete subsistence within the hypostatic union—it was *enhypostatic* in the Word. *Anhypostasia* and *enhypostasia* are inseparable. In the incarnation the eternal Son assumed human nature into oneness with Himself, but in that assumption Jesus Christ is not only real man but a man." *Scottish Journal of Theology*, 7/3, pp. 249 f.

side of man his understanding of revelation and his obedient response to it, to effect in man real meeting with God in revelation and to give him capacity for revelation. This capacity for revelation is not to be judged in terms of the receiver, as if he could achieve it on his own, but in terms of the Giver, the Father in Heaven, who acts by His Spirit upon man, from beneath and from within man, but who effects from the side of man and issuing out of man's life a really human understanding of revelation and a really human obedience to it. In other words, in revelation we have the divine assumption of our human word into union with God's own Word, effecting it as the human expression of the divine Word, and giving it, as such, real and full place as human word in obedience to the divine.

In revelation, therefore, we are not concerned simply with *anhypostatic* revelation and with human response, but with *anhypostatic* revelation and true human response *enhypostatic* in the Word of revelation. We are not concerned simply with a divine revelation which demands from us all a human response, but with a divine revelation which already includes a true and appropriate and fully human response as part of its achievement for us and to us and in us. Thus the incarnation shows us that the revelation of God fulfilled in Jesus Christ provides us with a truly human but divinely prepared response: and that is at once the divinely given objective reality of our knowledge and response, and the divinely appointed norm and pattern of our knowledge and response.

In the Humanity of Jesus Christ, in His mind and in His life, in the whole obedience of His incarnate being and knowing, we are given not only the revealed knowledge of God but the embodiment of that knowledge in our humanity. Jesus Christ the Word made flesh is not only the object of our theological knowledge but He is the Lord of it: as the Word become man, He is the criterion of our knowing and as the man assumed into oneness with the Word He is the pattern of our knowing. He is not only the content of our theological knowledge but He provides for us in Himself the way which our theological knowledge must take. "I am the Way, the Truth, and the Life. No man cometh unto the Father but by Me."

(c) The incarnation shows us that revelation and reconcili-

B

ation are inseparable, for revelation does not achieve its end in humanity apart from reconciliation. Obedient as He was throughout the whole course of His life, Jesus had yet to *learn* obedience. Though conceived by the Holy Spirit and born of the Virgin Mary, Jesus was yet born in the womb of a sinner, within the compass of our sinful flesh. As the Son of Adam He was born into our alienation, our God-forsakenness and darkness, and grew up within our bondage and ignorance, so that He had to beat His way forward by blows, as St. Luke puts it, growing in wisdom and growing in grace, before God as well as before man. He learned obedience by the things which He suffered, for that obedience from within our alienated humanity was a struggle with our sin and temptation; it had to be fought out with strong crying and tears and achieved in desperate anguish and weakness under the crushing load of the world's sin and the divine judgment. Throughout the whole course of His life He bent the will of man in perfect submission to the Will of God, bowing under the divine judgment against our unrighteousness, and offered a perfect obedience to the Father, that we might be redeemed and reconciled to Him.

That is the way which the Word of God made flesh takes in the midst of our sinful humanity, the way of vicarious suffering and judgment and atonement. Revelation does not achieve its end as revelation apart from reconciliation, for only through reconciliation can revelation complete its own movement within man, bringing out of our humanity the obedient reception of revelation which is an essential part of its very substance. Revelation involves a communion through the reconciliation of the estranged parties, a reconciliation of the will and mind of man with the Will and Mind of God. Revelation entails the entry of the Mind of God into our darkness and estrangement in order to redeem our understanding and to achieve its reconciliation to the Mind of God. Revelation is unthinkable, therefore, apart from the whole movement of divine humiliation from the cradle to the Cross, apart from the grace of the Lord Jesus Christ which means that the Word which was rich with the Wisdom of God for our sakes became poor, making our poverty His own, that we through His poverty might be made rich with the wisdom of God. It is only through that atoning exchange that God's revelation achieves its end as revelation to and within a sinful world.

Once again, the way which God has taken in His revelation and reconciliation, the way of the Son of Man, the way of humiliation, is the way which we must make our own, adopting it as the way of our thinking and speaking and of all our theological discipline. As God and yet as Man, Jesus Christ penetrated into the midst of our humanity in order to overcome our estrangement and to reconcile us to the Father. He who is God and Man in one Person acts from the side of God in the faithfulness of divine Truth and Love, and acts from the side of man in the faithfulness of a life wholly obedient to the Father. In that unity of the divine-human faithfulness the Word of God is spoken and the Truth of God is actualized in our humanity, in and through the whole assent of Jesus to the Will of God as it confronts the will of man: "Not my will but thine be done." That is the way in which revelation comes to us, in which the Word of God confronts us, so that we have no option but to follow it. Therefore to all discipleship, including all theological *disciplina*, Jesus Christ says: "If any man will come after me, let him deny himself and take up the cross and follow me."

The significance of the incarnation for dogmatic theology lies here: not only, though supremely, in providing our theological knowledge with its unique content, but in providing it with its normative pattern in the obedient humanity of Jesus Christ. In the incarnation we have a divine-human Word in the unity of the divine and the human natures in Christ, so that we are unable to separate out the human word from the divine, for the Word of God to us is precisely this one divine-human Word in the mutual involution of revelation and reconciliation. It is for that reason that the Humanity of Jesus Christ is of inescapable and essential importance for dogmatic procedure and method; for it sets before us the actual Way which the divine Word has taken and takes in our human communion with it and our human knowing of it. The Humanity of Christ provides us not simply with an externally imposed norm for theological understanding and articulation, but the actual medium in and through which God acts upon our thinking and speaking, giving them an inner obedience to His Word through our participation in the holy Communion of Father, Son, and Holy Spirit.

For too long in Protestant, as well as in Catholic, theology the full place of the Humanity of Christ has been neglected. The thinking together of divine revelation and human response, with inadequate attention to the *tertium datur* in the Humanity of Christ, in Catholic theology has meant the subordination of revelation to the natural forms of man's rationality and piety, and in Protestant theology has meant the transmutation of revelation into the subjectivity of the religious consciousness or Christian experience or faith. Against both tendencies we have to insist again that in the incarnation we are given not only the objective Word of God but the objective Word subjectively realized in complete and final form in the Humanity of our Lord. For Catholic theology that will mean the rediscovery of the Lordship of Christ and the radical inversion of all its thought-forms and patterns of piety, and their critical renewal in thorough and consistent conformity to Jesus Christ. For Protestant theology that will mean the rediscovery of the onto-logical and objective ground of faith, not only in the act of God for us in Christ but in the subjective embodiment of that act in the Humanity of Christ, and therefore it will mean the critical reorientation of faith in a repentant self-denial of its own subjectivity and a renewed subjection of itself to the reality of its object, Jesus Christ as true God and true Man. The crucial issue for Catholic and Evangelical theology is the disciplined grounding of it upon Jesus Christ as Himself the Truth: Truth as God is Truth, and that same Truth in the form of Man, Truth answering itself, Truth assuming its own true form from the side of man and from within man. The subjective reality of this Truth can never be made a separate theme for theology any more than the Humanity of Jesus in abstraction from the incarnation. That Humanity as the subjective reality of the Truth is already enclosed in the objective reality of the Truth: that is precisely the significance of the Humanity of Christ for the procedure of dogmatics. From end to end, therefore, dog-matic theology must be determined and shaped by the Human-ity of the Son of God.

2. *The Apostolic Foundation of the Church*

The incarnation shows us that the Word of divine self-revelation is objectively and subjectively fulfilled and complete in Jesus Christ: but as such it is objective to the Church and requires subjective realization within the mind of the Church. The Word of revelation declared to mankind achieves its end in that it is heard and understood, received and obeyed, in the Church, which is therefore given to share in the election and assumption of our humanity in Christ and which is assimilated to that Humanity in its own human life and thought. The incarnation shows us that the divine revelation is given not apart from reconciliation but is mediated within an atoning life and death offered on our behalf: but as such it is objective to the Church and requires subjective realization within the life of the Church. The Word of divine reconciliation proclaimed to mankind achieves its end in that it is accepted by sinners who allow themselves to be drawn into the sphere of its effective operation, in the Church which is given through the communion of the Spirit to share in the union of the Father and the Son. The subjective actualization of revelation and reconciliation is wrought out in the institution of the Apostolate, the foundation upon which the whole Church is built.[1]

In Jesus Christ the Word of God entered into the midst of our flesh of sin and worked out in our existence the perfect obedience of man to God. In Him alone we have the holy and perfect Word of God not only from the side of God to man but from the side of man to God. From beginning to end He is that Word in representative and vicarious action in our midst. But this pure and holy Word of God gathers round Him the apostles to be the inner nucleus of His Church, to be in a special way one body with Him, the Word made flesh, and to be the receiving end within our sinful history of the complete incarnate revelation. Here revelation assumes certain men and incorporates them in revelation from their own side and incorporates them not as co-revealers nor as co-redeemers, but as recipients of revelation and as ambassadors of reconciliation. They are the specially chosen witnesses, the specially appointed

[1] See *Royal Priesthood*, .J.T. *Occasional Papers*, no. 3, pp. 26 f.

vessels bearing the treasure of revelation and reconciliation. They are the apostles of revelation and reconciliation, put in trust with the Word of reconciliation. But they are sinners, they are Christians saved by grace, who come under the judgment of God and the cleansing of the blood of Christ. And it is as such, redeemed sinners, not as redeemers, that they are given apostolic function with regard to the Incarnational revelation.

As such the apostles stand over against Christ in entire contrast to Him. Jesus Christ was not a Christian. A Christian is a sinner saved by Christ, saved through Christ, for a Christian's relation to God is entirely through the mediation of Christ in revelation and reconciliation. Christ is Redeemer, Mediator. He is not Christian, not a sinner saved by God, but the Saviour Himself. He is both the author and the content of revelation and reconciliation, but as such He has instituted the Apostolate as the means whereby He passes His revelation and reconciliation into the world of sinners, that in that world His revelation may achieve its end as revelation subjectively realized in the mind of sinners, and His reconciliation may achieve its end as reconciliation subjectively actualized in the life of sinners. The Apostolate is elected and instituted as the specific point among sinners where revelation and reconciliation are, so to speak, earthed. Corresponding, therefore, to the particularity of the incarnation, there is in the Apostolate a particularity of fulfilled revelation and reconciliation within our sinful minds and our sinful lives. As such the Apostolate stands with sinners among sinners, and belongs to the sphere where salvation is bestowed. But within that sphere, within the perspective of redeemed sinners, the apostles provide us with the divinely appointed, the divinely prepared, and therefore the normative realization and actualization of revelation and reconciliation. It is as such that the apostles are given to sit upon twelve thrones sharing with Christ His authority and judgment over the Church. In other words, it is the point of view of the apostles which is the point of view which Christ means us to have of Him. Their point of view is the point of view of those who have been forgiven and reconciled by Christ, the specifically Christian point of view. And as such it is the divinely guided and inspired point of view from within the perspective

of redeemed sinners, providing us with the definite and normative pattern of response to revelation and reconciliation which
God Himself has willed and constituted in the Church.

This doctrine of the Apostolate belongs also to the doctrine
of the Holy Spirit. As long as Jesus was with His disciples in the
flesh He formed them round Him as His Body and taught them
as they were able to hear. He had yet many things to say to
them but they were unable to understand them then. He
promised, however, that the Father would send the Spirit in
His name, the Spirit of Truth, who would teach them all
things, remind them of what Christ had already taught them
and interpret it to them, leading them into all Truth. He would
not speak of Himself but speak of Christ and show Him to the
disciples. In fact, Jesus promised that in the sending of the
Spirit He Himself would return to the disciples and His Word
would abide in them. And that happened after the incarnational revelation was complete, after the reconciliation of man
to God had been carried out in the death and resurrection of
Christ. God poured out His Spirit upon the apostles and the
apostolic Church, and the risen Lord returned to them clothed
in the power of His Spirit and gave Himself to them to be
known and appropriated in His own Spirit, in His own Light,
and in His own Truth. Clothed with the historical facts of the
Gospel Jesus Christ now returns to shine with the light of His
glory within the apostolic mind and to fulfil in them His own
interpretation of Himself and His work. This is not any new
revelation, nor any new interpretation externally put by the
apostles upon the historical facts, but the actual unfolding of the
Mind of the risen Lord within the apostolic Church. The
Revelation of God objectively given and subjectively realized
in the Person and Work of Christ now through the Spirit subjectively takes shape in the mind of the apostolic Church in
final form.

We have to think of this also in terms of reconciliation, for
that which was atoningly wrought out in Jesus Christ on our
behalf is now through the Spirit subjectively actualized in the
apostolic foundation of the Church. In the apostles the mind of
the Church is so reconciled and joined to the Mind of Christ
that the Mind of Christ is not to be separated out from the

mind of the Apostolate, or the *kerygma* of the apostles to be distinguished from the Word of the Lord (except, of course, in those rare instances where the apostle himself may do so). The Lord reconciled the apostles to Himself and breathing upon them His Spirit wrought out that reconciliation in the inner obedience of their witness, and was pleased to control and assume that witness into oneness with His own Word, so that the apostolic word is Word of Christ. Thus the apostolic witness is incorporated by Christ into His own Word, so that through the apostolic *kerygma* it is Christ Himself who is at work testifying to the mighty acts whereby He has redeemed the world and offering Himself to men as their Saviour and Lord. This is the apostolic revelation of the Gospel in which the whole witness of the New Testament is delivered to the Church, and in which the Gospels as well as the Epistles are written as the Word of the Lord to the Church.

This doctrine of the Apostolate, therefore, belongs also to the doctrine of Holy Scripture. As bearers of the incarnational revelation, the apostles are the hinges where that revelation is folded out horizontally into history, but as such they are hinges in two senses: as disciples, in which they are the hinges between the Old Israel and the New Israel; and as apostles, in which the foundation of the Church is once and for all laid, and from which the Church is sent out into history. The revelation of God which selected Israel as the sphere of its prophetic operation in the world and the means of its translation appropriately into our human speech was fully and finally consummated in Jesus Christ in the midst of Israel. That entire revelation which was gathered up, transcended and fulfilled in Christ was once and for all bestowed upon the Church in the apostles. Thus in and through the medium of the apostles the Old Testament revelation belonging to Israel, made to shine out in its divine revelation as through the Spirit the glory of the crucified and risen Lord is shed over it, is subsumed under the New Testament revelation to form together, as the one apostolic-prophetic revelation of God in the language of our human flesh, the perpetual foundation of the Church as the Israel of God. The Scriptures of the Old Testament are therefore annexed to the Scriptures of the New Testament as the divinely appointed means in which there is folded out and delivered in written form to the Church the joining of the revelation of God with the corresponding reception which it requires from within the community of the redeemed, and therefore as the divinely instituted norm and pattern for the obedience of the Church to Jesus Christ from age to age.

That is the basic fact in the doctrine of Holy Scripture: that God has willed and constituted in the apostolic foundation of the Church a creaturely correspondence to His own Word, assuming it into union with His Word and effecting it as the human expression of His Word. As such the Holy Scripture, like the Apostolate, stands with sinners and among sinners, and belongs to the sphere where salvation is bestowed. That gives us the peculiar problem of Holy Scripture and its peculiar place. Holy Scripture is assumed by Christ to be His instrument in conveying revelation and reconciliation, and yet Holy Scripture belongs to the sphere where redemption is necessary. The Bible stands above the Church, speaking to the Church the very Word of God, but the Bible also belongs to history which comes under the judgment and the redemption of the Cross. That double place of Holy Scripture must always be fully acknowledged, else we confound the word of man with the Word of God, and substitute the apostles in the place of Christ.

On the one hand, then, we have to insist that the creaturely correspondence of the Holy Scriptures to God's Word is a correspondence which is actualized from within the perspective of redeemed sinners, but because it is a human expression corresponding to the Humanity of Jesus Christ, we have to understand it according to Him who as Word of God in our midst learned obedience to the Father. We can no more speak of dictation in the doctrine of the Scripture than we can speak of the life of Christ as dictated by the Father. Just as we speak of His life in terms of obedience, so we must speak of the Bible as obedience to the Divine self-revelation, in which the human word of Holy Scripture bows under the divine judgment just because it is part of His redemptive and reconciling work. In the Bible, therefore, the Word of God is not given to us ready-made. We see it growing in wisdom and grace before God and before man. We see it in the midst of our God-forsakenness and darkness, struggling with our temptations and our rebellious will. The Word of God comes to us in the midst of our sin and darkness at once revealing and reconciling, but it comes with strong crying and tears, pressing its way through the speech of our fallen flesh, graciously assuming it in spite of all its inadequacy and faultiness and imperfection, and giving it a holy perfection in the Word of God. The doctrine of verbal inspiration does not, therefore, mean the inerrancy and infallibility of the Biblical word in its linguistic and historical and other characteristics as human word. It means that the errant and fallible human word is, as such, used by God and has to be received and heard in spite of its human weakness and imperfection. The Bible has to be heard, therefore, as Word of God within the bi-polarity of revelation and reconciliation, in which we acknowledge that in itself, in its human expression, the Bible is word of man with all the limitations and imperfections of human flesh, in order to allow the human expression to point us beyond itself, to what it is not in itself, but to what God marvellously makes it to be in the adoption of His grace.

On the other hand, we have to insist that the creaturely correspondence of Holy Scripture to God's Word is so miraculously assumed and used by the divine revelation that even within the perspective of redeemed sinners it is adapted by the Spirit not only to mediate the Holy Word of God but to be the holy expression of that Word in human form. The word of God has wrought so effectively in and with the human language of the Bible that it has achieved from within it a true obedience to God. The Word has so imprinted its own image upon the human word as to make it a faithful reflection of its own revelation. Through the power of the Spirit the perfect obedience of Christ is so actualized within the humanity of the Bible that it is given to manifest the normative Humanity of Christ.

Although we cannot speak of a direct identity between the human word of Scripture and the Word that was made flesh in Jesus Christ, resting in the essence either of the divine Word or the human word, we must speak of an identity between the word of man and the Word of God in the Bible which rests upon the gracious decision of God to unite it with His own Word, and so to give it a divine perfection in spite of its human imperfection. Therefore the Bible has to be heard as the very Word of God in which we acknowledge that, although in itself, in its human expression, it is involved in the limitation and imperfection of human flesh under judgment, it is so inseparably conjoined with the divine Word as to be the written Word of God to man, and is brought into such a faithful correspondence with the divine revelation that it mediates to us in and through itself the exemplary obedience of Christ as the authoritative pattern and norm for the obedience of the Church in all its thinking and speaking. It is because the humanity of the apostolic Scriptures is already incorporated in the revelation and already enclosed within the reconciliation of Christ that these Scriptures are both the organ through which Jesus Christ from age to age conveys His Word to men with saving power and the canon by which He rules His Church, shaping its mind and forming it to be His Body.

3. *The Function of Biblical and Dogmatic Theology*

The Church that is built upon the apostles and prophets continues to be the Church as it continues in the apostolic tradition of obedience to Jesus Christ, that is, as it continues to be a follower of the apostles as the apostles were followers of Christ. But to be a follower of the apostles is to be bound to the apostolic Scriptures of the Old and New Testaments and through them to be schooled and moulded and incorporated into the apostolic foundation, for it is through those Scriptures that Jesus Christ the Word made flesh begets the Church from age to age as His own Body and forms it ever anew into His own Image. It is by listening to the Word of God speaking to us through the Holy Scriptures delivered to the Church by the apostles, by being drawn into, and by continuing in, the sphere of the apostolic community in which the risen and ascended Lord fulfils His own revelation and reconciliation among men, by submitting in the obedience of faith to the same revelation and reconciliation, that the Church continues to be ever the same, *semper eadem*, identical with itself in its sole foundation in Christ, living throughout all the changes of history and all temporal succession in such a way as not to be conformed to this world but to be transformed by the renewing of its mind and so to be conformed to Christ. It is within that whole movement of growth and change, continuity and identity, that we are to understand the significance of Biblical and dogmatic theology as the edification of the Church in hearing and appropriating the Word of God, and as the discipline of the Church in assimilating all its thinking and speaking to the Mind of Christ, that it may continue to become what it is, the One Body of the One Lord.

It is the perpetual duty of the Church to listen to the Word of God speaking in Holy Scripture, to accept and appropriate it through a true interpretation, that it may become the Church's own word in preaching and teaching. But the Word of God comes to us in Holy Scripture in human words which as such are always ambiguous and need faithful interpretation. That interpretation is faithful when we explain it according to the objective reality in the Word of divine Revelation to which they point us. "Why do ye not understand my speech (*lalia*)?" asked Jesus of the Jews. "Even because ye cannot hear my word (*logos*)." The *lalia* of Jesus, His human speech, is ambiguous, and is not to be understood except in terms of the *logos* that utters it and stands behind it, but on the other hand there is no revelation of the *logos* apart from the human *lalia*. It is the work of the *logos* to explain the *lalia* which it adopts, and the work of the *lalia* to reveal the *logos* which it serves. Thus the Word of God which speaks to us through Holy Scripture in human words is to be understood and appropriated as we interpret the human word (*lalia*) faithfully in accordance with the objective Word (*logos*) which adopted and moulded it as its instrument of communication, and which still uses it to communicate to us the divine revelation.

That confronts us immediately with several important considerations.

(a) We are not concerned here with the Word of God *in abstracto*, i.e. in abstraction from the *lalia*, but we are concerned with the Word of God *in concreto*, in the actual human situations in which the Word has addressed itself to men in the Old Testament and in the New Testament, in and through the actual humanity with which the Word has wrestled, achieving within it, in spite of its recalcitrance and intractability, an obedient

instrument for its revealing purpose. If we are to listen to that
Word and appropriate it to-day we must allow ourselves to be
drawn into the effective and creative operation of the Word in
its original sphere, in the witnesses of the Old and New Testaments, and in that original sphere subject ourselves to the
manifestation and sanctification of the Word and Truth of God.
This means of course that we have to give the most rigorous
attention to the actual text of the Scriptures and to their actual
setting in history, that we may stand in the place of the original
witnesses and go along with them in all that they suffer under
the impact of the Word of the Lord. Arduous exegetical study
is the foundation for all theological discipline in the Church.

(b) We are not concerned here, however, with the human
speech of the Bible as an independent theme of study, that is,
with the humanity of the original witnesses in themselves, all
of whom without exception point away from themselves to the
Word of the Lord which has laid hold upon them and drawn
them within its saving operation. That is to say, true hearing of
the Word of God coming to us through the human words of the
Bible which is faithful to those words can take place effectively
only within the sphere of reconciliation to God. Only then can
we stand in the place of the original witnesses and go along
with them in all that they suffered under the impact of the
Word. It is as we allow ourselves to be drawn into the community of the reconciled that the Word of revelation speaks to
us effectively by adapting us to its hearing, judging our sin and
darkness and restoring us into union and communion with
God's Word. In other words, we have to be drawn into the
place before God where our enmity to Him is exposed and
judged, where our opposition to His revelation is overcome,
where the lines of communication between God and man disrupted and damaged by sin are healed, where there is real
reconciliation so that there can be real communication. Just as
the doctrine of Scripture cannot be divorced from the doctrine
of Atonement, so Biblical interpretation cannot be genuinely
undertaken apart from reconciliation to God.

(c) All this means that to hear and interpret and appropriate
the Word of God speaking to us in the Holy Scriptures we have
to subordinate our own presuppositions and conceptions and

indeed the whole of our own humanity to the critical and creative activity of that Word effectively at work in the humanity of the Bible. We find ourselves at the bar of the divine judgment where we are summoned to repentance and are forced into ruthless self-criticism. Our great problem is that we are unable really to listen to the Word of God speaking in the Bible, for our listening is a strange mixture of listening and our own speaking, and it is our own speaking which is usually uppermost. The Word of God summons us to listen to it not as though we know already what it has to say, not as though it only confirms what we have already said to ourselves, but to listen in such a way that we are lifted outside of ourselves and hear what only God can say to us. How can we do that except in repentance? To listen and deny ourselves, to listen and to repent of what we want to make the Bible say, to listen in such a way as to let the Bible speak against ourselves, that is to listen indeed to the Word of God.

(d) We are confronted now with the problem of theology in relation to Biblical exegesis, which arises when the coherent pattern of our own conceptions and presuppositions conflicts with the coherent pattern of obedience to the Word of God revealed in the Bible. We all have our own schemes of thought which we inevitably bring to the interpretation of the Holy Scriptures. Doubtless it would be wrong for us not to have them, and certainly wrong for us not to realize that we have them, for then they would have supreme power over us as unconscious canons of interpretation imperceptibly determining and damaging our exegesis. But we have to face the fact that in faithful listening to the Word of God, we allow ourselves to be drawn into a sphere where human thought-forms are already shaped and knit together in a pattern of obedience to the Word of God, while faithful interpretation and appropriation of the Word of God mean that we allow ourselves to be schooled into this obedience, in order that we may yield to the Word of God the mode of rational activity which it requires of those to whom it gives itself to be known.

This is where the Old Testament has an incalculable importance for Christian theology. All through the history of Israel as a people brought into covenant relation with God, the Word was wrestling with our stubborn and rebellious humanity and dealing faithfully with it in judgment and mercy and truth to achieve a coherent pattern of obedience, a sphere in human understanding and human speech, with appropriate forms of thought and language, which could be used as the instrument of divine revelation to all men and at last as the sphere of actual revelation and reconciliation for all men. The Word of God comes to us in the Scriptures of the New Testament only through that schooling in the Old Testament, and we need that schooling too, not only to hear the Word of God in the Old Testament, but even to hear it in the New. We cannot do without the Old Testament if we are to acquire the obedient orientation of mind with which faithfully to apprehend the Word as it gives itself to us to be known.

Here then in the school of the Biblical world of communication we learn to yield to the Word of God that mode of rational activity which it is the responsible thing to do, if we are really to behave according to the nature of the Word of God in revelation and reconciliation. We have to allow the Word in its obedient humanity to impose itself upon us, and allow ourselves to go along with it, to be led and guided and corrected in all our thinking and speaking, so that it becomes our own. It is this activity which gives rise to Biblical theology which seeks to unfold the content of the Word of God as it has taken human form in the witnesses of the Old and New Testaments, and therefore to unfold the pattern of inner obedience to it which the Word requires of us. The Word of God comes to us in the Bible in such a way that the appropriate obedience to it from within our humanity is already enclosed within it, in such a way that the objective revelation already includes its subjective realization in the humanity of the Bible. We are not concerned therefore in Biblical theology simply with revelation and response, or with listening to the Word of God simply in the presentation of exegetical results, but with revelation and a divinely schooled, prepared and coherent response revealed not only in the thought-forms of the Biblical revelation but in the essential unity of their correspondence to the Word of God.

It is important, however, to insist that the Biblical thought-forms cannot be abstracted from their context in revelation and be interpreted and used as universally valid principles. They have their meaning and importance only within the concrete situations where the Word of God uses them, and in inseparable relation to the objective revelation which has given them shape. They belong to a coherent pattern of revelation and actualized response which is gathered up, transcended and fulfilled in the incarnation. It is Jesus Christ, the Word made flesh in the midst of Israel, in His exemplary obedience to the Divine Will, who provides us with the criterion for our interpretation of the thought- and language-forms of the Bible. They have their authority and significance not in themselves as such but as they point to Him and as they are ultimately made to cohere in Him.

There is a significant difference, however, between the theology of the Old Testament and that of the New Testament, for the theology of the New Testament gives rise to dogmatics as the theology of the Old Testament does not, except in so far as it is subsumed under the New Testament. The Old Testament thought- and language-forms receive their fulfilment in the incarnation where they are given critical reinterpretation, so that we can no longer stand with the witnesses of the Old Testament in precisely the same way that they stood under the impact of the revelation, for the revelation has moved on beyond that concrete human situation into the incarnation and the concrete human situation bound up with it in the apostolic Church. But when we stand within the pattern of human obedience actualized in the incarnational revelation we are able to stand in the place of the witnesses of the Old Testament in a profounder sense; for we are able to give an interpretation of their forms of thought and language in terms of their fulfilment in Jesus Christ, which is entirely faithful to the concrete human situation in which they were schooled in Israel.

All through the history of Israel in the Old Testament the Word of God which had bound Israel into covenant-union with itself insisted on being translated into the flesh of Israel so as to adapt Israel to its purpose, to fashion within it a womb for the incarnation of the Word and a matrix of appropriate thought- and language-forms for the reception of the incarnational revelation. But in the nature of the case, although the

Word of God and the existence of Israel are bound up inextricably together, the concrete form of Israel in the Old Testament is revealed by the incarnation to be a passing form which exhibits the judgment of our stubborn and rebellious humanity in its restoration to union with the Word of God, although the pattern of obedience already apparent in Israel, in the Servant of the Lord above all, points through judgment and death into resurrection, to the recreation out of Israel of a new humanity which, in the finality of the incarnation and the new concrete human situation begotten by it in the Church, exhibits the permanent form of the Israel of God, which will not pass away but will endure throughout all the changes of history into the glory of eternal consummation.

Here, however, within the sphere of the incarnational revelation and the new concrete human situation where everything reposes upon the finality of the incarnation and the foundation once and for all laid in the apostolic Church, we are concerned with a pattern of obedience which is completely coherent and of final authority, but we are concerned with more than a pattern, namely, with an actual *structure* of obedience inserted with its appropriate forms of thought and language into the midst of our humanity in the Church as the Body of Christ. As Biblical theology lays bare the inner coherence and structure of the Word of God as it has taken human form in obedient correspondence to it, Biblical theology passes over into dogmatic theology, which is concerned with an integrated and orderly unfolding of the content of the Word of God according to its own essential norms as they operate effectively and creatively within the mind of the historical Church, bringing it into conformity with Jesus Christ and into unity within its own understanding and appropriation of His Word.

Biblical theology passes over into dogmatic theology where two significant things happen: (a) Where our hearing and receiving of the Word of God is not in isolation either from our fellows in the contemporary situation or from our fathers in the context and continuity of history, that is, where it is a conjoint hearing with all saints in the life and growth of the Church in accordance with its apostolic foundation; (b) Where we have to assimilate all our thinking and speaking and acting in the

C

Church to the Biblical revelation so that it may be assimilated truly and faithfully into all our thinking and speaking and acting from age to age. That gives us two primary characteristics of dogmatic theology.

(a) Dogmatic theology acknowledges that all our hearing and thinking of the Word of God is conditioned by our place in the Church. Our hearing is determined by previous hearing of the Word in the Church, and our thinking is conditioned by the thought-forms which we have inherited in the traditional teaching of the Church. That is to say, dogmatic theology seeks to unfold and present the content of the Word of God within the limits of the Church prescribed for it by the incarnation and the apostolic foundation, and to articulate that content to-day through an examination of the doctrinal decisions in the past which have shaped and moulded the listening of the Church in the present. Dogmatic theology operates not only within the sphere of the Church as the sphere of revelation and reconciliation, but within the historical continuity of the Church in its learning obedience to the Word of God, and in its growing up into the full stature of the Humanity of Christ. It is undertaken in reliance upon the promise of Christ to send His Spirit upon the Church to lead it into all truth concerning Himself, and is undertaken in the constant prayer that faithful expression of the Mind of Christ may be given in and through the mind of the Church. In all this, dogmatics is the instrument whereby the Church inquires whether its traditional teaching is in conformity with Christ, and is the means whereby as far as possible it is emancipated from the *Zeitgeist* which always threatens the thinking and teaching of the Church with historical relativity, and is the discipline whereby the Church is prevented from imprisoning the Truth in definitive dogmatic formulations of any age. Thus the Church is kept ever open to the renewed understanding of Christ the Truth who alone can renew the mind of the Church from age to age.

(b) Along with all this belongs the duty of dogmatic theology to bring the thought- and language-forms used by the Church in its preaching and teaching under the review and judgment of the Word of God, that they may be so assimilated to the obedient Humanity of Christ as to become proper and adequate instruments for the proclamation of the Gospel and for the instruction of the Church. The constant task of dogmatic theology is thus to test the mind of the Church in accordance with the Biblical revelation, to protect the Church from becoming independent and self-willed (i.e. heretical) in its teaching, to protect the preachers of the Church from preaching themselves and their own preconceptions or merely private interpretations of the Gospel, and so to direct the Church back to the self-unfolding of the divine Truth within the Body of Christ and to help the preachers of the Church to point away from themselves to Jesus Christ, the Way, the Truth and the Life.

Dogmatic theology is able to undertake this critical task only if behind it all it engages in a great positive attempt to expound and set before the Church the whole movement of obedience to God's Word in the incarnation, in the apostolic foundation, and in the history of the Church, and in the light of that to articulate afresh in the thought- and speech-forms of the present a coherent account of all the doctrines of the Christian Faith. In undertaking this task, dogmatic theology will show the Church not only where our forms of thought and language conflict with the Word of God and the Humanity it assumed in Jesus Christ, but how these forms can, and must, be bent to meet the needs of theological articulation. Dogmatics is not primarily interested in the forms of thought and language which the Church must use from age to age to proclaim the Gospel. It is primarily concerned to unfold the objective content of revelation and is only interested in the forms of thought and language as the expressions of that content. Dogmatics must show the Church, therefore, how the objective content of the Word of God transcends the forms of our thought and language from age to age and from nation to nation, but also how it can make abundant use of them, adapting them to its purpose, while preserving its own freedom and sovereignty over them. But dogmatics can do this only as it expounds the objective content of the Word of God in and through the subjective form which it has already taken in the Humanity of Christ and assumed into its own objectivity. The objective reality of the Word and the subjective actualization of it in the obedient Humanity of Christ together, in their inseparable union, form the objective content of revelation which is delivered to the Church for its understanding and appropriation. The task of dogmatic theology, therefore, is above all to expound the doctrine of Jesus Christ as true God and true Man, but also to show how in obedient conformity to Him a Christological pattern is made to appear in the forms of thought and language which we are bound to use of Him.

It is thus that there emerges a twofold criterion of theological procedure prescribed to us by the very nature of the Word and the control which it exercises over our knowing and articulation of it. Not only must the content of our theological knowledge be determined and controlled throughout by its object, the Word made flesh in Jesus Christ, but the modes and forms of our dogmatic activity must exhibit an inner structural coherence reflecting the nature of the object. This twofold criterion or norm can be described as *correspondence* to the Word of God speaking to us through the Holy Scriptures in the midst of the Church, and the *coherence* of our doctrinal forms in an essentially Christological structure. Though these may be distinguished they are not to be regarded as two norms, for they cannot be separated from one another. They work together as one norm in the inseparable relation of *kerygma* and *dogma*, of Biblical theology and dogmatic theology.

We have already seen how Biblical theology lays bare and operates with a pattern of obedience to the Word of God revealed in the humanity of the Holy Scriptures, and as it seeks to articulate that in the understanding of the Church it passes over into dogmatic theology. Dogmatic theology, on the other hand, lays bare and operates with a pattern of doctrine prescribed to it, in its unfolding of the whole content of the Word, by obedience to Jesus Christ as true God and true Man; but in the nature of the case this pattern of doctrine cannot be abstracted from the self-disclosure of Jesus Christ through the Biblical revelation and be erected into an independent norm with its own inherent authority. In itself it is only a formal pattern, but it derives from, and reposes upon, the actual structure of the incarnation. This pattern of doctrine, therefore, can be used as a dogmatic norm only in conjunction with correspondence to the Biblical revelation and in subjection to it. Within that subjection, however, and within the subordination of all our thought- and language-forms to the critical and creative activity of the Word of God, dogmatic theology must proceed to lay bare the essential inter-relation of all the doctrines of the faith, and their integration within the one Body of Christ, within the whole structure of obedience to Christ. This is the *interior logic* of dogmatic theology which is in the object of our knowledge before it is in our thinking, but which imposes itself upon our thinking as our minds seek to behave in terms of the nature of the object, that is, to be conformed to Jesus Christ.

In other words, dogmatic inquiry discovers that there is a structural and essentially Christological pattern running throughout the whole body of our theological knowledge, which can be studied and used as a norm or criterion for helping to shape the true form of each doctrine, for testing and proving the different doctrines to see whether they really fit into the essential structure of the whole. This cannot be undertaken in any arbitrary and authoritarian fashion but only in the form of a humble inquiry, for the thought-forms used in the expression of the structural pattern are subject throughout to the review and judgment of the Word of Revelation. Thus, for example, when we take the doctrines of the *hypostatic union* and of *anhypostasia and enhypostasia* which arise out of the Church's articulation of the doctrine of Christ, and use them as dogmatic norms, we have to remember that these doctrinal forms have no inherent authority and are themselves subject all the time to modification by our hearing of the Word of God in the Holy Scriptures. They can be used only in humble obedience to that Word and in coherence with the whole body of Biblical theology; but within that coherence and along with correspondence to the Word of God speaking to us in the Holy Scriptures they may be used legitimately, and can be used with the greatest gain in understanding and clarification of our theological knowledge. As such, this is a specific but important illustration of the dogmatic procedure in which we adopt and make our own, in our thinking and understanding, the way which the Word of God has taken in human form in Jesus Christ.

I

CHRIST IN THE OLD TESTAMENT

by JOHN MARSH

Principal of Mansfield College, Oxford

CHRIST IN THE OLD TESTAMENT

by

JOHN MARSH

Patrum omnium foedus adeo substantia et re ipsa nihil a nostro differt, ut unum prorsus atque idem sit. Administratio tamen variat.

Calvin, Institutes II, 10: 2.

The covenant made with all the fathers, so far from differing from ours in reality and substance, is absolutely one and the same. Yet its execution is different.

Denn dies ist die Schrift, die alle Weisen und Klugen zu Narren macht und allein den Kleinen und Albernen offen steht. . . . Hier wirst du die Windeln und Krippen finden, da Christus inne liegt, dahin auch der Engel die Hirten weist. Schlecht und geringe Windeln sind es, aber teur ist der Schatz, Christus, der drinnen liegt.

Luther's Vorrede auf das Alte Testament, Abp 3.

For this is the Scripture which makes all the wise and prudent into fools, and is plain only to the child and the simple. . . . Here you will find the cradle and the swaddling-clothes in which Christ is laid, to which also the angel sent the shepherds. The swaddling clothes are poor and mean, but the treasure they contain, Christ, is precious indeed.

FROM the very earliest days the Christian Church has been obliged to take a difficult, dialectical, paradoxical, almost self-contradictory attitude to the Old Testament. The Christian Church soon recognized that it was by no means identical with Judaism, and therefore rejected the Old Testament as the Jews interpreted it. But the Church also claimed continuity with the old Israel after the flesh, and therefore claimed the Jewish scriptures as its own. The tension can be seen in the pages of the New Testament itself. On the one hand

Matthew can write of Jesus saying: "Think not that I came to destroy the law or the prophets: I came not to destroy, but to fulfil";[1] while on the other Paul can affirm: "Christ redeemed us from the curse of the law."[2] And even if we remember that Paul goes on to say that "the law hath been our tutor to bring us unto Christ"[3] we must also bear in mind his further comment: "Now that faith is come, we are no longer under a tutor."[4]

This same tension is reflected in Christian writings from the very beginning. Barnabas is emphatic in his rejection of the Jewish interpretation of scripture, and all the religious life that followed from it, but he goes to what seem quite fanciful lengths to illustrate the point that the Old Testament foretells our Christian situation in every detail. The Lord, he says, "hath made manifest to us by all the prophets that he wanteth neither sacrifices nor whole burnt offerings, nor oblations." And what fanciful, if pious, exegesis it is which takes the scripture: "And Abraham circumcised of his household eighteen males and three hundred,"[5] and makes this comment on it: "Understand ye that he saith the eighteen first, and then after an interval three hundred. In the eighteen ($18 = IH$) I stands for ten, H for eight. Here thou hast Jesus ($IH\Sigma OY\Sigma$). And because the cross in the T was to have grace, he saith also three hundred ($300 = T$). So he revealeth Jesus in the two letters, and in the remaining one the cross."[6] Justin makes the same two points in his dialogue with Trypho the Jew. First, "The law given at Horeb is already antiquated and belongs to you alone, but that other (a final law) belongs to all men absolutely. And a law set over against a law has made the one before it to cease. . . . And as an eternal and final law was Christ given to us."[7] And second, "I am not unaware that you dare to expound this Psalm (110) as spoken of King Hezekiah, but that you are in error I will at once prove to you from the words themselves. We find: 'The Lord sware and will not repent, and thou art priest for ever after the order of melchizedek,' and the context both before and after. But that Hezekiah has neither been, nor is, a priest of God for ever, not even you will dare to contradict. But that it is

---

[1] Matt. 5: 17   [2] Gal. 3: 13   [3] Gal. 3: 24
[4] Gal. 3: 25   [5] Gen. 14: 14, 17: 23   [6] Barn. 9
[7] Justin, *Dialogue*, 11: 2

spoken about our Jesus, even the phrases themselves show."[1]
It would be a superfluous task to seek to quote, in one short
essay, all that the Fathers have said on this matter in order to
show how universally the paradoxical tension has been felt.
Perhaps Augustine gives it its most succinct formulation when
he wrote: "The New is concealed in the old, and the old is
manifest in the New,"[2] a sentence which affirms the identity
and the difference between the two Testaments.

But we must not suppose that this mode of thinking of the
relation of the two Testaments is peculiar to "reformed"
theologians, or to those who, like Augustine, may be thought
to be of the same sort of mind. It is common, with varying
modifications, to all types of theologians in the Christian
Church. It will perhaps suffice to quote St. Thomas Aquinas to
show how the Roman tradition comes to much the same
general conclusion as Barnabas, Augustine and the Reformers.
It is true, of course, that the problem is not conceived in quite
the same terms in St. Thomas, who has no place for it in his
great *Summa Theologica* where the relationship of the two Testaments is considered as such: but in 1.2.106.3 he discusses
"whether the New Law is contained in the Old". Aquinas says:
"One thing may be contained in another in two ways. First,
actually; as a located thing is in a place. Secondly, virtually, as
an effect is in its cause, or as the complement in that which is
incomplete; thus a genus contains its species, and a seed contains the whole tree virtually. It is in this way that the New Law
is contained in the old."[3] This is not quite unambiguous.
Clearly Thomas means that the Old Law is contained in the
law "virtually" and not "actually". But if he thinks of both
"genus-species" and "complement-incompleteness" as examples
of virtual inclusion, his suggestions are not as useful as he
believes. For the inclusion of a species in a genus is surely as
much actual as virtual, if not completely actual. Nor can the

---

[1] Justin, *Dialogue*, 33: 1

[2] Augustine, *Quaest. in Heptateuchum*, 2: 73: "Quanquam et in vetere Novum
lateat et in Novo vetus pateat."

[3] St. Thomas, *Summa Theologica*, 1.2.106.3: "Aliquid continetur in alio *dupliciter:
uno modo* in actu, sicut locatum in loco: *alio modo* virtute, sicut effectus in causa, vel
complementum in incompleto: sicut genus continet species potestate: et sicut tota
arbor continetur in semine: et per hunc modum nova lex continetur in veteri."

cause-effect relationship throw any helpful light on the relationship of the Old Testament to the New. But if by "in this way" St. Thomas meant not virtual inclusion in general, but the kind of inclusion that a tree has in its seed, then he has somewhat overstated his case, for the application of such an analogy permits of no new act of revelation, like that on which the New Testament scriptures rest. But that may be to press the analogy too far, though it is difficult, unless we go that far, to derive much help from it. And lest it be urged that in any case Thomas is writing here of the New Law and the Old, and not of the two dispensations as such, we must remember that only a little later he writes: "Whatsoever is set down in the New Testament explicitly and openly as a point of faith, is contained in the Old Testament as a matter of belief, but implicitly, under a figure. And accordingly, even as to those things which we are bound to believe, the New Law is contained in the Old."[1] Thomas is evidently thinking more widely than of the relationship of legal codes!

If we now consider these statements together with the quotations from Luther and Calvin at the head of this essay, we can perceive a clear agreement in asserting an identity as well as a difference between the Old Testament and the New. It is when the various authors try to specify in what the nature of the unity consists, and wherein the difference lies, that opinions diverge. It is surely inevitable that there should be a formal agreement, as long as the Old Testament is in any sense accepted as Christian scripture. But none of the authors so far examined seems to have found a satisfactory basis for specifying in what the unity and difference consist. Not even Karl Barth, in the view of the present writer, is fully satisfying here. Barth says that God has revealed Himself to us in an event, the reality of which is the presence of Jesus Christ. This revelation, this event, this presence of Jesus Christ is God's time for us—the time, that is, which God has for us. In the revealing act itself God's time is "fulfilled time"; but the Old Testament and the New are

---

[1] Thomas, *ibid*.: "Quod omnia, quae credenda traduntur in novo testamento explicite, et aperte, traduntur credenda in veteri testamento, sed implicite, et sub figura: et secundum hoc etiam quantum ad credenda lex nova continetur in veteri."

times of witness to the "fulfilled time", that is to say, the revealing event itself, and the Old Testament witnesses to the fulfilled time as a "time of anticipation" while the New Testament witnesses to it as a "time of remembrance". It would seem therefore that for Barth Christ's presence is something anticipated in the Old Testament, and remembered in the New.[1]

But, illuminating and profound as such an analysis is, it seems to be unsatisfactory. For if *Christus praesens* is characteristic of the fulfilled time, to which other times witness either by anticipation or remembrance, we surely have no option but to describe Old Testament time in the words *Christus absens*. Can Christ be present if He is expected, or expected if He be present? We may say of the New Testament time of witness that it involves Christ's presence in some sense since it is a time of remembrance. There are certainly Biblical usages to support this view: but whether Barth's formulation is meant thus seems at least questionable; and in more normal language we should think ourselves relieved of remembering someone who was actually present.

These difficulties are not eased when we consider the three ways in which Barth finds the Old Testament like the New. First, it is like the New in being a witness to a revelation which can be understood only as a free, once-for-all, concrete act of God. Second, it is like the New Testament in being a witness to a revelation in which, paradoxically, God remains hidden. And third, it is like the New Testament in its witness to a revelation in which God's presence is near as the one who is to come. These three propositions seems unexceptionably true, but they surely constitute a "philosophizing" and "universalizing" of what is essentially particular, concrete and incapable of reduction, without distortion, into general propositions. In any event, the three propositions would be equally true of preaching or the celebration of the sacraments, which also bear the same threefold witness as scripture, but which yet must differ from it,

[1] Barth, *Dogmatik* I/2, p. 50: "Gottes Offenbarung in dem Ereignis der Gegenwart Jesu Christi ist Gottes Zeit für uns. Sie ist die erfüllte Zeit in diesem Ereignis selbst. Sie ist aber als die alttestamentliche Zeit der Erwartung und als die neutestamentliche Zeit der Erinnerung auch die Zeit des Zeugnisses von diesem Ereignis."

since scripture stands over them in some sense as canon and norm.

From this all too brief review of Barth we may conclude that in order to formulate a satisfactory doctrine of the relationship of the Old Testament to the New, we need to fulfil at least two conditions: we need to find a formulation of the relationship which will enable us to state some identity between them, and not leave, as Barth does, *Christus praesens* as a reality only in the "fulfilled time" of the revelatory event. And we need to find a formulation which will do that without abrogating from the particularity of the historical. The rest of this essay will attempt a prolegomenon to this twofold task, and seek to illustrate its thesis by reference to Scripture.

We must begin by making a distinction which by now is commonplace enough—between history as event and history as record. As event, history is what happens; as record it is a report on what happens. But history cannot be located in the mere "happening" of an event, in its bare occurrence, but only in events as related to each other. A brief musical melody makes a useful illustration. Its constituent notes do not form a melody in isolation from each other, nor yet if they are sounded in sudden simultaneity, but only if and when they are played one after another in a certain series and rhythm. So it is with events constituting a piece of history. The various human actions which together constitute the French Revolution would not be "a piece of history" if they occurred in isolation from each other, or if they all occurred simultaneously. They formed a piece of history precisely because they followed one another as they did. Out of their occurrence in a certain order *and in certain relationships* an historical episode resulted.

We wrote of a brief melody. But melodies cannot but be brief. This is no doubt due in some measure to the character of the minds that know them. There is a limit to the length of melodic line that any human mind, however trained and skilled, can synthesize into an whole. But even if we could suppose an indefinite extension of man's power to hear a melody, we should still have to say that melody belonged to finitude, if only for the reason that an infinitely long melody could never be heard. But while melodies must be brief to be apprehensible, we can hear and understand much longer musical compositions as synthesized wholes. This is possible only because we can break such compositions down into their component melodies, counter melodies, contrapuntal and harmonic treatment and so on. The same things have to be said about history. We can only know history "episodically". History, like melody, belongs to finitude—and conversely infinity can have no history. Further, the episodic nature of our apprehension of the historical is the means by which we can come to a synthesis of great sweeps of history, and even speak, without complete non-significance, of universal history. We may note that in this process, as in that of apprehending say a symphony, it is the thematic recurrences of history that enable us to link historical eras together—a point well illustrated in Professor Toynbee's *Study of History*.

It is possible to distinguish three chief ways in which historical unity and continuity may be realized. If we continue to make use of the musical analogy, we may think of some periods of history as a mere continuation of the same melodic line. These are "conservative" periods, characterized by stability and uniformity. Other periods may be characterized as reformative or evolutionary, as if a basic melody were subjected to elaborations of shape or variations in stress or rhythm. A third form of historical unity and continuity is exhibited in times of revolution and swift change—times of upheaval. In such times there may seem to be no observable continuity between the status and the *status quo ante*, save that the former is in some ways conditioned by the latter. Musically we may compare such periods to the appearance of a counter melody which, though discontinuous from the melody, is in some degree conditioned by that to which it is counter. Historically we may say that a revolution, though seeking, and often achieving, discontinuity from the *ancien régime*, is yet in a real sense, its child. There is unity in and behind such an apparent disunity. So history is never, in Masefield's titular phrase, "One Dam Thing After Another", never a number of random notes quite disconnected from each other, but always a series of inter-related events. Nothing, that means to say, merely "happens" in history. All events bear some relation to what has gone before, over and above their mere subsequence. The unity and continuity is, of course, at once apparent in conservative eras; it is discernible to the trained observer in reformative periods; and it demands unusual insight to perceive continuity in times of sudden or drastic change, so much so that it is given to but few men to be able thus to understand the history of their own times.

Events, then, must be related if we are to know them as history. They beget meaning by being related to each other. An isolated event, which is strictly speaking inconceivable, would have no meaning, and would indeed be unknowable. But if this be true of one particular event, it is surely true of complexes or series of events. Indeed, since any event is itself a plurality of events, we do not need to argue from the particular to the general, but only to pass from the smaller to the larger aggregates. The execution of a Charles Stuart outside the Banqueting House in Whitehall on January 30, 1649, could not be known at all unless it were part of a whole human situation. In particular, it could never be known as an historic act unless it were seen related both to the antecedent despotism of the Stuart Monarchy and to the subsequent experiment of a Parliamentary Commonwealth. But the whole "Story of the House of Stuart" is likewise incomprehensible and meaningless save as it is known as one chapter in the *History of Britain*. And the story of Britain is significant only against the background of European and American (to say nothing of African, Asian and Australian) histories. And so on—but not *ad infinitum*! for to carry the series *ad infinitum* would be to say that what we know as meaning or significance in history was at best provisional and intra-historical. We should have to confess to the impossibility of ever knowing whether history itself had a meaning apart from the events which make it up. And that seems to be a nonsensical basis for asserting significance of what happens within history. But if we think that history is not itself an infinite series, we can only suppose it to have meaning if we are ready to seek its meaning outside itself. The many events which in such a supposition would go to constitute the finitude of history would be like any complex of events within the whole—either meaningless if unrelated to something else, or significant if related to a reality beyond itself. If the meaningfulness of history be asserted in these terms, then there is no previous as there is no subsequent event to which it can be related. Its significance can only be asserted in relation to some non-temporal, non-historical reality, some eternal being, God. History is either meaningless in itself, or it "makes sense" in relationship to the eternal. The temporal must be related to the non-temporal, the eternal, if it is to bear any meaning at all.

We have claimed that all events bear some relation to what has gone before over and above their mere subsequence. This is involved in the very possibility of history and of our knowing it. Suppose, for example, that from the very day of his birth some infant were to be subjected daily to as nearly total changes of environment as was possible. On the first day English parents in Sussex, on the second German in Westphalia, on the third Icelanders in Reykjavik, on the fourth Bantus in South Africa—and so on throughout his life. It is conceivable that at long last some dawn of intelligence would appear in the child, but it would be very long delayed, if not completely inhibited. There would be a lack of knowledge because of the absence of the factors essential to it—continuity and identity. Continuity is the basis of historical judgment whenever the story of a changing human society is told. The French Revolution is something that happened to the historical entity we call "France" because the whole process from before to afterwards was continuous. Identity is the basis of historical judgment whenever the story of one human episode is used to understand or interpret another. Professor Toynbee uses this principle extensively in his discovery of certain morphological laws in history. In the former case historical episodes are joined together in a continuity of time and some substantial identity between them is affirmed on that basis. In the latter case some substantial identity is observed between events which are not contiguous in time, and they are used, on account of the alleged identity, to throw light on each other's meaning. This principle underlies the Biblical and Christian use of typology.

It is important to realize that in any interpretation of history some such substantial identity is affirmed—either the bearer of history remains identical (France in the French Revolution) or the events that occur to the same or different subjects have some substantially identical elements. History, we must repeat,

D

is not simply a succession of different and merely subsequent events, but a relationship between them resting upon continuity and identity. But in saying this we must utter a warning, lest it be thought that the meaning of history can be quickly reached by finding some universal propositions to assert as its general principle. Identity in history is not that known to the mathematician or logician; it is much more akin to that familiar to the biologist or the zoologist. But with that warning uttered it remains true that events cannot just "happen" and find themselves just "pointing" to each other for their meaning and significance. If one event "points to" another as its meaning or explanation then it is because of some continuity or identity between them. There is thus always some embodiment of the future in the present, if that future is in any way to bestow significance on the happenings of the present. We can see this principle being applied in the Prologue to the Fourth Gospel. The writer tells us in v. 14 that the Word became flesh for the first and only time in history. Nevertheless, He had been substantially present as the reality of preceding events. This is not mere paradox, but a situation with which we are quite familiar; for we often do not know what is "going on" in the events that take place. A policeman on his beat may come upon two men fighting, and may ask his usual question: "What's going on here?" That is to say, he realizes that until he has discovered with what continuum and in relation to what identities he is to envisage the things he sees, he cannot really know what they are. The two men may be engaged in a street brawl; but conceivably they could turn out to be cinema actors in some outdoor shooting for a film, or it may be that their brawl is the focus point of a fateful political struggle, as many fights in Germany were before Hitler came to power.

Some such considerations lie behind the common view that one cannot write a history of one's own time. Two things indeed seem necessary before good history can be written: a certain distance from the events recorded, that they may be seen in due perspective; and some element of common experience, some identity, between the age recorded and either the historian's time or the historian's own interest, that there may be a basis of historical sympathy and some guide to interpretation. Both are illustrated in the history of the Jews. They knew well enough what had happened in their history, and they wrote what they knew, mostly in long perspective. They also had some idea as to "what had been going on", and their own prophetic knowledge of God enabled them to see the saving mercy of God as the reality of their people's history. For human history this might be enough, but for sacred history it is inadequate. To interpret history aright one must see events in their proper continuities and identities, and when the Messiah came, whom the Jews expected on the basis of their own interpretation of history, they denied the claim he made that his life and its outcome were the real continuity with their own history, and his belief, and the belief of his followers, that God's saving mercy was to be fully and finally identified in him.

In our treatment of history as event we have reached the point where we must pass over to think of history as record. We may begin by making a literary point parallel to our first point about historical events, and distinguish between "annalism" and "history". The annalist writes down events as they occur, without any conscious attempt at interpretation. No doubt not even annals can be written down without some measure of interpretation, even if it be no more than the inevitable selection of events to be recorded. No doubt also the very existence or appointment of an annalist implies some perhaps unformulated interpretation of history: the ancient oriental monarch who employed an annalist was doubtless saying in effect: "The history of my time means me", and doubtless the annalist concurred, as he was paid to do. Nevertheless, as an annalist, the scribe would seek to record the events of each year as "One Dam Thing After Another". Indeed the common form is "I did this" (he writes in the first person for his monarch) "and I did that and I did a third thing". This is not history. The historian, when he appears, sees more than a mere series of conjunctions in history. Writing from some temporal perspective the historian can look back and see continuities and complexes of events, and identities reaching across the boundaries of event complexes, across ages and eras and cultures. So the historian is concerned with "patterns" and "meanings" in history, with connecting one event with another, and with the discovery thereby of the meaning of one event in terms of another.

The Biblical writers who record the past are all historians: none is an annalist. They never attempted anything save to write history. Their work, like that of all historians, is a blending of the annalist's "fact" with the prophet's "interpretation". They wrote, as we have said, for the most part at a considerable distance from the events they recorded, and they were able to see that some past events had special significance as bearers of meaning, and those events were used very much as the norms of historical interpretation. It would seem that sometimes the whole people which cherished the memory of these normative events as a great national memory were able to approach new events in the light of the past—as, for example, when they crossed the Jordan and picked up some unmistakable features from the great deliverance at the Red Sea.[1] This whole incident may be questioned by some critics as to its historicity: but whatever the verdict on that might be the essential point would remain, viz., that in order to understand what was happening when the Israelite tribes crossed the Jordan, the reader must recall what happened at the Red Sea. I am not myself persuaded that some such conception was impossible to at any rate some of the Israelite tribes who entered Canaan by this route. Contemporary Englishmen can surely enter into such a possibility by imagining what might well happen if another world war were to break out on the Continent of Europe. Suppose that the British and allied forces were once again pushed by their enemies to the Channel ports. Suppose that once more little boats set out to operate a mass evacuation of troops. And suppose that once more hundreds of thousands of men were rescued in time, due in no small measure to quite abnormally fair weather. No Englishman would fail to understand a newspaper that printed a headline "Another Dunkirk". Surely a tribe, close-knit and history-conscious as the Israelite tribes were, would be capable of thinking "Another Red Sea", and of doing something to symbolize that inspiring historical insight.

Whatever we may say of this particular incident as history, there is no doubt about Hebrew historiography. It uses such a

[1] Joshua 3: 17; Exod. 14: 29

method extensively. The New Testament historians make frequent use of it in order to point out the significance of an event which they record, to indicate what they believed was "going on" in what they knew was "happening" in their history. Sometimes they use an actual historical event to express the meaning they discern, and the complex of events at the Exodus from Egypt is a favourite source for them. Elsewhere the New Testament writers will use a prophetic comment on history or a prophetic anticipation of history to indicate the meaning of a recorded event. If we find their historiography difficult we must not blame them. Their historiographical tools were suited to their day as well as to their task: it is our duty to understand their tools and their usages and so come to appreciate the meanings they meant to convey.

The function of all such historiographical devices is to point out what we have referred to as "identities": it is a way of saying: "This is really, at bottom, only that." We must not ourselves be so unimaginative as to suppose the sacred writers were affirming a merely phenomenal identity; there is clear evidence to the contrary. Sometimes historical details were "written up" to make such identity possible, but even then the real point was not in the mere repetition of historical detail, but in the identity of meaning which the repeated details were meant to signify. Thus in Joshua 3: 17 we read that "all Israel passed over [Jordan] on dry ground", a statement which echoes Exod. 14: 29: "the children of Israel walked upon dry land in the midst of the [Red] sea". The writer of Joshua means to affirm some identity of detail in the two historical events, not in and for itself, but only that the discerning reader might know what the historian knew, and believed the tribes crossing the Jordan knew—that at the Jordan the same God was working out the same deliverance of the same covenant people of God as He had wrought in the surpassing wonder at the Red Sea. We can see very plainly from the prophecies of Second Isaiah that such phenomenal identities are by no means the essence of such historiographical devices. This anonymous prophet addresses his fellows during their exile in Babylon, and he consistently seeks to persuade them that their captivity is shortly to be terminated by Cyrus, who, though a Gentile monarch, is nevertheless a servant of their own God. Many times Isaiah pictures what will happen on the way from Babylon back to Jerusalem, and each time he uses images drawn from their national history, from the story of their first journey from Egypt's slavery to Canaan's freedom. "When thou passest through the waters I will be with thee, and through the rivers, they shall not overflow thee: when thou walkest through the fire, thou shalt not be burned; neither shall the flame kindle upon thee" (Isa. 43: 2; cf. Exod. 14: 22, 29; 19: 21–24; 24: 17). "I will open rivers on the bare heights, and fountains in the midst of the valleys: I will make the wilderness a pool of water and the dry land springs of water" (Isaiah 41: 18; cf. Exod. 17: 1–8; 15: 23–25). Or again, in a passage predicting the fall of Babylon: "Thus saith the Lord, which maketh a path in the sea, and a path in the mighty waters: . . . Behold, I will do a new thing; now shall it spring forth; shall ye not know it? I will even make a way in the wilderness and rivers in the desert" (Isa. 43: 16, 19). It is quite clear that Second Isaiah used the phenomena of the first Exodus to predict the imminence and certainty of the second. But in doing this it is surely quite past belief that he really meant that each phenomenon would be literally reproduced. He knew very well, as one who had made the sad journey from Jerusalem to Babylon, that there was nothing equivalent to the Red Sea to be faced on the return. His use of the image is therefore not literal, but religious and theological. He intended his first hearers, as the compilers of the Bible meant us, to understand that there would be a deliverance from Babylon, and that in that happening the same thing would be going on as went on in the great deliverance at the Red Sea, and as went on in the various wonders during the years of wandering. In a word, the same God Jehovah would be securing the same salvation for his same people Israel.

In providing an illustration of an unmistakable "writing up" of an identification we pass to a New Testament assertion of a fulfilled prophecy. The instance is in Matthew's version of the Triumphal Entry into Jerusalem, where Matthew, in distinction from the other evangelists, reports that Jesus told his disciples to bring both an ass and her colt to Him. They did so, Matthew informs us, and Jesus (*per impossibile!*) rode on both

(Matt. 21: 1–7). It has been suggested that Matthew was either ignorant or careless of a principle of Hebrew poetry with which every first-year student of theology is familiar—the repetition, or near-repetition, of one idea in the two halves of a verse of poetry.

> "Declare his glory among the nations
> His marvellous works among all the peoples"
> (Ps. 96: 3.)

is a verse chosen at random, but it illustrates the feature admirably. The suggestion is that Matthew took as matter for literal phenomenal fulfilment what the ancient prophet-poet intended as poetry, and so introduced both an "ass" and a "colt, the foal of an ass", into his story of the Triumphal Entry. But that is surely to underestimate Matthew's capacity quite gratuitously; and, which is worse, seriously to misconceive his purpose. We need suppose no more than that Matthew wanted to ensure that his readers' attention would be fixed, not upon the singular achievement of riding two beasts at once, or upon the literal phenomenal identity between prophecy and fulfilment, but upon the identity of meaning between prophetic word and messianic action. It is highly probable that Jesus had many times ridden into Jerusalem on a donkey. This is not another such incident. This ride links up, not with the immediately preceding events, nor with previous rides (if any) into the capital, but with the hope of Zechariah's vision. The deliberate, premeditated act of Jesus constitutes a claim to Messiahship, and Messiahship of a certain kind. Matthew is not one whit interested in *Picture Post* reporting—"A Sunday Afternoon in the Life of Jesus"; he is concerned to demonstrate, by methods familiar to himself and his first readers, that the incidents of the first Palm Sunday are seen in their true depth and their right perspective only when the prophecy of Zechariah (9: 9, 10) is applied to them. A careless or uninstructed reader of Mark's Gospel might be excused if he mistook the story for just a story; Mark makes no explicit reference to Zechariah. When Matthew retells Mark's story, here and in other places, he tries to make sure that the real meaning is made explicit. This he does most frequently by introducing to Mark's material, or underlining in it, certain events or prophetic sayings which he believes are related to it, as we now say, "typologically".

We may, in the light of this examination, draw a not unimportant distinction in the New Testament use of typology. There are times when the identities pointed out belong undoubtedly to the historical occasion, as did the fact of Jesus riding into Jerusalem on a donkey provide an actual historical identity between the conceived hope of Zechariah and the action of Jesus. There are times when a "phenomenal" identity is applied to an event in order to emphasize an identity of meaning, as when Matthew writes of a colt and a foal. There are times when we cannot easily decide whether the typology is "real" or "applied". But in each of these three classes of typological allusion the fundamental intention remains the same—to assert an identity of meaning.

Typology is a matter of much contemporary debate. Many dispute the typological exegesis of Scripture which is offered by some modern interpreters: but none can dispute that the authors of Scripture used the device. It may not have been the only way open to them to indicate the meaning of the events they recorded, but it was certainly the most potent. For them it was historically and theologically indispensable. Historically so, because by an appeal to an event in the past whose meaning had already been fixed and set in the national memory, or to some hope or anticipation consciously cherished by the nation, they could tell their contemporaries the meaning of an event. Theologically indispensable because by an appeal to some event which the nation accepted as manifestly the activity of God, they could indicate in terms understood by all, their own conviction that God was also active in the events which they were recording. There is, of course, a limitation to the usefulness of this early device to communicate historical meaning—it was understood only by those who stood inside the national tradition that cherished the historical memories supplying the typological material. But history, at any rate history in the Bible, was written for those inside the life of one people—the people of God. Thus Matthew's intense concern that the prophecy of Zech. 9 should be applied to the story of the Triumphal Entry is enlightening only to those who stand within the

historical community of the "two" peoples of God—the Israel-
ites of the Old Testament and the Church of the New. And on
us who are less likely to understand fully the hope which
Zechariah expressed there falls a duty of becoming familiar
with the whole prophetic tradition and movement, if we are to
understand our New Testament narrative aright. Similarly
when Matthew reproduces at the beginning of his Gospel a
number of features lifted straight out of the story of the Exodus
under Moses, when God first called, gathered, chose and constituted His people, the meaning was doubtless plain to those
who were brought up in a tradition where such allusions would
be understood. To-day they seem quite "odd". Matthew tells
us, as he begins his story of Jesus, that there was a "descent into
Egypt" (2: 14), a "return from Egypt" (2: 21), a going down
into the waters and a coming out of them (3: 15–17), a sojourn
in the wilderness and a temptation (4: 1–11), a victorious entry
into the land of Promise (4: 12–25) and a giving of a New Law
(5: 1–7: 29). Dull indeed is the mind that knows the story of the
Old Israel even in bare outline, and yet cannot hear what
Matthew is saying in his typological allusions, viz.: "In the
events I am describing there was another Exodus, another, *the*
other, calling, gathering, choosing and constitution of the new
People of God." Of course the events forming the typological
reference do not exactly fit the story of the Gospel, but that is
no more than we have seen in Second Isaiah's use of the Exodus
phenomena. Matthew, for all his insistent assertion of a theological identity by typological allusion, is fully aware of the
newness of the Gospel story. The Sermon on the Mount leaves
us in no doubt about the transcendent newness and authority
inherent in the new act of God. Nevertheless there is a theological identity between the first Exodus of the Old Israel out
of Egypt and the New Exodus of the New Israel embodied in
the person of Jesus Christ.[1]

Typology may be inherently difficult. It may present very
considerable difficulties to modern scholars as they seek to
establish proper criteria for its detection and interpretation.
But it has this one manifest and immense advantage—it leaves

---

[1] cf. Matt. 2: 15: "Out of Egypt have I called my son." By "son" the prophet
Hosea (Hos. 11: 1) meant the people of God, Israel after the flesh.

history history. The difficulty for modern western man is that he is beset with metaphysical concepts and language. His speech and his ideas have largely come down to him from Greece and Rome; Israel has played but a small part in providing his intellectual equipment. Consequently when he tries to state what things mean he tends to seek some universal proposition, which will be applicable to all occasions and from which, therefore, the temporal, and therewith the historical, has disappeared. When Plato, Aristotle and Cicero discourse of God, their speech is abstract and their thinking metaphysical, logical, timeless. They say or conclude "God exists", or "God is good", and the proposition is held to be true at all times and places. But how different is the Hebrew mind! It does not discuss the existence of God, but affirms belief in Him, belief which is not just an intellectual assent to an argument and its conclusion, but a committal of the self to the providential care of a living, active God. It is, indeed, much more than that. The Hebrew does not characteristically profess belief in God, not even in a living God, nor yet in a God who acts. What is most characteristic of the Hebrew is that he proclaims specific mighty acts that God has done, and commits himself in trust and obedience to such a God.

Typology thus keeps faith with history in a way that no philosophy of history can. It brings no universal propositions to historical events, so rendering them, in some aspect at least, "timeless"; but it keeps the historical as the historical, and whether as event or hope or person, it will bring nothing but the historical to the interpretation of the historical. On the face of it, this is a weakness, for, as we have seen, we cannot reach meaning for one historical event by even an endlessly repeated reference to other historical events. Is not typology the historian's equivalent to "seeing faces in the fire"?—the fireside dreamer sees his faces, no doubt, but they belong to the ephemeral flame, and when the fire is out they are seen to have had no substance at all. Is not a similar fate reserved for typology, even if we accept it as a useful pointer to intra-historical identities? What is the significance of discovering typological affinities of historical occasions if in the end we find ourselves without any reference beyond the historical order itself? Is the historical order no more than the flame in whose ceaseless change we "see patterns" that are not real, even if they are "real to us"? Is history no more than the swirl of the waters of time's stream, in which we "see likenesses and forms" but which will in the end demonstrate our error to us in "bearing us away"? Can typology provide the extra-temporal, the extra-historical reference that is necessary if history itself is to have a meaning? Is not the Graeco-Roman way of philosophy to be preferred?— for it at least takes us outside the prison house of time.

But it would be foolish to be so persuaded. For one thing, philosophy invites us to pass from our imprisonment in time through the gate of one finite mind: and it may well prove to be, if we may continue the figure, that what the philosopher has done is no more than to paint a vast landscape on the walls of his prison cell. And for another, typology is by no means so impotent to bring the eternal to us as its consistent historicity suggests. To realize this we need only to examine the difference between an historical metaphor and a typological application. In the Trial scene in *The Merchant of Venice* Shylock is at first enthusiastic about the legal insight of "Balthazar", and greets Portia's apparent justification of his plea with the words:

> "A Daniel come to judgment: yea, a Daniel!
> O wise young judge, how I do honour thee!"

This is clearly "mere metaphor": "*A* Daniel come to judgment." Shylock is not in any way asserting an ontological or personal identity between the person known to Hebrew tradition as Daniel and the young "lawyer" whose gifts he wished to praise. Neither did Gratiano, who later mocked the Jew with his own metaphor, nor anyone else in the court, ever seriously imagine that the Daniel of Hebrew tradition was present or, by one party or the other, believed to be present. But contrast with this the attitude of Jesus and His contemporaries to Elijah. Elijah was, like Daniel, a figure in Hebrew history and tradition. According to the tradition, he not only had miraculous powers that really belonged to the Deity (such as that of resuscitation of life) during his lifetime, but his death was different from that of ordinary men.[1] He was therefore distinguished

[1] 2 Kings 2: 11

among the figures of Hebrew history in that he was expected to return, and his return, so Jewish tradition claimed, would herald the coming of God's promised Messiah. It is therefore plain that if we were to find some expectant Jews saying "An Elijah come to prophesy" we should at once see more in it than we could read into Shylock's metaphor; and it is unavoidable, if we are to be honest with such thinking, that we should have to suppose them to be asserting some kind of personal identity between the historic Elijah and their own contemporary.

Outside the Gospels Elijah is mentioned in the New Testament but twice,[1] and as both of these are ordinary references to an historical figure they need not concern us here. Thus we are left with the usages of the four evangelists for a study of the typological application of this Old Testament figure. It is doubtless difficult for us to imagine how Elijah could be thought of as "present" in the time of Jesus; but the evidence for this idea is irresistible. We may classify the Gospel usages into three main types. To the first we may assign the reports of the crucifixion in Mark and Matthew,[2] where, on the cross, Jesus cried out: "Eloi, Eloi, lama sabachthani?" Some of the bystanders, when they heard this, said: "Behold, he calleth for Elijah," and they waited to see if Elijah would come to take Him down from the cross. This is not an actual identification of Elijah as present in a time long after his "historical" existence, but it serves to show that there was a well-known and accepted belief that Elijah could appear in person and even intervene with supernatural power in some historical episode. Such a belief is incorporated, without any self-consciousness, in the story of the Transfiguration, which constitutes the second class of references to Elijah. The story presents many difficulties for the sophisticated critic of the twentieth century, but if we try to enter into the thought world of the evangelists and the disciples, it is clear that for them it was not an impossible way of talking about a transcendent religious experience to say that they had seen Jesus and Moses and Elijah together on some Galilean hill. That is the "phenomenal" record they give of their experience. Its reality and intention is that they understood and the evangelist wants us to understand that there was a real identity

[1] Rom. 11:2; James 5: 17   [2] Mark 15: 34; Matt. 27: 46

between Moses and Elijah on the one hand and Jesus on the other. If men's eyes were to be opened to see the reality of the incarnate Son in a way that conveyed meaning to them they would see Him in this illuminating and revealing identification —law and prophecy are both fulfilled in Him. Indeed, we may think that law and prophecy were singularly joined in both the companions of Jesus on the Mountain, for Deuteronomy says of Moses the great law-giver that "there hath not arisen a prophet since in Israel like unto Moses, whom the Lord knew face to face"; and Elijah, the first of the great prophets, was clearly a great reviver of Mosaic religion, the initiator of that school of religious reformation that eventually found expression in the avowedly Mosaic reform of Josiah.[1] At the Transfiguration Elijah was present, and the significance is surely that his work and that of Jesus are really one.

The third class of reference to Elijah may be instanced, strangely enough, by Matthew's account of what took place coming down from the Mount of Transfiguration. In common with Mark, Matthew tells of a question the disciples put to Jesus: "Why then say the scribes that Elijah must first come?"[2] The question is intelligible only if we suppose that the disciples are now convinced, by what they have seen and heard on the Mount of Transfiguration, that Jesus is the hoped-for Messiah. Elijah, according to the traditional interpretation of Malachi 4: 6,[3] would appear before Messiah and restore everything to God's ordering, so that the world should be ready for Messiah's reign. How can Jesus be Messiah if Elijah has not come and fulfilled his predicted role? The answer Jesus gives in both Mark and Matthew is capable of the same answer in principle, though Mark's text has some difficulties of its own. Jesus replies that Elijah has come, but that he was not recognized as such and that instead of acting as the great reformer to prepare for Messiah's reign, he prepares for it in quite another way. They "did unto him whatsoever they listed" he goes on to say. This refers back to what the "Old Israel" intended to do to the historical

---

[1] 2 Kings 18: 4　　　　　　　　[2] Matt. 17: 10

[3] "Behold, I will send you Elijah the prophet before the great and terrible day of the Lord come. And he shall turn the heart of the fathers to the children, and the heart of the children to their fathers."

Elijah—Jezebel sought to have him killed. But when Elijah came a second time and was not recognized, the "old Israel" at last had its way with him and put him to death. Salome achieved what Jezebel failed to do, but in his death the second Elijah had pointed more clearly than he knew to the Messiah, and to the way He must take to ascend His throne. It was no wonder that Matthew could add what Mark does not report: "Then understood the disciples that he spake to them of John the Baptist." Here typological identification is explicit and complete; and, whether in the minds of disciples or in the view of the evangelist, is a perfectly natural way of seeing and experiencing the meaning of historical occasions.

The remaining references to Elijah are of this kind. Sometimes Jesus is Himself identified with Messiah's herald. When Herod heard of what Jesus was doing, he imagined that John the Baptist had returned from the dead. "But," Mark tells us, "others said, It is Elijah."[1] Similarly when Jesus asked the Twelve with whom men had identified Him ("Who do men say that I am?") they tell Him "John the Baptist: and others, Elijah."[2] Sometimes John the Baptist is identified with the ancient prophet, though the one direct statement is ascribed (surely with some probability) to Jesus, when Matthew reproduces His witness to John: "And if ye are willing to receive it, this is Elijah, which is to come."[3] Luke reports a similar identification in the message of the angel to Zacharias about the son who is to be given him: "He shall go before his face in the spirit and power of Elijah. . . ."[4] The only other reference in the Synoptics is made by Luke in his record of the preaching in the Synagogue at Nazareth. While it may be granted that the dominant motive of the references there to Elijah and Elisha was in all probability a desire to pave the way for the Gentile Mission recorded in Acts, it is surely also in keeping to suppose that the reference to Elijah and Elisha, who received a double portion of Elijah's spirit, was connected with Jesus' claim, made explicit on other occasions, that His own Messiahship was in some sense authenticated because Elijah had now been sent again in the person of John the Baptist.

There are but two references to Elijah in John. They both

---

[1] Mark 6: 15   [2] Mark 8: 27   [3] Matt. 11: 14   [4] Luke 1: 17

point to the same identificatory character of typology, though they take a different view of the person of John the Baptist. But, as many scholars have observed, John is anxious, for quite new reasons, to make it plain that the Baptist made no claims that could in any way be thought to rival those of the one who came after him. So it is not surprising that when the priests and levites asked him "Art thou Elijah?" he should reply, "I am not."[1] Nor is that answer inconsistent with the typological identification made by Jesus. It is not given to ordinary men to know the place and meaning of their own lives in the divine economy. That is an insight reserved for very few indeed.

We may conclude, then, that typology is a species of historical identification between events which either indicates or applies phenomenal identities between events in order to indicate their identity in meaning. This does not mean that the typologist historian abstracts from history some timeless truth or principle which the historical order merely illustrates. On the contrary, typology involves quite a different relationship of the eternal to the historical. As we have seen, Biblical typology is concerned to identify for man the historical acts by which God has wrought his salvation. This is the real purpose behind the typological use of the Exodus events in the Old Testament. Whether the historian records the crossing of the Jordan, or whether the prophet anticipates a return of exiles from Babylon to Jerusalem, the fundamental thing to which expression is given is the amazing belief that the same God who wrought a wonder at the Red Sea is at work again now, at the selfsame work of the redemption of the world. In any historical occasion we can know only "in part", as Paul put it; yet, by the aid of typological illumination, we are enabled to see beyond and beneath the phenomena of the present into the fullness and depth of what God is doing. But the same is true of the New Testament. All the evangelists write their account of the crucifixion with at least some help from the typological allusions provided by the Exodus from Egypt. In the Synoptic Gospels the Last Supper is a Passover meal, and since it appears that even before the disciples asked Jesus about it He had made preparations for it, and since He uses the festival meal to inaugurate a new feast of

[1] John 1: 21

the fulfilled, the real "Passover", we cannot but suppose that the Synoptics are trying to tell us both that the first Exodus is the antitype of the second and that the typological relation derives from Jesus Himself. John tells us that Jesus died as the Passover lambs were being slaughtered. Again it is clear that the evangelist is telling us that the Exodus typology applies; and further, since Jesus Himself initiates the moves that ensure His being crucified at that particular time, we may assume that John, too, conceives this typological connection to have a dominical origin.

But whatever the origin, the content is for the moment the more important thing. The use of typology in the Bible is not just a device of patriotic historians, but the witness of prophetic insight into the revealing and saving acts of God. The writer of the Book of Joshua is doing more than shout "another Exodus"; he is confessing his belief and trust in one God who is active for the salvation of man in His historical actions that, for all their differences, and indeed in them, are essentially one in meaning and content. The prophet of the Exile who prophesied a return to Jerusalem is not simply promising his fellow-captives another return through a desert to Palestine; he is, like the author of Joshua, asserting the unity of God's salvation and revelation, the unity of God Himself, in and through the acknowledgedly different historical occasions. So with the New Testament. The Synoptists are not simply saying "another Exodus" when they depict the cross partly in Exodus terms; they are saying "here is the same God, the same revelation, the same salvation, the same fundamental 'thing that is going on' in these otherwise markedly different and temporally separated events". So all the typology of the Bible is theological. If typology is written in the lines of the narrative, then theology and religious trust and faith are therewith written "between the lines". He who runs may read.

But clearly typology of this sort is possible only if there be already one event which has been recognized as God's action, and, therefore, as more than historical, in the sense that it asserts the reality and activity of supra-temporal, supra-historical agents. But how did the first action of God come to be known? The answer is that somewhere, at some time, God's action must have been known for what it was without any previous reference. If historical events are to be explained and understood typologically, there must be one not so known and explained, or else the series of theological interpretations could never begin. This need not trouble the Biblical reader unduly. For it is plain that, in the Old Testament, Moses is the person who is given an insight into events which is contemporaneous with them. This explains the stories of Moses' leadership which occasioned so much murmuring by the people. He had been given to know the meaning and reality of the Exodus, to know what was to "go on" in it, even before it happened. The people did not know, and would not fully believe and trust what Moses taught them; hence their "rebelliousness". The same witness is borne by the great and decisive position accorded to Moses in Hebrew tradition. He is credited with legislation that could not have derived save from a settled civilization; he is called the greatest of the prophets—a double tribute to this insight which he was granted into the meaning of the Exodus before it happened and as it took place. His knowledge of the fundamental meaning of this event was not derived by any identification with a past event, but came before and with the event itself. He did not need to wait for time to put it into perspective but saw what were the basic meanings as they were enacted. Or, to use Deuteronomic language, "the Lord knew him face to face".[1]

Moses' presence at the Transfiguration may well indicate, among other things, that Jesus in the New Covenant has the same place as Moses in the Old. Whatever may be said of the historicity of the predictions of the Passion in the Synoptics, or the conscious awareness of His fate from the very start of the Fourth Gospel, Jesus is clearly presented as knowing His destiny and discerning its meaning quite a time before it was upon Him. Recent studies of Christ's teaching on His death have largely emphasized this anew. But is New Testament typology different from the Old? Assuredly: for in the New Testament all the antitypes of the Old Testament are present in the Type Himself. The events of the past certainly throw light on those of the New Testament and show them to be acts of God: but

[1] Deut. 34: 10

E

they are also transcended there, because in the incarnation of Jesus Christ we have not only a revelatory event, not only an act of God, but God Himself present and acting, the very presence of the saviour-revealer to complete and fulfil the salvation of the world.

God's salvation, however, is wrought in history; and therefore, only as history permits. That God lets history remain history is clear from the very fact of incarnation. And because God acts in history when He accomplishes our salvation, time is not ended, history goes on. We are not yet in God's eternal kingdom. And yet, such is the meaning of Biblical typology, when we at last reach the final and eternal kingdom we shall find its reality the same that we have known, believed, loved, adored and obeyed *sub specie historiae* as our Lord and Saviour, Jesus Christ. This is the final consequence of the Bible's refusal to find meanings for history in metaphysical propositions, but to see them only in other events. The event which gives meaning to all that goes before and all that comes after, the event which is the meaning of all other events, is this central event of the presence of Jesus Christ as historical man in history. Once the cross has taken place it is the reference of meaning backwards for us, and forward for the Jews. Paul tells us that the reality of our baptism is that we died with Christ and were raised with Him to newness of life. He tells us that we have been "made to sit with Him in the heavenly places"[1]—so complete is the typological application of His life to ours. Our life is hid with Him in God. We seem to our fellows to have the reality of our life with them in this visible, tangible, audible world; in fact, its reality is where Christ is—with death past and victory won, at the right hand of the majesty on high.

So we claim that Christ is the reality of both events before and events after His incarnation. And that statement must be taken in full historical and ontological seriousness. It is doubtless a persistent difficulty for human minds to understand how Christ could be a known reality, even before His incarnation. But there are considerations which may help us to understand how that could be. For one thing, we must rid ourselves of the notion that the difference between Old and New Dispensations

[1] Eph. 2: 6

can be put like this: that before the incarnation no one could see Christ because He had not been born: therefore no one could know Him: that during His incarnate life He could be seen because He had been born, and so men could know Him: and that after the incarnation, because He was born, seen, known, and written and spoken of, we may know Him as a figure of history. We must remind ourselves that Jesus Christ has never been known as such by ordinary sight. When Peter, who had "seen" Him for some time, confessed Him as Christ, Jesus replied (according to Matthew): "Blessed art thou, Simon bar-Jonah, for flesh and blood hath not revealed it unto thee, but my Father which is in heaven." Paul says that none can confess that Jesus is Lord save by the Holy Spirit. The story of the man born blind in John 9 shows how impotent mere sight is. He received sight from Jesus "that the works of God should be made manifest in him."[1] The work of God is more than physical sight, and the evangelist skilfully develops the quality of vision. The man's first comment on the "miracle" was "I went away and washed, and I received sight."[2] When he was questioned about Jesus who healed him, he said: "He is a prophet—"[3] a confession which joins Jewish theology to his own experience. This same combination of sight and Judaism produced the further assertion that Jesus must be from God, or He could work no such wonder on a man born blind.[4] That led to his excommunication. Then *the* miracle happens. Jesus seeks the man again and asks him whether he believes on the Son of God. The man replies that he does not know who he is. Jesus then answers: "Thou hast both seen him, and he is talking with thee." The man worships Him. And that is the miracle—that this man could see a figure who to normal eyes was quite rightly a Nazarene carpenter, an itinerant evangelist, a stirrer-up of trouble, or what not, but who to the eye of faith, to the eye of faith alone, was the veritable Son of God.

The same situation persists, with the necessary modifications, until this day. Two men read the Scriptures, or hear a sermon: the one is "converted" and confesses Jesus Christ as Lord, the other remains untouched. The difference between B.C. and A.D. is not that B.C. could not see Him but A.D. can; rather

[1] John 9: 3   [2] John 9: 11–15   [3] John 9: 17   [4] John 9: 32, 33

are we all B.C., religiously and theologically speaking, until God has "manifested His work in us". Are we to say, then, that God did not do His work upon great prophets and the humble faithful of the old dispensation? Surely not. They knew Christ in expecting Him; not indeed as they might have known Him had they seen Him in the days of His flesh (though they might well have failed to see Him then!) but really and in the depth of knowledge. The prophets and patriarchs may not have been able to describe what the Incarnate Lord looked like in His appearing in history: we are no better than they in that respect. But they did know that He would come, as we know that He has come, and as some confessed that He had come during His own historical lifetime. They did not know "all" about Him, but neither do we, nor did His contemporaries. But they knew Him well enough to trust Him in His future coming. And dying in that faith, they may be said to have "fallen asleep in Christ". But how far can we push this kind of argument? It seems necessary to answer: "as far as we may find identities of meaning between Christ's coming at the Incarnation and the histories of men." That, at any rate, is the principle on which John wrote the Prologue to his Gospel, and in it the presence of the Eternal Word is traced back through history, through the act of creation to the very eternity of God.

But another set of considerations helps us to understand how we may think of knowing Christ before the Incarnation. Our quite ordinary and short-term anticipation of events can be either fairly rich in content or almost devoid of it. In the years between 1933 and 1939 I believed that another war was inevitable though I worked as I could to obviate it. Others shared the view. And as the years went by the "shape of things to come" became clearer. Yet when it came the reality was different from all our expectations: indeed some of them looked almost comic beside the reality. And yet we all had apprehended beforehand the reality which was the world war of 1939-45. Some of our knowledge was false—but so it was during the war, and so it is still! This does not put aside the difference that historical occurrence makes, but it lets us see that knowledge can be called knowledge quite properly in advance of as well as alongside of or even past historical occurrence. Or again, we may remind ourselves of the way in which we know any historical person or movement. If we know Mr. X as a baby we really know him, and we may speculate—as we do—upon his future: the older he grows the more, for a time, will our anticipations increase. The flow of events will prove us right or wrong; but if we are wrong we shall not say we never knew Mr. X as a child. So it would be improper to argue that because the knowledge of Christ is anticipatory knowledge it is not knowledge at all. It is knowledge which must wait upon the passage of events for its verification or falsification.

But with all this said, it is necessary to point out that we do not think ourselves to have made the Christological interpretation of the Old Testament an easy or an automatic thing. In the Old Testament and in the New there are persons and occasions over against which He appears as Judge and yet which can occur only, in a real sense, in Him, by His will and for His purpose. But what we have done is to point to a certain general outlook, certain principles by which we believe ourselves to have shown that Christ was not only an expectation, to be known in reality in the future, but that He was really present, though His full nature and the full wonder of His work for man could only be revealed in its completeness in the incarnation. Our gain may seem trivial and verbal; but the issue is whether we are to have a Christ who is an unique intrusion into history, with no other historical occasions which by way of typological identity can illuminate the wonder for us, or a Christ who is the reality of the whole extraordinary process of history with all its light and shade, joy and sorrow, life and death. We have not tried to give examples of exegesis on this basis, but they can be provided. And the more one comes to understand even the "strange" things of the Old Testament the more one is impressed by the extraordinary foresight and insight which the authors showed in recording what they did and as they did. To avoid quoting a personal and therefore possibly subjective example, we may remind ourselves how even the strange and arbitrary-sounding word of God "I loved Jacob, but Esau I hated" becomes a pointer forward to the unmerited grace and forgiveness of God, a power that, for all its seeming arbitrariness in history, is part of God's plan to include both all Israel and the fullness of the Gentiles in His salvation in Christ.[1] Doubtless the principles we have enunciated require to be tested in actual exegesis; but it would have been open to equal objection had we tried exegesis without first stating the principles. Both could not be done in one essay and we have chosen to deal with what we believe to be the prior issue.

But, however much we emphasize the reality of Christ in the Old Testament, we can never turn the Old Testament into the New. On the contrary, it is only if we can affirm that the substance of both Testaments is the same that we can have both an Old Testament and a New comprising the one Christian Bible. The only alternative to this, as the Church has known since the days of Marcion, is to have, in effect, two different Bibles, a Jewish and a Christian. But all through its history, from Clement of Rome to Calvin of Geneva, from Barnabas to Karl Barth, the Church has insisted, and rightly insisted, that, though the administration is different, the substance of the two covenants is one and the same.

[1] cf. Rom. 9–11.

2

THE WITNESS OF
THE NEW TESTAMENT TO CHRIST

by C. E. B. CRANFIELD

Lecturer in Theology, University of Durham

THE WITNESS OF THE NEW TESTAMENT TO CHRIST

by

C. E. B. CRANFIELD

The witness of the New Testament to Christ is summed up concisely in the primitive confession contained in Rom. 10: 9; 1 Cor. 12: 3: "Jesus is Lord" (cf. 2 Cor. 4: 5; Phil. 2: 11; Col. 2: 6; also 1 Cor. 8: 6).

I

JESUS NAZARENUS

WHEN the early Christians confessed that *Jesus* was Lord, they were speaking about someone who had lived in Palestine in the reigns of the Emperors Augustus and Tiberius (being distinguished from other bearers of what was then a common name among the Jews by the mention of His home town) and had been put to death by the governor of Judea, Pontius Pilate. The fact that the name Jesus occurs well over a thousand times in the New Testament, and in every book with the single exception of 3 John, is itself an indication that the New Testament witness to Christ is inextricably bound up with the memory of this particular historic life. Specially important in this connection are the historical passages of the speeches in the earlier chapters of Acts. In other parts of the New Testament this testimony to the historic Jesus is all the time implicit, and again and again it becomes explicit in touches which are often all the more significant for being almost accidental. (The Epistle of James, which at first sight seems an exception, is perhaps to be explained as a consciously marginal comment, in which the author has purposely avoided saying things he knew he would be expected to say in the hope of thereby startling the Gospel-hardened complacence of those who made pious professions all too easily while denying them by their lives.) But, while the whole New Testament clearly points

73

to the historic Jesus, only the Gospels purport to give the history concerning Him in any fullness.

But what of the validity of this claim of the Gospels to give us *history*? It must be said at once that in them we see Jesus not through the coldly objective depositions of neutral observers but through the testimony of people who believed Him to be the Son of God. An element of interpretation is thus involved. Most apparent in the fourth, it is also present in the first three Gospels. Compare, for instance, Mark 1: 1 with John 20: 31. The Gospels were written from the point of view of faith—the faith that Jesus is Lord. It is also true that there is a gap of some thirty-five years between the events recorded and the writing of the earliest of our Gospels. In view of these two facts, can this claim to give history be sustained?

It is well known, of course, that according to Dr. Bultmann and others a great deal of the narrative material is legend and ideal construction, many of the sayings attributed to Jesus are similarly the creation of the primitive community, and, while the Gospels are evidence for the faith and interests of the early Church, of the historic Jesus we can now know next to nothing.[1] But there are many considerations which lead other scholars[2] to believe that the Gospels do give us a substantially reliable picture of the historic Jesus, among them: the survival of eye-witnesses, hostile as well as believing, throughout the oral tradition period; the prominence in the New Testament of the idea of witness, implying that the community was conscious of the obligation to tell the truth (their sense of responsibility in the matter is illustrated by 1 Cor. 7, where Paul distinguishes more than once between that for which he has the authority of a definite word of the Lord and that which he is saying on his own account: it was all the greater because they believed it was about God's mighty acts that they were speaking, as 1 Cor. 15: 15 indicates); the fact that the main outline of events must have been constantly repeated in preaching and liturgy—especially the story of the Passion; the easily memorable form of much of Jesus' teaching; the fact that the Church grew up inside the Jewish community with its long-standing tradition of oral preser-

[1] cf. R. Bultmann, *Jesus and the Word* (Eng. trans. 1935), p. 8.
[2] e.g. C. H. Dodd, W. Manson, V. Taylor.

vation and transmission of rabbis' teaching by their pupils; the
tradition of Mark's association with Peter which is not just to be
ignored; the respect shown by the later evangelists for Mark's
Gospel, which we should hardly expect if the Christian community was really as creative of material as Dr. Bultmann would
have us believe; and the presence of material which by its very
nature not only authenticates itself but also goes a long way
toward guaranteeing the general reliability of the tradition and
the frankness and honesty of the early Church, e.g. material dis-
creditable to Peter and the other apostles, and sayings of Jesus
like His admission of ignorance of the date of the Parousia or
the cry of dereliction on the cross, which we know perplexed
and embarrassed the early Church.

These and other considerations are enough, we believe, to
justify us in thinking that by and large at any rate the Gospels
give us history and that Dr. Bultmann's historical scepticism is
not so much the result of a rigorously scientific as of a thoroughly doctrinaire approach. He has made the evidence fit his
presuppositions by a wholesale use of the methods of Procrustes.
The nature of these presuppositions has been made abundantly
clear by the culmination of his work in the much-discussed
demythologizing project, according to which the "mythological" features of the New Testament message which he supposes to be unacceptable to the modern man are to be reinter-
preted non-mythologically in such a way that, while the essential offence of the Gospel will remain, what Bultmann regards
as unnecessary offences will be eliminated. But, while it is a
little naïve to assume that one's own world-view is *the* world-
view of the century, it is extremely rash to make the world-
view of any century the criterion of how God must have acted.

To reject, for example, the miracles out of hand is too rigid
and dogmatic a procedure to be truly scientific. Since there is
good reason to suppose that the Gospels embody a tradition
derived from honest and responsible and not unintelligent
people, and since there is—for the most part at any rate—a
notable reserve about the miracles attributed to Jesus (contrast
the apocryphal gospels!), it seems more reasonable to accept
their historicity generally, while allowing for the possibility of a
heightening of the miraculous here and there.

With regard to the Incarnation, Resurrection and Ascension, it is important to distinguish between the event itself and the accompanying outward sign or signs. Whereas the last, though miraculous, was witnessed by men, the first was unseen of human eyes and, so to speak, of an altogether different texture from the rest of history and therefore not verifiable by ordinary historical methods. To fail to distinguish between the unseen event and the accompanying sign leads to serious misunderstandings. For instance, to identify the outward sign related in Acts 1: 9–11 with the Ascension itself is to make of the Ascension merely an upward journey through space. But, while it is important to recognize that these events are of an altogether different texture from the rest of history, it is also essential to recognize their historicity in the sense that they actually happened at particular times.

It is also important to recognize picture-language as such. The New Testament is using picture-language when it speaks, for example, of the Son sitting at the Father's right hand. This Calvin saw clearly. "A similitude borrowed from princes" is his comment, and "the subject here considered is not the position of His body, but the majesty of His empire".[1] Here is a legitimate demythologizing! But this is one thing. To deny that the Incarnation, Resurrection and Ascension actually took place is quite another. If that is what Bultmann is doing—and it certainly seems to be—then it must be said (humbly and with all due respect for the undoubted sincerity of his motives and for his great ability, but at the same time quite firmly and bluntly) that he is preaching "a different gospel, which is not another gospel";[2] for "if Christ hath not been raised, then is our preaching vain, your faith also is vain".[3] The demythologized Gospel is not the heart of Christianity, but rather a Christianity from which the heart is gone, and to welcome it is not to enter upon a brave new freedom but to return to a quite old-fashioned and unromantic bondage.

But our opposition to Dr. Bultmann must not mislead us into glossing over the gaps, ambiguities, disconnectedness and discrepancies of the Gospel material. These we ought neither to exaggerate with Bultmann, nor deny with the "fundamental-

[1] *Inst.* II, 16, 15   [2] Gal. 1: 6 f.   [3] 1 Cor. 15: 14

ists", nor seek to by-pass, as do some "Biblical theologians" who are apt to fancy that to ask what is the theological meaning of an episode is an excuse for ignoring the question of historicity. The New Testament insistence that the Word really became flesh itself compels us to seek to know the historical truth as exactly as possible. Only where the historical problems are wrestled with, in proper seriousness, does their theological significance become apparent. The scantiness and scrappiness of the record are of a piece with the indirectness of the revelation itself (that Messianic hiddenness to which we shall have to refer later), which, while summoning men to decision, at the same time left them sufficient room in which to make a personal decision, without which faith would be impossible. Moreover, these gaps, ambiguities, etc., are a means by which the Lord of the Church maintains His freedom over against us, keeping the Word which is His sceptre in His own hand and not allowing it to fall under our control.

DOMINUS JESUS

That Jesus was sometimes addressed by His disciples during His ministry as *mari* (my lord) or *maran(a)* (our lord) seems to be indicated by Matt. 7:21 = Luke 6:46; but used in the vocative this was a respectful form of address that need not mean any more than "teacher", "rabbi", "sir". Whether the word was actually used of Him in the third person during His ministry is uncertain—Mark 11: 3 may or may not be an instance. But it is quite certain that, after the Resurrection, "Lord" (no longer in the weak sense the vocative can have) became the characteristic title of the exalted Jesus. The Gospels here and there reflect this post-Resurrection use. In Acts the title is frequent. In Paul it occurs well over two hundred times, no other name for Jesus being anything like so common. It is used in all the other books of the New Testament except Titus and 1, 2 and 3 John.

That the use of the title did not originate with Paul is suggested by its occurrence in the early speeches in Acts, and is confirmed by its appearance in the earliest of Paul's letters without any hint that it is an innovation, by his use of it in credal formulae (e.g. Rom. 10: 9), in a name for the eucharist

(1 Cor. 11: 20), in what appears to be a liturgical fragment
(Phil. 2: 6–11), and in a passage where he expressly says he is
repeating what he himself has received (1 Cor. 11: 23 ff.), and
also by the preservation of the Aramaic liturgical formula
Marana tha (1 Cor. 16: 22). This last piece of evidence is the
rock on which the theory that the title was first used in the
Greek-speaking church at Antioch comes to grief. A further
important indication that the title belongs to a very early stage
is the extraordinarily widespread use of Ps. 110: 1—it is quoted
or referred to in the New Testament more often than any other
Old Testament passage.

If we ask what it was that caused "Lord" to become the
characteristic title of Jesus, the answer must certainly be that
the decisive fact was the certainty of the disciples that Jesus had
been raised from the dead and exalted (cf. Acts 2: 32–36;
Rom. 10: 9, 14: 9; and also Matt. 28: 18, where "all authority"
is the correlate of lordship). The fourth evangelist's use of the
word suggests that he may have felt it appropriate to refer to
Jesus as "Lord" after the Resurrection but not before. That
Jesus had actually quoted Ps. 110: 1 with reference to Himself
during His ministry (Mark 12: 35 ff., 14: 62) may have helped
to encourage the post-Resurrection use of the title.

The significance the title had for the first Christians is shown
by the fact that they prayed to Jesus. Christians may in fact be
referred to as those "that call upon the name of our Lord Jesus
Christ".[1] Stephen addresses to Jesus in Acts 7: 59 f. two peti-
tions closely similar to those which Jesus had Himself addressed to God (Luke 23: 34 longer reading and 23: 46), while
Paul again and again joins the name of Jesus with that of God
(e.g. 1 Cor. 1: 3, 8: 6; 2 Cor. 1: 2). It was therefore not un-
natural that Old Testament passages in which *Kyrios* stood in
the LXX for the divine name *YHWH* should be referred to the
exalted Jesus. So "the day of the LORD" (e.g. Amos 5: 18;
Joel 2: 31) is used in 1 Thess. 5: 2; 2 Thess. 2: 2 of the expected
Parousia of Jesus; the prophet's promise that "whosoever shall
call on the name of the LORD shall be delivered"[2] is understood to refer to calling on the name of Jesus (Rom. 10: 13);
and the statement, "unto me (i.e. *YHWH*) every knee shall

---

[1] 1 Cor. 1: 2 cf. Acts 9: 14   [2] Joel 2: 32

bow, every tongue swear",[1] is refashioned: "that in the name of Jesus every knee should bow . . . and that every tongue should confess that Jesus Christ is Lord, to the glory of God the Father."[2] Compare also 1 Pet. 3: 15 with Isa. 8: 13, 29: 23 and Rev. 17: 14, 19: 16 with Deut. 10: 17. So too in Rev. 1: 17 f., 22: 13, formulae based on Isa. 41: 4, 44: 6, 48: 12, are applied to Jesus. From the above examples it becomes clear why the name *Kyrios* which has been given to the exalted Jesus is referred to as "the name which is above every name";[3] it is because it is God's own name. In the LXX it is used more than six thousand times to represent *YHWH*, and when used in a religious connection is exclusively used of the true God.[4] To sum up this section we may say that the New Testament confession "Jesus is Lord" ascribes to the exalted Jesus the name, holiness (1 Pet. 3: 15), majesty (Rev. 17: 14), authority (Matt. 28: 18) and eternity (Rev. 1: 17) of God.

We must now attempt to draw out its implications more fully.

II

CUM ESSET DIVES

The New Testament witness to Jesus Christ is witness to One who was from all eternity. It declares that He whom men knew as Jesus of Nazareth did not originate in His mother's womb, but had from all eternity shared the life of God. The "yesterday" of Heb. 13: 8 refers not merely to the historic life of Jesus but to a pre-existence without beginning.

Pre-existence is probably implied by Jesus' self-designation "Son of Man"; for in Eth. Enoch 48: 2 ff., 62: 7, the Son of Man is apparently a pre-existent heavenly being. It is perhaps also implied by the sayings beginning "I came" or "the Son of Man came" (e.g. Mark 2: 17, 10: 45; Matt. 5: 17, 10: 34 f.; Luke 12: 49, 19: 10; cf. the variant readings at Matt. 18: 11; Luke 9: 56).

That Paul asserts the pre-existence of Christ is clear from such passages as "For ye know the grace of our Lord Jesus Christ, that, though he was rich, yet for your sakes he became

---

[1] Isa. 45: 23   [2] Phil. 2: 10 f.
[3] Phil. 2: 9   [4] cf. G. Quell in Kittel's *TWzNT*, 3, 1057.

poor . . .";[1] "Christ Jesus, who, being in the form of God, counted it not a prize to be on an equality with God, but emptied himself . . .";[2] and "who is the image of the invisible God, the firstborn of all creation; for in him were all things created . . .; all things have been created through him, and unto him; and he is before all things, and in him all things consist".[3]

So also the writer to the Hebrews can speak of the "Son, whom he appointed heir of all things, through whom also he made the worlds . . ." (1: 2) and apply Ps. 102: 25 to Jesus: "Thou, Lord, in the beginning hast laid the foundation of the earth, and the heavens are the works of thy hands" (1: 10). And the author of the Fourth Gospel can say: "In the beginning was the Word, and the Word was with God, and the Word was God. The same was in the beginning with God. All things were made by him; and without him was not anything made . . ." (1: 1–3) and represent Jesus as speaking of "the glory which I had with thee before the world was" (17: 5).

That it is the pre-existence of the Divine Subject of the Incarnation and not the pre-existence of Jesus Christ as man that is meant is fairly clear. But it is to be noted that the New Testament does actually refer to the Son of God in His pre-Incarnation existence as "Jesus Christ" (e.g. 2 Cor. 8: 9; Phil. 2: 5; Heb. 13: 8), and this has its justification in the fact that from all eternity the Son of God was He who in the eternal plan of the Triune God should in the fullness of time take upon Him human nature. In God's foreknowledge He was already that which He was to become. So it comes about that Rev. 13: 8 can refer to "the Lamb that hath been slain from the foundation of the world".[4]

EGENUS FACTUS

But "the Word became flesh" (John 1: 14). The ground (διό) of Christ's exaltation in Phil. 2: 9 is His prior self-abase-

---

[1] 2 Cor. 8: 9

[2] Phil. 2: 5–7. The suggestion that this does not refer to the pre-existent life seems to the present writer most unlikely.

[3] Col. 1: 15–17; cf. 1 Cor. 8: 6

[4] On the subject matter of this paragraph see the discussion in Barth, *Kirchl. Dogm.* III/2, 580–2

ment. The New Testament bears witness to a condescension of ineffable graciousness, the descent of the Son of God from the glory which He had with His Father before the world was, to the very lowest depths of human suffering and shame. This downward movement, indicated in 2 Cor. 8: 9 by the pregnant expression "became poor" and traced in more detail in Phil. 2: 6–8 in language strongly reminiscent of Isa. 52: 13–53: 12, was a real and thorough-going self-identification with sinful men. The words "became flesh" mean that, without ceasing to be God, He took upon Himself not a human nature uncorrupted by man's fall, but the selfsame human nature that is ours, that is, a fallen human nature.[1] It was with that altogether unpromising material—what Paul calls σάρξ ἁμαρτίας (Rom. 8: 3)—that He wrought out His perfect obedience to the Father, being "in all points tempted like as we are, yet without sin".[2] "Became flesh" and "became poor" are not adequately interpreted unless we go as far as this.

His obedience was the obedience of the Servant who "bare the sin of many"[3] and on whom "the LORD hath laid the iniquity of us all".[4] (See especially 1 Pet. 2: 21–25.) It involved not only death, but death under the curse of God (Gal. 3: 13; Deut. 21: 23). The cry of dereliction (Mark 15: 34) is not to be glossed over or explained away: it denotes a real abandonment by God endured by Christ on our behalf and in our stead (though to assert this is not to deny that the unity of the Blessed Trinity was even then unbroken). And the burial is the seal on that abandonment—the becoming a mere thing carried about and put away out of men's sight. The cup of God's wrath was not removed from Him (Mark 14: 36; Isa. 51: 17 ff.): He had to drink it to the dregs.

Why? The New Testament gives a clear answer. It was "for your sakes . . . , that ye through his poverty might become rich",[5] or "that he might bring us to God",[6] or, in His own words, "the Son of man came . . . to minister, and to give his life a ransom for many".[7] (Compare also Mark 14: 24; Luke 19: 10; John 1: 29; 3: 14–16, 10: 10 f., 11: 51, etc.)

A necessary part of His self-abasement on our behalf was that

---

[1] cf. Barth, *op. cit.* I/2, 167–9   [2] Heb. 4: 15   [3] Isa. 53: 12
[4] Isa. 53: 6   [5] 2 Cor. 8: 9   [6] 1 Pet. 3: 18   [7] Mark 10: 45

F

He should lay aside every externally compelling evidence of His divine glory, everything in the way of a proof, and submit Himself to a situation in which His claim to authority could only appear to the world problematic and paradoxical. Thereby men were placed in a position of crisis but given sufficient room in which to make a personal decision.[1] Thus Jesus resists the temptation to provide a display of divine power (Matt. 4: 5–7), rejects the request for a sign (Mark 8: 11 f.), and refuses to come down from the cross "that we may see and believe" (Mark 15: 32). He avoids, in fact, what would have the effect of rendering assent inevitable and therefore faith impossible.

It is important to see that the miracles were not exceptions to this. They were not compelling proofs. For one thing, miracles were attributed to others besides Jesus, including unbelievers. Moreover, it is clear that the miracles of Jesus are not represented in the Gospels as having the effect of compelling assent—not even the raising of Lazarus. They are represented rather as, so to speak, chinks in the curtain of the Messiah's hiddenness, which are an effective manifestation of His glory only for those who already believe (note that in John 2: 11 it is only the disciples who are said to have believed), while for others they are unconvincing. The light let through the chinks is real light, and failure to discern it is without excuse (Matt. 11: 20–24); nevertheless the revelation is not so direct as to make assent inevitable. Among unbelievers the amazement caused by the miracles is counterbalanced by the apparent weakness and unimpressiveness of Him who works them, and the contradiction or paradox involved becomes an offence or stumbling-block. In harmony with what we have been saying is the fact that the Resurrection appearances were limited to people who already in some measure believed.

The New Testament witnesses to the utterly unique significance of this particular human life and death as God's mighty act for the salvation of the world. In this Man the kingdom of God had come. It was at hand in the sense that it had come near and was actually confronting men. And it had come in its fullness;[2] (for the kingdom of God is, as Marcion and Origen

[1] cf. the present writer in *Scottish Journal of Theology*, 5: 60–3.

[2] *Pace* R. H. Fuller, *The Mission and Achievement of Jesus* (1954), pp. 20 ff.

saw, Christ Himself, and in the Incarnation He had come Himself fully. The contrast between the Incarnation and the Parousia is not between partial and complete so much as between veiled and manifest). At the same time the New Testament testifies to the fact that the unique significance of this life and death was veiled—a μυστήριον, as Mark 4: 11 calls it. It is something which can only be recognized by faith—faith which is, on the one hand, God's miraculous gift (δέδοται, Mark 4: 11) and, on the other, man's free personal decision.

AD DEXTERAM DEI

Phil. 2: 6 ff. not only traces the downward path of the Son of God; it goes on to say: "Wherefore God also highly exalted him, and gave unto him the name which is above every name. . . ." The New Testament speaks of His being received up (into heaven), exalted, of His ascending, and of His sitting at the right hand of God. And, if we agree with Professor Cullmann that the element that is common to the oldest credal formulae to be found in the New Testament must be the focuspoint of the Gospel as the earliest Christians understood it, we may say with him that it is this "present Lordship of Christ, inaugurated by His resurrection and exaltation to the right hand of God, that is the centre of the faith of primitive Christianity".[1]

The New Testament bears witness to Jesus Christ as the One who is Lord *now*, the One to whom "all authority hath been given . . .".[2] The kingdom of God's beloved Son is a fact of the present.[3] He is already "the ruler of the kings of the earth",[4] "Lord of Lords, and King of kings",[5] the One to whom angels and authorities and powers have already been made subject.[6] But, while Heb. 2: 8 says: "Thou didst put all things in subjection under his feet. For in that he subjected all things unto him, he left nothing that is not subject to him", it goes on: "But now we see not yet all things subjected to him." Christ is already King, but the universal acknowledgment of His Kingship is still future; already seated at the right hand of God, He

---

[1] *The Earliest Christian Confessions* (Eng. trans. 1949), p. 58.
[2] Matt. 28: 18   [3] Col. 1: 13   [4] Rev. 1: 5   [5] Rev. 17: 14
[6] 1 Pet. 3: 22

is "expecting till his enemies be made the footstool of his feet".[1] The devil has been bound, but not yet destroyed (Mark 3: 27); the demonic forces defeated and dethroned, but not yet annihilated.

Jesus Christ is Lord of the *Church*. The very use of the title "Christ" is testimony to His kingship over the people of God. According to Luke 1: 32 f., "the Lord God shall give unto him the throne of his father David: and he shall reign over the house of Jacob for ever; and of his kingdom there shall be no end". Though it is probably a misunderstanding of the narratives of the first Palm Sunday to regard Jesus' action as an *overt* claim to Messiahship (see John 12: 16), it is clear that the evangelists mean their readers to see its Messianic significance: Zech. 9: 9 with its "Behold, thy king cometh unto thee" is actually quoted by two of them. According to all four Gospels it is as the King of the Jews that Jesus dies (Matt. 27: 37; Mark 15: 26; Luke 23: 38; John 19: 19–22). But Israel rejects its King, and so the true Israel, "the children of the promise",[2] "the Israel of God",[3] becomes distinguishable from "Israel after the flesh".[4] The beginnings of this new Israel go back to the ministry of Jesus. His choice of the Twelve is the foundation of the new twelve-tribe people and it is as the nucleus of the new Israel that He calls His disciples "little flock".[5] As the new Israel replaces the old, it appropriates the names and descriptions that the Old Testament had applied to Israel (e.g. the word "church" itself).

The Messiah's relation to the new Israel is indicated in various ways, e.g. by the metaphors of master and slaves, shepherd and sheep, vine and branches, head and body, husband and wife. It belongs to Him (Matt. 16: 18; John 21: 15; Rom. 16: 16). It is His, because it owes everything to Him (Acts 20: 28; 1 Cor. 6: 19 f., 7: 23; 1 Pet. 1: 18 f.). It is altogether dependent on Him and apart from Him can do nothing (John 15: 4 f.). His claim to its allegiance is absolute. The mark of the true Church is that it recognizes His voice and will not follow any other (John 10: 4 f.). He and only He is His people's Teacher and Master (Matt. 23: 8, 10). He is not content with

---

[1] Heb. 10: 12 f., cf. 1 Cor. 15: 24–8, esp. 25.   [2] Rom. 9: 8
[3] Gal. 6: 16   [4] 1 Cor. 10: 18   [5] Luke 12: 32, cf. Isa. 40: 11, Ezek. 34.

pious protestations, but expects His Church to do what He commands (Luke 6: 46 ff.). Only those who obey Him can rightly be said to love Him (John 14: 15, 15: 14). His claims must take precedence over the most sacred of human obligations (Matt. 8: 21 f., 10: 37). To be His disciple is to be utterly committed to Him, to follow Him with all that entails (e.g. Mark 2: 14, 8: 34 ff., 10: 21). The witness of the New Testament may here be summed up in the words of Eph. 1: 22 f: God "gave him to be head over all things to the church, which is his body".

But this same passage which speaks of Him as the "universal and supreme Head of the Church", as Weymouth translates it, also asserts His lordship over the *world*: God "put all things under his feet". With authority over all mankind (John 17: 2), King of kings and Lord of lords (Rev. 17: 14, 19: 16), He is also Lord of the whole creation (Matt. 28: 18), "upholding all things by the word of his power" (Heb. 1: 3). The Church is but the inner circle of His dominion, the area in which His authority is already known and confessed: beyond its frontiers His authority is no less real.

Here the State must be mentioned as an instrument of His kingly rule. 1 Tim. 2: 1–7 makes clear the connection between the State and the divine reconciliation of men through Christ. State authority has its origin in the mercy and patience of God who wills that all men should be saved and therefore provides means for the limitation of human self-assertion, so that even in a world disrupted by man's sin there may be room for the Gospel to be proclaimed and heard. The similar passage, Rom. 13: 1–7, is no erratic boulder in its context but an integral part of the specifically Christocentric exhortation in the midst of which it is set. The "powers"[1] which are active in the State are powers which have been made subject to Christ (Eph. 1: 20 f.; Col. 2: 15; 1 Pet. 3: 22). The State's authority must therefore, whether consciously or unconsciously, willingly or unwillingly, subserve the purposes of Christ the King. (So, for example, it cannot avoid honouring "the good work" of a faithful Church, either by its protection or by a martyr's crown, just as it cannot

---

[1] It is probable that angelic powers are meant. cf. Barth, *Church and State* (Eng. trans. 1939), pp. 23 f.

help but punish "the evil work" of an unfaithful Church,
though it may be by loading it with shameful honours.) Since
the State serves, though more or less unconsciously, the same
Lord as the Church, the Christian cannot withdraw from his
political responsibilities; for to evade them would be rebellion
against Christ's kingship. Their fulfilment is an inescapable part
of the obedience he owes to Christ and has therefore to be
undertaken "for conscience sake". But the criterion of these
responsibilities, of the "subjection" owed by the Christian to
the State authority, is not what a particular State authority
may choose to demand, but what Christ commands. In the
circumstances of a modern democracy this "subjection" involves an active and responsible (and therefore not uncritical)
co-operation and a resolute and unambiguous defence of justice, mercy and truth both by the Church as a whole and by its
individual members. Such responsible service of the State
is a part of the Church's confession of Christ, whereby "the
manifold wisdom of God" is "made known through the
church" "unto the principalities and powers in the heavenly
places".[1]

But the New Testament bears witness not only to the royal
authority of the exalted Jesus but also to His *High Priesthood*.
This comes to its clearest expression in Hebrews, though it is
hinted at and implied elsewhere. Having "offered one sacrifice
for sins for ever" (10: 12), even "himself" (7: 27; cf. 10: 10) and
having by virtue of that one sacrifice "entered in once for all
into the holy place" (9: 12; cf. Mark 15: 38?), that is, "into
heaven itself, now to appear before the face of God for us"
(9: 24), He continues "a high priest for ever" (6: 20). Through
Him we may "draw near to God" (7: 25; cf. 10: 19–22; Rom.
5: 2; 1 Pet. 3: 18, etc.); through Him we are to pray and offer
up our worship to God (John 15: 16; Heb. 13: 15). As High
Priest He intercedes for us (Rom. 8: 34; Heb. 7: 25; cf. 1 John
2: 1), and He is "not a high priest that cannot be touched with
the feeling of our infirmities; but one that hath been in all
points tempted like as we are" (Heb. 4: 15), "a merciful and
faithful high priest" (2: 17). That He intercedes not only for
believers but for all men is suggested by Matt. 5: 44; Luke 23: 34

[1] Eph. 3: 10

(longer reading); John 1: 29, 3: 16 f., 4: 42, 12: 32; 1 Tim.
2: 1 ff.; 1 John 2: 2 among other passages. (John 17: 9 is certainly not to be taken to imply that He will never pray for the
world.) It is in the light of the High Priesthood of Christ that
the oft-recurring formula "in Christ" can best be understood,
and also such passages as 1 Cor. 1: 30, Col. 3: 3, and perhaps
1 John 3: 6, 9, and 5: 18.

Closely connected with the thought of Jesus as High Priest is
that of Him as our *Forerunner*. In Heb. 6: 20 the two are linked
together. He goes away from us in order to prepare a place for
us, "that where I am, there ye may be also".[1] Compare the
similar, though distinct, ideas of 1 Cor. 15: 20, 23; Col. 1: 18;
Rev. 1: 5. For Him the resurrection, for which we must wait
till His Parousia, is already accomplished.

The Ascension was not only the transition to the heavenly
glory: it was also quite definitely a going away from us. In a
real sense the Church has an absent Master. Matt. 26: 11 =
Mark 14: 7 = John 12: 8 must be taken seriously as well as Matt.
28: 20! Compare Mark 13: 34–36. Between the Ascension and
the Parousia His presence with us is indirect, hidden and unseen, though none the less blessedly real. He is present through
the Holy Spirit as our Helper. He is present in the Word and
Sacraments. The New Testament bears witness most clearly to
His presence with us, or comings to us, in the words of Scripture
by authenticating itself to us through the Spirit as the medium
of His conversation with His Church. Again, the New Testament bears witness to His comings to us in the Sacraments.
And there is yet another way in which the exalted Lord comes
to us in the interval between His Ascension and His Parousia,
and that is by His self-identification with the least and weakest
of men (Matt. 25: 40, 45). It is in them that He wills to be
thanked and served, in them that He gives us the gracious gift
of the opportunity to thank and serve Him.

ET VENIENTEM

The New Testament bears witness to Jesus Christ also as the
coming Lord. Jesus in His teaching often contrasts the present
hiddenness and apparent weakness of the Kingdom of God with

[1] John 14: 2 f.

its future manifestation. So, for example, in Mark 4: 30–32 His meaning seems to be that, whereas in His own earthly life and also in the subsequent witness of His disciples the Kingdom of God is outwardly weak and inconspicuous, the time will come when the veil will be lifted once and for all and the Kingdom made manifest. Similar is the point of the little parable of the lamp (Mark 4: 21). No one in his senses would go to the trouble of carrying a lighted lamp into a house simply in order to hide it. The intention would of course be to place it on the lamp-stand. No more must it be supposed that God's whole purpose in sending His Son into the world was that He should be concealed. True, the Light of the world is for a while hidden —Jesus must be rejected and killed and even after His resurrection His disciples will have to "walk by faith, not by sight"— but this painful veiledness will not be for ever; for God's ultimate intention in sending His Son was not to conceal Him but to manifest Him to all. Faith will then be needed no longer; it will be replaced by sight—"then shall they *see* the Son of man",[1] and in that "they" all men are included.

It will not do to refer this contrast between present veiledness and future manifestation to the contrast between the small beginnings of the Gospel in our Lord's own lifetime and the subsequent spread of the Gospel by the Church. The reference is to His Parousia. All four Gospels bear witness to the fact that He spoke of it. There are Johannine sayings like John 14: 3 (cf. 14: 18, 28, 16: 16–22) to be set beside the more obvious Synoptic sayings such as Mark 8: 38, 13: 26, 14: 62.[2] In the rest of the New Testament Christ's future glorious coming is again and again referred to.

It is not to be explained away in terms of a "timeless fact".[3] Paul in the most systematic of his extant letters underlines quite unmistakably the historical nature of the Parousia (i.e. historical in the sense that it will actually happen at a particular time), when he speaks of our salvation being nearer now than when we first believed (Rom. 13: 11). And it is a misunder-

---

[1] Mark 13: 26.

[2] The fact that the "coming" is mentioned *after* the "sitting" shows that the coming referred to is not exaltation.

[3] C. H. Dodd, *The Parables of the Kingdom* (rev. ed., 1936), p. 108.

standing of the Fourth Gospel, we believe, which sees in it what might be called a "dehistoricizing" of the Parousia.

But, while it will be historical in the sense that it will actually happen, it will be, like the Resurrection, of an altogether different texture, so to speak, from ordinary history; for it will be the End of history (both termination and consummation)—"the end" (Mark 13: 7), "the end of the world" (Matt. 24: 3), "the end of all things" (1 Pet. 4: 7) and also the establishment of God's New Order (1 Cor. 15: 24–28). Therefore we cannot describe it directly, but have to use picture-language. It is foolish to ask such questions as how can the elect be gathered together from the four winds; for an event which we could neatly and satisfactorily explain could certainly not be *the* End. To try to compress the picture-language to a literal interpretation is vain. While holding fast to the truth that the Parousia will be a real Event, we must not forget its otherness, its absolute uniqueness.

The New Testament insists on the imminence of the Parousia[1] (e.g. Mark 13: 29; Rom. 13: 12; 1 Cor. 7: 29; Phil. 4: 5; Heb. 10: 25; Jas. 5: 8 f.; 1 Pet. 4: 7; 1 John 2: 18; Rev. 22: 20; cf. the repeated "a little while" in John 16: 16 ff. and the conviction that they are living in the last days indicated in Acts 2: 17). This presents us with one of the most difficult problems in New Testament studies; for it is clear that nineteen hundred years have passed and the Parousia has not yet occurred. Did the primitive Church read into Jesus' teaching apocalyptic ideas that were alien to it? Or was Jesus Himself mistaken? Or is the solution to be found in a more theological understanding of what is meant by the nearness of the End? We believe that this last alternative is the right one and that the paradoxical nature of the New Testament material itself invites us to explore in this direction. If we realize that the Incarnation–Crucifixion–Resurrection–Ascension, on the one hand, and the Parousia, on the other, belong essentially together and are in a real sense one Event, being held apart only by the mercy of God who desires to give men opportunity for faith and repentance, then we can see that in a very real sense the latter is

---

[1] On the subject matter of this paragraph see further Barth, *Kirchl. Dogm.* III/2, 560–616, and also an article by the present writer in *Scottish Journal of Theology*, 7, 284 ff.

always imminent now that the former has happened. It was, and still is, true to say that the Parousia is at hand—and indeed we may say that this, so far from being an embarrassing mistake, is an essential part of the Church's faith. Ever since the Incarnation men have been living in the last days, and the only thing that holds back the end of history is God's patience that waits to give men time to hear the Gospel and to believe. But this insistence on the nearness of Christ's coming is not the same thing as insisting that He will necessarily come within a few months or years or decades. The passages which are often taken to imply this are, we believe, patient of other interpretations. For example, in Mark 13: 30 "all these things" (as also "these things" in v. 29) may be taken to refer to the signs mentioned in vv. 5–23; Mark 9: 1 is perhaps best regarded as referring to the Transfiguration (in which both the Resurrection and the Parousia are foreshadowed); Matt. 10: 23 may perhaps mean that the conversion of Israel will not be complete before the Parousia; in 1 Thess. 4: 15–17 and 1 Cor. 15: 51 the first person plural need only mean "we Christians" (it need not imply that Paul was sure he would be included, any more than the "you" in Amos 2: 10 implies that Amos thought the people addressed had been alive at the Exodus); and it is very much to be doubted whether 1 Cor. 7 could only have been written by someone who thought the End must necessarily come within a short time (it is rather that Paul was taking absolutely seriously the possibility that it might come at *any* time).

Christ's coming will be sudden and unexpected, like a thief in the night (Matt. 24: 42–44; Luke 12: 39 f.; 1 Thess. 5: 2; cf. Matt. 24: 37 ff.). Not even Jesus Himself knew when it would be (Mark 13: 32). The disciples must therefore be ready all the time (Mark 13: 33–37). Such readiness or watching is the whole duty of the Christian. It certainly is no mere waiting around for something to happen, but a going forth in the power of the Spirit in active and resolute faith and obedience to meet the coming Lord. Its character is indicated by the three parables of Matt. 25, which draw out the implications of the preceding discourse and which have been so magnificently expounded in the *Kirchliche Dogmatik*.[1] To watch for Him is to

[1] III/2, pp. 607–12.

make sure that our faith is no counterfeit which at the last crisis will vanish, but that true faith that will enable us to take our place beside Him. It is to use the time that remains before His coming in the work of winning others for Him. It is to recognize and to serve Him in the persons of the least of His brethren. To expect the coming Lord every moment is to be enabled and obliged to love (cf. Rom. 13: 8–14; Phil. 4: 4–7; 1 Thess. 5; Heb. 10: 24 f.; Jas. 5: 7–11; 1 Pet. 4: 7–11).

And He will be the Judge (e.g. Matt. 25: 31 ff.), before whom all without exception will have to appear—Christians and non-Christians alike, for "all the nations" in v. 32 is all-inclusive.[1] Then those who by their failure to care for their fellow men, who needed their service, have shown that all the time their faith was counterfeit, will hear His sentence, "Depart from me" (v. 41).

Though His coming will be unexpected, it is nevertheless heralded by signs (Mark 13: 5–23). For Christians the events of history are reminders and pledges of His coming and of its nearness and therefore reasons for lifting up our heads (Luke 21: 28). As our faith recognizes them, we are again and again put in remembrance of our Hope, and our gaze which is so easily distracted and diverted from its proper Object, our coming Lord, is again and again directed back to Him. The function of the signs is not to enable us to predict the date of His coming, but to keep us faithful to our task of watching.

---

[1] cf. K. L. Schmidt in Kittel's *TWzNT*, 2, 366 f.

3

ON BEHALF OF CHALCEDON

by J. L. M. HAIRE

Professor of Systematic Theology, Presbyterian College, Belfast

3

ON BEHALF OF CHALCEDON

by

J. L. M. HAIRE

THE Fathers at Chalcedon bore testimony to their Lord as both true God and true Man, one Person in two Natures. Many theologians in the nineteenth and early twentieth centuries have expressed strong dissatisfaction with this Chalcedonian Christology. Others are now defending it in ways which seem to endanger the very truths it stood for. Thus many have wanted to offer a new solution of the relation of the divine and the human in Jesus Christ. They have abandoned the two-nature formula because they believe that there is a better one-nature hypothesis. For them the human at its best is itself divine. Jesus Christ was the perfect man and for that reason divine. Such a theory is monophysite, but in a very different way from the original monophysites. At the same time, other theologians have seen Jesus Christ as the consummator rather than the restorer of human nature. By His incarnation He makes human nature what it could never have become, even apart from sin. This new human nature is human nature divinized. Their position seems very difficult to distinguish from that of the original monophysites. Both solutions are much less adequate than the solution reached at Chalcedon. The purpose of this essay is to defend these dogmatic assertions.

I

We must state at the beginning the Biblical basis from which we start. The New Testament writers bear testimony both to Jesus Christ's human life and to His divine authority. Both appear clearly in the Fourth Gospel. Those who find its witness to His Lordship unacceptable, claim that the writer has introduced the conception of His authority to heighten his picture of a divine Son of God. But this high Christology is already in the Apostle Paul, with his assertion that his Master is both behind creation and the one in whom creation is to reach its fulfilment. And Paul's conviction about the divine authority of Christ is already implied by the writers of the Synoptic Gospels. "The whole ministry of Jesus, according to Mark, is the advent precisely of those things which were sighed for in the Messianic hope."[1] John the Baptist is contrasted with a greater. Already at the baptism Jesus is revealed as the Son. He forgives sins. He acts with authority in overthrowing the powers of evil. He is the stronger who binds Satan. At the transfiguration He stands between Moses and Elijah, and prepares Himself to perform a greater work than the law and the prophets. His eschatological triumph and His place at the right hand of God are foretold.

What is true of Mark is of course true of Matthew and Luke. This high view of the Man, Jesus of Nazareth, is not however the creation of the evangelists. It is already in their sources. For the sources themselves teach a suffering and triumphant Messiah. This high Christology is already in the individual stories which may well have circulated separately. Finally it is in the words of Jesus Himself, in His "But I say unto you", His knowledge of His Father, and His victory over the powers of evil. This authority is the authority of One who is meek and lowly of heart, a real man, to whom nothing human—except disobedience—is alien. But He who is humble and lowly does call men to Himself, does make clear to them that their final destiny depends on the way in which they listen to Him, and does teach His final triumph in the glory of the Father.[2] This may well seem unduly to emphasize the authoritative side of our Lord's life, but this emphasis is necessary because many in the last seventy years have glossed over this clear New Testament conviction.

Is it not also this failure to recognize both the human and the divine in Jesus Christ, which has made many modern writers from Gibbon to Henry van Loon treat the long orthodox struggle for a true definition of the Person of Christ as if it were a mere verbal quibble? The Fathers of the first five centuries were convinced that it was the divine in Christ and not the

---

[1] Hoskyns and Davey, *The Riddle of the New Testament*, p. 119.
[2] cf. Kierkegaard, *Training in Christianity* (trans. Lowrie), pp. 9–72.

human by itself which saved men. Against Gnostic and Arian beliefs in an intermediary as revealer of God they fought for a revelation which was the revelation of God Himself. As the Bringer of truth, Christ was the divine Logos and the divine Son. The powers of evil were conquered by one whose divinity the devil could not endure or could not capture or on which he could not establish a claim. Human nature was restored by a second Adam who was not less than divine. Expiation was made by the Son of God. There was of course the division between the schools of Antioch and Alexandria. There was the tendency at the former so to emphasize the divine element in the human life as to change the human into the divine. Eutychianism is already latent in some teaching on the deification oı human nature in Clement and Origen.[1] Equally Diadore and Flavian in the other school come near to teaching that our restoration is achieved by the victory of a man over death, and Apollinarius does not find it difficult to reply that such a victory would save only that one man and not the race.[2] But the orthodox position stands quite firmly in the middle. The divine comes to save in a real human life, but it is the divine in the human life that saves. Chalcedon restores the balance. It is not simply a victory for Antioch. It may well be too static in its expression. It may well fail adequately to relate the person of Christ to those acts of His life, death and resurrection, through which the revelation is given.[3] But it does not teach that the human is itself the source of our deliverance because it is at its best itself divine; equally it does not teach that the divine so overshadows the human that the human is transformed and that this transformed human nature in Christ is then communicated to others, who are thereby deified.

II

When we turn to the second half of the nineteenth century, we find that this doctrine of the two natures in one person now appears as what Luther called "sophistical" knowledge, a form of words that perhaps at one time averted heresy, but which

[1] H. E. W. Turner, *The Patristic Doctrine of Redemption*, pp. 82–3.
[2] *ibid.*, pp. 67–8.
[3] See T. F. Torrance in *Scottish Journal of Theology*, 7/3, pp. 245–6.

made the person of Christ quite unreal. This is true even of otherwise orthodox theologians like Charles Gore and H. R. Mackintosh.[1] The view of Chalcedon "now fails to satisfy the great bulk of evangelical theologians." "In its traditional form it imports into the life of Christ an incredible and thorough-going dualism." "It gives two abstractions instead of one reality." "It hypostatizes falsely two aspects of a single concrete life, not in themselves distinctly functioning substantialities."[2] What men want is "a new and better way" of expressing who Christ is, for to these men "it is impossible to believe that the human intelligence has made no progress since the fifth century in the precision and delicacy of its instruments of expression." Men want now to express their belief about who Jesus is by using terms that seem to them "more spiritual than nature and substance". "It is more than possible", writes Mackintosh again, "that by the ethicizing of the divine attributes we may relieve some of the foremost problems of the incarnation, parti-cularly those which are due less to the ascertained facts of his-tory than to the physical and all but mechanical thought-forms employed by the early Church." We need "the restatement of Christology in fully personal and spiritual terms." "In ethical terms, the highest terms available, we must affirm his onto-logical unity with God."[3]

The Nineteenth-Century Alternatives

What we are now going to maintain is that a great deal of this criticism is misdirected. It really arises because certain great and influential nineteenth-century philosophers and theologians believed not so much that the technical terms used at Chalcedon were inadequate, as that the solution itself was false. For them there is one human-divine nature in Christ and not two natures. As has been said recently: "What formerly was called nature is now accepted as person." "What formerly was defined as person is now regarded as non-existent."[4]

For Hegel, mind or thought is the highest thing in the

---

[1] Charles Gore, *Belief in Christ*, ch. 7.
[2] H. R. Mackintosh, *The Person of Christ*, pp. 293, 295.
[3] *ibid.*, pp. 297, 303, 304.
[4] Lewis B. Smedes, *The Incarnation, Trends in Modern Anglican Thought*, p. 3.

universe and is at its highest itself fully divine. As man has evolved, the divine has been expressed better and better in him. This world is the necessary counterpart to God, through which He is enabled to express Himself. Thus the divine is realized in this world and in man and is realized most fully in Jesus Christ. He is the human-divine who surrenders Himself to the infinite divine. Thus you have no problem of two natures in Christ. You have one human-divine nature, possessed by all men, in a more undeveloped form and in Him in its most developed form. Under His influence we can surrender ourselves to God and so become one with Him, and in this act we manifest our own divine nature which has now become mature.

For Schleiermacher the greatest thing in the universe is not intellect but deep and noble passion. And the deepest and noblest passion is the feeling of utter dependence on God. Such utter consciousness of dependence is wholly visible in Jesus. In Him it is perfect and in its perfect form is divine. His perfect filial response is the response of a Son of God. This response can be awakened by Him in others, so that they too completely depend on and are united with God. Thus perfect obedience and dependence is itself divine. There are not two natures in Christ but the one perfectly obedient and trusting human nature, which in its self-expression is the nature of a son of God and so is divine.

The third thinker who shared this general nineteenth-century approach is Ritschl. For him it is neither intellect nor noble passion which is divine, but rather the enlightened conscience. Perfect love of what is morally good is the highest thing in the world. Such devotion to goodness is itself divine. We see such goodness, such holy love in Jesus Christ, and when we see it, we recognize it as both perfect and divine. There is thus in Jesus Christ one perfect moral nature which is perfect human nature and so a perfect expression of the divine nature. We are moved by such a vision to imitate Him, and so become members of the kingdom and family of God.

Ritschl's theory found a special application among the Kenosis school of Christologists. For them, love and righteousness are the essentially divine attributes which can be manifested under all conditions. When they are perfectly manifest in the human life of Jesus, they reveal that life as being divine. Thus perfect human goodness is itself the differentia of the divine.

These nineteenth-century attempts to state the person of Christ in terms of one nature, human in a perfect way and for that reason divine, do not really do justice to the New Testament conviction that Christ is the unique Son of God. For Hegel Jesus speaks authoritatively, because He manifests the divine under human limitations in the same way as others do less fully, but He speaks no unique word of God to men. For Schleiermacher Jesus wins His influence over men by His perfect God-consciousness, but whether this God-consciousness is unique or simply the most perfect form of a general human God-consciousness remains ambiguous. For Ritschl the Reformation classification of the person of Christ as that of Prophet, Priest and King is reduced to the picture of the kingly prophet and the kingly priest, and kingly means not divine but speaking with the authority of perfect human moral insight. In all three the unique divine authority is merged in a perfect human authority.

III

These three very influential nineteenth-century interpretations of the person of Christ in terms of one perfect human-divine nature reappear in a great deal of modern English Christological writing. In most of the English writers however in the last fifty years the influence is not that of Hegel or Schleiermacher or Ritschl separately, but a general influence in which the teaching of all three plays its part. Here the human at its best is itself divine in its intellectual, emotional and moral self-expression.

The influence of the three great Germans is to be seen in so distinguished a Christian philosopher as Pringle-Pattison, in such great orthodox thinkers as William Temple and Charles Gore, and quite recently in the very penetrating book on Christology by D. M. Baillie. Pringle-Pattison, in his chapter on Creation in his Gifford lectures, claims that the world is necessary to God, in order to give Him opportunity to express His nature which is perfect love. As the human responds to this love, the divine realizes itself in man. Jesus Christ is then pre-

sumably the perfect human life which perfectly responds and is
for that reason divine. Already in 1918 Baron von Hügel pro-
tested that this solution means the playing down of the divine
transcendence in favour of a complete divine immanence.[1]

For William Temple, will is the centre of human personality;
will is the only substance in a man. To be of one mind with
another is to be of one substance with him and to be of one
mind with God is to be of the same substance with Him. This
we find to be historically true in the case of Jesus Christ. In
Him there is to be seen the one human-divine substance of perfect willing fully in harmony with the will of God.[2] Such unity
of will may be one way of expressing the unity between the
human and the divine, but such a conception taken by itself,
without another proposition which asserts the uniqueness of
Christ's unity of will with the Father, leads to a denial of the
truth of the Chalcedonian statement about two natures. It
offers no way of expressing the unique divine authority with
which Jesus Christ confronts mankind.

In Temple's writings, as in those of C. C. J. Webb and many
others, the concept of personality plays an important role in
the attempt to state a more adequate Christology than that
which Chalcedon offered. It is in this concept that, I believe,
H. R. Mackintosh saw a great advance in human thinking on
that of the fifth century.[3] The universe is viewed as a proper
place for the perfection of personality and the incarnation is
looked on as this process fulfilled.[4] The perfect personality, integrated by the power of holy love, is itself divine. Chalcedon
seemed to destroy the unity of such a personality. "In tradition
human nature is taken as real apart from personality."[5]

Two types of criticism have recently been directed against
such a solution. (1) Personality is a description of human nature
by use of an important psychological term. Unless therefore we
believe for other reasons that the human and divine are one by
nature, this term itself will not explain the whole person of

[1] A. S. Pringle-Pattison, *The Ideal of God*, p. 295; H. von Hügel, *Essays and Addresses*, Second Series, Essay on the Idea of God.

[2] William Temple in *Foundations*, pp. 248–50; cf. *Nature, Man and God*, pp. 445–6.

[3] H. R. Mackintosh, *op. cit.*, p. 297.   [4] Smedes, *op. cit.*, p. xiii.

[5] H. R. Mackintosh, *op. cit.*, pp. 296–7.

Christ. It may be quite possible to say that the one perfectly integrated personality was His. If however we do so, we must remember that it was the divine in Him which achieved this, not the human by itself; so that we have still to postulate a divine behind the human. And we must not like Schleiermacher so portray a unified personality as to deny the reality of His temptations and His experience of dereliction. For it is our human nature which He shared, that of "the seed of Abraham", and in it He remained fully obedient. Whether His life on earth can therefore be accurately described simply as "a perfectly integrated personality" remains a question, unless by this is meant a person who did not sin.

(2) It may also be argued that the whole nineteenth-century concept of personality is based on certain questionable Idealistic assumptions. Because man is a sinful being, "personality" often really describes his outward appearance, the self which he presents to others. Thus it has been argued by Sir Harold Nicholson that in the nineteenth century a scientist like Darwin or a poet like Tennyson believed himself called to act as a scientist or poet ought to act and to appear as a great and impressive personality, overawing others by the power of such personality. A personality so conceived would lack that humility which is the Christian mark of the perfect man. Such a picture of personality might also lead to a conception of Christ which was very impressive but which was very unlike the One who was humble and lowly of heart and whose authority at the same time was felt to be the authority of God. For here it was not the power of His personality (in which he then surpassed a Socrates or a Cato) which impressed men. It was the divine in the human life. He was not divine because He was a perfect and so a very forceful personality. He was divine because through a real human life God was drawing near to men.

We have therefore to ask whether the nineteenth-century idea of personality is not based on the presupposition that the human at its best is itself divine. The concept of personality may enable us better to state the nature of the human in Christ, but does it really explain the relation of the human and the divine, unless we assume that the perfectly integrated human personality is in itself divine?

Just as there is a tendency in some of William Temple's writing to define the perfectly human as itself divine, a similar tendency may be detected in the important work on Christology of D. M. Baillie. For him the key to the understanding of the person of Christ is to be found in the human experience of grace. Through grace man himself acts, yet knows that all the good in his action is from God. Similarly in Christ the human referred all to the divine. This seems akin to the old orthodox view of the two natures and two wills. But at times the same ambiguity appears as in Schleiermacher, and one is not quite sure if by the human Baillie means the human nature or the man Christ Jesus. Clearly it is not his intention to state an Adoptionist Christology, but his method of approach by beginning with the human experience tends in this direction. For example, he writes: "We see the man in whom God was incarnate surpassing all others in refusing to claim anything for Himself independently and ascribing all the goodness to God." "We see Him also desiring to take up other men into his own close union with God that they might be as He was." "In the Jesus of the Gospels it is not His (Messianic) self-consciousness that strikes us but God consciousness."[1] This tends to suggest that playing down of the Messianic consciousness of our Lord which many scholars to-day believe to belong to the words and work of Jesus Himself. Baillie defends his position by quoting those passages which state the dependence of the Son on the Father rather than those which state His claims to speak with divine authority and call for obedience. He believes that this is also the view of Barth. While he can quote "the God-man is the only man who claims nothing for Himself but all for God", he does not quote also the other side which is equally clear in the same volume of Barth where he distinguishes the relation of the Son to the Father from that of the Saints to God, and implies that obedience alone is not the complete differentia of the Son.[2] Yet Baillie can say also: "In Christ the divine prevenience was nothing short of Incarnation and He lived as He did because He was God Incarnate" which seems to emphasize a greater distinction between Christ and us than is illustrated by

---

[1] D. M. Baillie, *God was in Christ*, pp. 117, 129.
[2] Barth, *Kirchl. Dogm.*, I/2, 171 f.; contrast I/2, 177-8.

the paradox of grace.[1] Must we not say both that Christ is the second Adam and so the only truly obedient man, and also, and before this, that He is the Word and Son of God? And if we do this, are we not reaffirming the doctrine of the two natures?

A similar view, and I think a less guarded one, is stated by Dr. W. R. Matthews. For him the key to Christology is to be found in the idea of inspiration. Jesus' whole personality is the personality of one who is not sporadically inspired like the prophets but is inspired continually. This inspiration is not only in His conscious experience but in His subconscious life, and is also mediated through suprasensory perception. "Because He is completely inspired, He is the temporal manifestation in human life of the eternal Word."[2] Complete inspiration appears therefore to be a way of expressing the relationship of Son to Father. It seems, however, to differ only in degree from the inspiration of the prophets, and so implies that that which distinguishes Christ is simply the possession of something human in a perfect way.

IV

Some Recent British Reactions

If much recent British Christology, like that of the great Christological writers in Germany in the nineteenth century, has been monophysite in the sense just described, recently there appears to have been a very understandable reaction which is in danger of monophysitism at the other extreme. If Christ's divinity is not simply perfect humanity, neither is it a divinity which deifies human nature as well as restores it. Yet this seems to be the tendency expressed in the works to which I must now refer. We all know how difficult it is to appreciate those who belong to traditions very different from our own, and many of us have learned in the ecumenical movement how often our views of other traditions are merely caricatures. It is therefore with some hesitation that I describe the books of L. S. Thornton and E. L. Mascall as writings which appear at the other extreme to deny the two-nature doctrine of Chalcedon.

[1] Baillie, *op. cit.*, p. 131.
[2] W. R. Matthews, *The Problem of Christ in the 20th Century*, p. 82. For a similar criticism of Matthews see W. Joest in *Ecumenical Review*, Vol. 7, No. 1, p. 91.

Father Thornton sees in Christ the founder of a new humanity which stands in the same relation to our original human nature as humanity stands to the animal creation below it. The new humanity is a stage higher in the evolution of life. This *saltus* is brought about by the Incarnation of the Son of God. By taking on Him our human nature He creates a new humanity higher than that which has existed in any form before. The state of unregenerate man is therefore not a state of humanity in the true sense of the word, and the truly human never exists till Christ comes.[1] We may well agree that we do not know what true human nature is till we see it in Christ, but is it correct to call this the creation of a quite new order of life and not the restoration of a humanity which has been lost? Can Christ in this case be said to restore the nature of that Adam who according to St. Luke was the son of God (Luke 3: 38), to take on Him the "seed of Abraham" (Heb. 2: 16), or to renew the image of God in man (Col. 3: 10)? Does this not appear to be the raising of humanity to the sphere of deity, even if some distinction is still preserved between the human and the divine? Is this not really to teach that Christ's nature is a divine human nature in which the humanity has been altered in being assumed by the divine? Can this view be said to be compatible with the intention of the Fathers at Chalcedon? In a recent review Father Thornton so expounds 2 Pet. 1: 4 on our "being made partakers of the divine nature" as to appear to give this text a central importance, interpreting the rest of the New Testament by it rather than it by the general teaching of the New Testament.[2] He clearly seems to teach that the human is made akin to the divine through the Incarnation.

A similar type of Christology seems to be implied in the writings of Professor Mascall. In his important book on Christology, *He Who Is*, he begins by drawing the valuable distinction between the various qualities which a person has and the individual person who has them. There is *what* a man is, the sum of his qualities, and *who* a man is, the unique individual in whom these qualities are united. In other men the *what* and the *who* are indistinguishable. In Christ the *what* is the human

---

[1] L. S. Thornton, *The Incarnate Lord*, pp. 32 ff., 362.
[2] *Journal of Theological Studies*, Vol. 5 (Oct., 1954), p. 302.

qualities but the *who* is the eternal Son. Mascall then proceeds
to argue that the union of the *what* with the *who* brings about a
new Being. The human through its relationships to the divine is
not made identical with God, but is transformed. Once again
we must ask if this really does justice to the real humanity of
Christ and does not in fact deny the reality of the two natures.

Both of these distinguished theologians are intent on upholding the full Christian faith as stated in the classical creeds over
against the liberal position we have just been examining. Both
consciously aim at being true to Chalcedon, even if Father
Thornton does not aim at stating the faith in the exact Chalcedonian terms.[1] Both display a spirit of Christian devotion above
criticism.

Yet both of these writers appear to make assumptions which
lead them to a view of our Lord's person and work hard to
reconcile either with the main teaching of the New Testament
or the intention of the Fathers at Chalcedon. They both are of
opinion that the Incarnation was necessary to make man what
God intended him to be, quite apart from man's sin. Creation
itself for them involved Incarnation. Creation without Incarnation would have been incomplete. By the Incarnation humanity
is raised to a new position to which it could not have attained
without the coming of the eternal Son of God. Human nature
is therefore raised to a higher metaphysical level and undergoes
an ontological change and is "taken up into a higher principle
of unity".[2] While they state this at times in the Biblical terms of
new creation, they appear to interpret this as a new kind of
creation; a conception which I shall attempt to show is not
Biblical at all. This new status they both also describe as if it
were divinization, though they seek to maintain some distinction between the divinity of God and that divinity imparted to
human nature through unity with the new higher human
nature of Christ.[3]

It is possible to appreciate the motives which have led men
to such a statement as this. There is the desire to show that man

[1] L. S. Thornton, *The Incarnate Lord*, p. 253; E. L. Mascall, *Christ, the Christian and the Church*, pp. 6–7.

[2] Mascall, *op. cit.*, pp. 51, 53, 77, 203; Thornton, *op. cit.* p. 362.

[3] For divinization: Thornton, *op. cit.*, p. 237; Mascall, *op. cit.*, pp. 3, 109. For modification of this, Thornton, p. 102; Mascall, p. 116.

is offered real communion with God and given a nature adequate for such communion. There is equally the desire to show how modern evolutionary theories of human development are not an alternative to, but may be the handmaid of a true Christian understanding of the universe. Both motives were at work in the minds of earlier theologians who favoured such a statement, like F. D. Maurice and B. F. Westcott, Charles Gore and R. C. Moberly. But this assumption raises at least two serious difficulties: Is there any basis for such a conception in the Biblical testimony? And does such an assumption really take seriously the sharing of our human nature by the eternal Son of God, or does it not lead inevitably to some sort of monophysitism of the Eutychian type? If our Lord brings a human nature such as never existed before, one which unites us with God as our human nature, even if sinless, never could have done, then does He really take on Him the seed of Abraham or renew the image of God, and does He in any sense act as our Representative, bearing our burden and making expiation for us? Is His not rather a new human-divine nature such as the original monophysites believed in? Is there not here a *communicatio idiomatum* which alters the human nature in the very way resisted by the Fathers at Chalcedon?

This view can be defended in two ways—by appeal to Scripture and by appeal to the Fathers. We must now consider how far either defence is tenable.

It has been argued that when God (in the first chapters of Genesis) breathes into man the breath of life, He thereby imparts to man something of Himself. Here the Atman of God in man is identical, so to speak, with the divine Brahman behind all things. But whatever may have been the origin of the idea of the divine "inspiration", it is clear that the writer in Genesis looks on it as completely compatible with the idea of creation, where Man is God's creature and not an emanation from the divine. This questionable exegesis is then connected with a second which does not seem quite consistent with it. This holds that the real divinization for the Old Testament is not in the present but in the future. The Messiah is to possess the gift of the Holy Spirit which will be the mark that He is divine, and this divine gift He will then impart to His people. Is this, however, at all akin to the New Testament? We have certainly come to accept the conception of Christ as a corporate personality, so that Christians are "in Christ". But at the same time the divine Spirit does not take the place of men's minds in the Church or divinize men. He guides, enlightens, leads into all truth, prays for men. As a New Testament scholar has recently shown convincingly, "neither side of this paradox can be neglected; when that has been done, false views of the nature of the Church have resulted".[1]

Reconciliation rather than divinization is at the centre of the Biblical teaching on the work of Christ for Man. God was in Christ reconciling the world to Himself; our Lord is said chiefly to have ransomed us from the powers of evil and made expiation for us. It is in the light of this that we naturally interpret the only text in the New Testament that might serve as the basis for a doctrine of divinization, with its statement that we are to become partakers of the divine nature (2 Pet. 1: 4). This is true also of the interpretation of the Fourth Gospel. In it eternal life is gained by believing in the name of the only begotten Son of God, and men fail to believe, not because their natures are by themselves inadequate and need divinization, but because they prefer darkness to light. The new creation and the new birth in the Bible are not a creation and a birth to a new level. The former is a new act of creation by which the original creation is restored. The new birth from above makes men not something more than human. Rather it makes men free again and true sons of Abraham (John 8: 31–47). The lost image is restored (Col. 3: 10). God reconciles all things to Himself in Christ rather than raises them here to a new metaphysical level (Eph. 1: 7; 2: 1, 5, 16).

The nature which our Lord shares with us is our nature, not some higher one. He takes on Him, not the nature of angels, but the seed of Abraham (Heb. 2: 16). His ignorance of the day and hour of the consummation or of the burial place of Larazus is not what E. L. Mascall would make it, simply His inability to put into human language a divine knowledge, but is a mark of His real human nature. His cry of dereliction is His very sharing in our misery. It is not only a sign of complete obedience and a

---

[1] Ernest Best, *One Body in Christ*, p. 186.

sacrifice in that sense. It is an obedience which involves a sharing of our very nature and a unique sacrifice in making expiation for us. It is this that Chalcedon affirmed against any suggestion that His human nature was of a higher ontological
status than ours.

If the conception of the divinization of human nature is not
easily discoverable in the New Testament any more than in the
Old, can it be said that this is due to the Hebrew fear of idolatry
and of confusing the Creator with the creature, while the truth
of our real position as Christians is better expressed by the
Greek Fathers with their teaching about our sharing the Divine
nature? This can be said, but what more truly ought to be said
is that either the Greek Fathers generally are sufficiently controlled by the Biblical witness as to avoid teaching divinization
without considerable qualifications,[1] or that where they do in-
dulge in such teaching without qualification they move straight
towards monophysitism of the Eutychian type. Professor Turner,
who cannot be said to be without sympathy for mysticism in
religion, as the conclusion of his book shows, has made this
strikingly clear. When we come to such teaching "we are here
[in Clement and Origen] at the beginning of those traditions in
devotion which ultimately went hand in hand with the rise of
Eutychianism and the Monophysite tradition. . . . This devotional attitude had a corresponding repercussion in the sphere
of Christology. If the aim of the Christian is to cease to be
'human, all too human', it would be a natural corollary in
Christology to regard the humanity of our Lord as problem
rather than datum. If Christians were seeking through the
grace of God to become *primum quidem homines, tunc demum Dii*,
then naturally the *homo* aspect of the *Cur Deus Homo?* was soon
to become a scandal to be undervalued and overridden as soon
as possible."[2]

v

What has been said of the liberal theologians might also, I
believe, be said of these more orthodox writers who, reacting
from liberalism, move towards a monophysitism of the opposite

[1] David Cairns, *The Image of God in Man*, ch. VII.
[2] H. E. W. Turner, *The Patristic Doctrine of Redemption*, pp. 82-3.

kind. Both bodies of Christian thinkers have sought to *explain* how God can become man. The former have done it by the assumption that human nature at its best is divine and so have argued that Christ had one nature, a perfect human and so a divine nature. The latter have done it by the assumption that there is a higher human nature which is capable of union with the divine as our human nature is not. Such a human nature they have attributed to Christ who then confers it on His people. What the Fathers at Chalcedon did was something quite different. They did not attempt to explain how the divine and the human are united. They rather *affirmed* that there is one Lord Jesus Christ, one *prosopon*, one *hypostasis* in two natures. The same person is both really God and really man. How this is so is beyond explanation.

In conclusion, therefore, let us look at their phraseology. Their aim is to support the faith expressed at Nicaea and Constantinople and to defend it from subsequent errors. These errors include the idea that "He who was born of the holy Mary was a mere man" and "the wrong opinion of Eutyches".[1] In opposing the latter they will have "no mixture or confusion of the two natures of Christ" and refuse to teach that "the form of a servant taken by Him from us is of a heavenly or any other essence". Thus they will neither have a Christ who is simply a perfect man united to God nor a Christ whose human nature is not as ours. Though they have been criticized for dividing the person of Christ by their terminology, they do, in fact, do their best to emphasize the unity of our Lord's person by repeating again and again the phrase "the same". Thus the first part of their statement on Christ's person runs: "*One and the Same* Son, *the same* perfect in Godhead, *the same* perfect in manhood ... *the same* of a rational soul and body, 'homoousios' with the Father as to His Godhead and *the same* 'homoousios' with us as to His Manhood."[2] He is perfect both in Godhead and Manhood, truly God and truly man. This humanity they further emphasize by saying that He is of a rational soul and body, as we are. He is as divine as the Father (homoousios) and as human as we

[1] The text and translation of the Chalcedonian Definition of the Faith are from T. H. Bindley, *The Oecumenical Documents of the Faith.*
[2] R. V. Sellers, *The Council of Chalcedon*, p. 212.

are, except for our sin. He is both the eternal Son of God, they conclude in this first part of their statement, and the real Son of Mary, who bore not only a man but the one who is divine also.

So far the definition has stressed the unity of His person in its two natures. Now it goes on to emphasize the two natures in the unity of the Person. He is "made known" or "recognized as one and the same Christ, Son, Lord, only-begotten in two natures".[1] While earlier statements had mostly said "out of two natures" Chalcedon says "in two natures" to rule out any monophysitism. He is made known and recognized as one in two natures in a way which excludes both Nestorian division and Apollinarian and Eutychian mixture and confusion—one in two natures without division or separation and equally without confusion or change. The defence against Eutychianism is further driven home by the words which follow: "the difference of the natures is in no way removed because of the union. Rather the property of each nature is preserved."

All this, however, is said of the *one* Lord Jesus Christ. Both natures concur into *one* prosopon or person and *one* hypostasis. This, the conclusion, is then repeated and finally confirmed from Scripture and the Fathers, who follow it, in the earlier ecumenical councils.

We may differ in our opinion about the extent to which the technical terms used at Chalcedon are final. We may wish more explicit reference in a statement on the person of our Lord to His Messianic acts. We may well desire to use the best modern scientific terms to describe our Lord's human nature. But can we go beyond the conclusion reached here, beyond the *vere Deus, vere homo*? To do so will, I suspect, tend to an Adoptionism or a monophysitism of the Eutychian type. I do not believe that the theologians whom I have dared to criticize intended to reach either of these positions. Indeed most of them make explicit disclaimers. But I believe that their assumptions lead them in the one direction or the other.

[1] Both shades of meaning are in *gnorizomenos*!

4

CHRIST AND CREATION

by W. A. WHITEHOUSE
Reader in Divinity, University of Durham

4

CHRIST AND CREATION

by

W. A. WHITEHOUSE

SINCE the repudiation of Marcion in the second century, the Church has firmly professed its belief in God as the Maker and Preserver of all things both visible and invisible. There has been little, if any, serious controversy about the bearing of this doctrine. It had to be pressed with particular force, and sometimes in new terms, whenever the Church had to meet the ancient counter-belief that the natural world springs from an evil root. For the rest, at any rate in Western Christendom, the chief interest in this part of Christian doctrine seems to lie in the possibility of establishing and illuminating the belief by way of natural science or philosophy, though errors of a dualist or of a pantheist kind have always been available as targets for the conscientious theologian. The impression given (and perhaps in these circumstances it is hardly surprising) is that the doctrine seemed to be complete in terms of the Creed's first article. The texts which speak of Christ as the mediatorial agent of creation were not essential to its statement. Their proper bearing is in the second article, where the clause "by whom all things were made" underlines the uniqueness of Christ but is not intended to have any decisive effect on the doctrine of creation. With the growth of the modern world-view, these texts have become something of a puzzle, even when the doctrine of creation has not been questioned.

This situation has altered, suddenly and remarkably. In Biblical theology the attention paid to eschatology has brought a new interest in the theme of creation as its necessary counterpart. This has entailed much learned discussion of the affinities and disparities between New Testament thought-forms and those current in the Hellenistic and Rabbinic environments. The same kind of problem has been raised about the Old Testament and the "Myth and Ritual" patterns of the Near East. The Bible is now being expounded by typological exegetes who claim to find in it a widespread "ktisiological pattern" which suggests that "the six days of creation are renewed in all the redemptive events of history".[1] In the field of Systematic Theology there is Barth's massive restatement of the doctrine in Christocentric terms, offered in the course of his *Dogmatik* (Vol. III, 1). There is the highly significant Roman Catholic response from H. U. von Balthasar (*Karl Barth: Darstellung und Deutung seiner Theologie*) which has much to say about the handling of the creation theme. And from Lutheranism there is a most impressive chapter in Edmund Schlink's *Theologie der lutherischen Bekenntnisschriften*. All this may be viewed as part of the Churches' effort to recover the full measure of faith and of theological understanding. But the effort, at any rate in respect of the doctrine of creation, is no more than under way, as two observations may demonstrate.

First, there is plenty of room for scholarly debate about the form and the place of a specific "theology of creation" both in the Old Testament and in the New. Does the Old Testament "doctrine of creation" develop simply in the form of a presupposition which is ultimately subordinate to a central theology of election and covenant? Or is it a major theme, one which "cannot reasonably be relegated to a subordinate place" and became a twin focus for religious life and thought alongside the Exodus theme when the foundation of the kingdom in Israel brought the cult of the divine king into Yahwism?[2] Is there in the New Testament a profound and deliberate doctrine of creation, expressed in a widespread pattern of images, or does

---

[1] L. S. Thornton, *The Dominion of Christ*, p. 48. The phrase "ktisiological pattern" comes from the essay by Gösta Lindeskog in *The Root of the Vine* (ed. Fridrichsen). I have not see Lindeskog's *Studien zum N.T. lichen Schöpfungsgedanken*, but I assume from the anticipatory essay that it has affinities with Thornton's work and also with Austin Farrer's *Rebirth of Images* and *A Study in St. Mark*.

[2] Lindeskog adopts this second point of view (*The Root of the Vine*, p. 4) and brings a charge of inconsistency against Gerhard von Rad who, on my reading of his Genesis commentary (*Das Alte Testament Deutsch* 2/4), does not. Lindeskog seems anxious to have the best of all possible worlds and has hardly managed to produce an integrated account. Lionel Thornton has firmly made up his mind about the form and place of a creation-cycle of imagery conflated with the redemptive history, but like his beloved Greek Fathers he does not expose the technical weighing of pros and cons to the full light of day.

the topic occur only in a few passages whose bearing is Christo-logical rather than cosmological? In either case, have we fully entered into the use made of Gen. 1–2, Prov. 8, and associated passages by the Christian writers? Was a Christocentric doc-trine of creation a major theme of early Christian thought be-cause "Christ's resurrection is effective not only in the redemp-tion of mankind, but in the true and perpetual creation of the world"? If so, what precise steps were taken, and why, to mark off this doctrine from current political mythology on the one hand and from Greek philosophical speculation on the other?[1] There is no room to take up these problems in detail in an essay of this character, but the implications of accepting one kind of integrated account rather than another may appear from what follows.

A second observation suggests that matters have not yet come to a head so far as modern discussion of the doctrine of creation is concerned. It is taken from the field of ecumenical discussion. The Bishop of Durham, in a somewhat disgruntled report of the Evanston Assembly of the World Council of Churches, said that in his opinion both the theologies dominant in the discussion of the "Main Theme" "lacked the right starting point in the *doctrine of creation* and the right goal in the *Beatific Vision*, with the call to holiness as the way to it. . . . It was a happy thing that Anglicans, Eastern Orthodox and English Methodists found themselves joining hands in a plea for a more comprehensive theology of creation, incarnation and sanctification."[2] It is a healthy thing that there should be injected into ecumenical debate the theme so notably stated by an earlier scholarly Bishop of Durham, B. F. Westcott, in his essay *The Gospel of Creation*. We have remarked that the doctrine of creation has not played a lively part in Christian thought and imagination for some time past. It has been formally professed in much the same way by Churches of all traditions, but it has not been ex-plicitly related to the person and work of Jesus Christ, nor to the doctrines of the Holy Spirit and of the Church. Westcott chose to dwell upon a subject which some, he knew, would

[1] The quotation is from a most illuminating essay criticizing the formula *creatio ex nihilo*, by Arnold Ehrhardt in *Studia Theologica*, Vol. IV, Fasc. I, 1951.
[2] In *The Bishoprick*, published at the Diocesan Office, Durham, Nov. 1954.

regard as "a mere matter of speculation, or a curious fancy of a past age". His conclusion was: "The thought that the Incarnation, the union of man with God, and of creation in man, was part of the divine purpose in creation, opens unto us, as I believe, wider views of the wisdom of God than we commonly embrace, which must react upon life."[1] This theme has been taken up by Anglican theologians of our own day, notably by those otherwise very different thinkers Lionel Thornton and Charles Raven.[2] We shall return to Dr. Raven's work at another point. But it will not be readily agreed, on the ecumenical scene, that here the Anglicans—or anywhere else their fellow petitioners—can supply a ready-made "right starting point" for the discussion of all other theological matters. Nor, of course, does the Bishop say so. The point, with which I agree, is that false or impoverished understanding of the doctrine of creation may be among the factors which keep the Churches apart. But when the time is ripe for this to be examined on the ecumenical level there may be much that we all have to learn.

Having noted some points at which the Church is beginning to show a lively concern with the doctrine of creation, we can turn to look at secular thought, for there too the situation has altered. It was a fairly safe assumption, until very recently, that any religious person (which means most people for some of their time) would subscribe to the first article of the Christian creed in some form or other. But when that article is expounded in the penetrating terms of Luther's *Larger Catechism*, those who would still confess it with their lips can at best only faintly believe with their mind that:

This is what I mean and believe, that I am a creature of God; that is, that He has given and constantly preserves to me my body, soul, and life, members great and small, all my senses, reason and understanding, food and drink, clothing and support, wife and children, domestics, house and home. Besides, He causes all creatures to serve for the necessities of life—sun, moon, and stars in the firmament, day and night, air, fire, water, earth, and what-

[1] *The Epistles of St. John*, published by Macmillan, 1884, p. 328.
[2] *Experience and Interpretation.* The second series of Gifford Lectures, published 1953; particularly cc. IV–VI.

ever it bears and produces, birds and fishes, beasts, grain, and all kinds of produce, and whatever else there is of bodily and temporal goods, good government, peace, security.

This belief has worked almost with the strength of an intuition in the lives of religious persons, even in those who would not regard themselves as committed or instructed Christians. But now, even for some instructed Christians, it is a form of pious words which has to maintain itself with difficulty against a curious alliance of rival intuitions: first, that the things enumerated come to us through a history of nature in which inscrutable Fate plays a considerable part; and secondly, that it lies within man's power and destiny to master the raw material of history and of nature in whatever way seems good to him. Only those who have great piety can now trust God to give; the rest of us take for ourselves as best we can and put up with mishaps with such dignity as we can muster. This is not the place to analyse the acids of modernity which have corroded simple faith in the Creator and His work. Among them, no doubt, there is the new scientific view of the world. But there we must take into account the paradoxical situation exposed by Mr. Michael Foster, who has shown how much the rise of modern natural science owes to the Christian doctrine of creation.[1] This particular acid is not a recrudescence of the notion that the natural world springs from an evil root. Historical scepticism, which became the handmaid of Nihilism, is perhaps a different matter. Two main positions have been established, outside the paths of traditional Christian thinking, which offer alternative ways of dealing with historical existence. Both of them are based on a complete rejection first of Greek cosmology and ontology, and secondly of the Christian doctrine of creation. In dialectical materialism, to borrow a phrase from A. C. Craig's *Preaching in a Scientific Age*, there is "the vision of man's mind displacing God as the creative intelligence of the world". In atheist existentialism, there is a defiant acceptance of "being here" without knowing the whence or the whither. Neither of these positions involve any decision about the origin of the world, though Communist dialecticians would presumably be ready to pronounce on the matter in scientific terms if it should become important to do so. The professed

[1] *Mind*, Vol. XLIII, p. 446 ff.; Vol. XLIV, p. 439 ff.; Vol. XLV, p. 1 ff.

Christian doctrine has been rejected as dogmatism in a field where men have no basis for being dogmatic, and this rejection cannot, as I suppose, be challenged on philosophical grounds. It is true that some scientists advance, as the more probable hypothesis, a theory of an origin in finite time for the natural universe in its present state. But some British astronomers are working out what they hope is a better hypothesis to explain the past out of which the universe has come. They are testing the possibility of a law for the continuous creation of matter. Aristotle would not have been disturbed by this; nor would Heraclitus:

> This world, the same for all of us, none of the gods nor of the humans has made; it has always been, and is, and will be, an ever-living fire, flaring up in parts, in parts dying down.[1]

It still seems unlikely, as it did to Aquinas, that any doctrine of creation can be established philosophically. The question is whether the full Christian doctrine can still be established theologically and whether it is our duty to God and to the world that we should do this again. If there is such a pressing duty, our power to fulfil it, like that of the early Christians, may depend very much on a renewed conviction that all things have been created by God *through Christ* the eternal Son who was incarnate and who suffered under Pontius Pilate and rose from the dead on the third day.

But the secular thinker, confronted by what he must regard as polemical theology, will at once make a further point which the theologian should heed for his own good. There are good reasons for suspicion about religious dogmatism in matters of this kind. We can look back to the ancient civilizations of Egypt and Babylon, where considerable knowledge about the constitution of the world and the technical manipulation of its resources was held in the form of religious secrets. There was also "an official mythology, transmitted in priestly corporations and enshrined in elaborate ceremonial, telling how things came to be as they are".[2] The scientific approach to what exists, in contrast with the religious, is often traced back to the "Ionian Enlightenment" of the sixth century B.C., and it is mentioned

---

[1] fr. 30 Diels I, 84, 1 ff.   [2] Benjamin Farrington, *Greek Science*, pp. 27–31.

as a favourable circumstance "that these communities, to put it briefly, were not priest-ridden".[1] Thales was able to shake off priestly fetters and talk constructively about the world, its constitution and its origin, *"without letting Marduk in"*. Now the point is not to be irreligious for the sake of being irreligious, nor yet because religion necessarily makes a man a poor scientist. It is the political significance of priestly corporations and of religious mythology which draws down well-merited suspicion. The political character of the term *cosmos* (*mundus*) in Graeco-Latin thought was doubtless appreciated by early Christian writers. "The Hellenistic theologians stated it quite plainly that 'the king is the last of the gods and the first of men', the connecting link between the supra-lunar *cosmos* and the sub-lunar *chaos*." When the king was acclaimed as *Epiphanes* (the present god) and *Soter* (the saviour), this "was not rank flattery but religion, the result of strong sentiments based upon a genuine and, in its way, competent theological and philosophical attempt at understanding the universe as a political system with a monarchical constitution".[2]

The religious leopard does not change his spots, and Christianity has in this world the form of a "religion", often without showing any serious self-criticism in this respect. Further, a critical observer of the British scene, to go no further afield, might conclude that an official mythology enshrined in elaborate ceremonial with royal personages at its heart has not lost its religio-political usefulness. The same critical observer would also be inclined to say that the New Testament witness to Jesus Christ as Lord and Saviour of the world looks like the supreme and consummating example of religio-political mystery-mongering, an impression which seems to be confirmed by extravagant attempts to commend Him as one who acted within the Godhead at the creation of all things.

I do not suggest that these secular observations should frighten the theologian away from a clear New Testament theme, nor that they should influence his handling of it, except perhaps in one respect which does not impair the proper substance of his work. The quotation from Luther's *Catechism* shows more clearly than do most of the available formal statements

[1] E. Schrödinger, *Nature and the Greeks*, p. 54.   [2] Ehrhardt, *op. cit.*, pp. 18–22.

that what is professed in the first article of the Creed reaches down to the simplicities of which a man is most conscious when he lives humbly in this world. But it has an equally intense bearing on the great complexities of historical and political organization. If it is to be treated as one of the great themes of Christianity, as undoubtedly it is one of the great themes of "religion", it must be expounded with care and responsibility, the emphases placed where the Bible places them, and perhaps with a reserve which matches that of the Biblical writers in both the Old and the New Testaments.

"God has spoken to us in a Son, through whom also He made the world."[1]

"He has delivered us from the dominion of darkness and transferred us to the kingdom of his beloved Son, in whom we have redemption, the forgiveness of sins. He is the image of the invisible God, the firstborn of all creation; for in him were all things created . . . through him, and for him."[2]

That is the particular theme, to be proclaimed "in faith", with which this essay is concerned. In the remainder of the essay I shall consider its presentation under some aspects which call for well-informed theological decision. This piecemeal approach, on the basis of two isolated statements of the theme whose exegesis I am taking for granted,[3] is perhaps excusable if I am right in supposing that current discussion of the doctrine of creation is still in the exploratory stage.

The theme has to be proclaimed "in faith" and it is "by faith" that it must first be held true. It is necessary first to explain how, when we say "by faith", we are not saying "by the speculative imagination" or "by the superstition which produced the ancient creation-myths of Babylon or Egypt or even Greece". The faith of Israel, which produced the very unmythical confessions in Gen. 1 and 2, and the faith by which Christians understand the worlds to have been framed by the

---

[1] Heb. 1: 1–2
[2] Col. 1: 13–16
[3] For the exegesis of the second passage I would acknowledge a particular debt of gratitude to W. D. Davies, *Paul and Rabbinic Judaism*, especially c. 7: *The Old and the New Torah: Christ the Wisdom of God.*

Word of God, are not of that order. In both cases, no doubt, it is
a matter of holding an intellectual opinion on grounds which
lack theoretical certainty. In Israel's case, however, it is a
matter of acknowledging that the whole of life has been set in a
pattern and direction for which no sufficient natural reason can
be discovered. The pattern, like the direction, is one of *gratitude*;
gratitude to one who is not to be counted among natural factors
but who calls for divine worship as Israel's *wholly gracious God*.
This gratitude was evoked in Israel by the calling and the
deliverance from Egypt and by the covenant relationship
offered and accepted at Sinai. Historically it may be true that
this characteristic faith of Israel was not fully articulated until
the promised land fell wholly under the control of the early
monarchy, and by that time other factors—notably the pattern
of Canaanite religion—had their part to play. It was at that
period most probably that the response of gratitude took concrete form in the production of an integrated tradition depict-
ing the past out of which David's kingdom had come. This
tradition included God's earlier call and covenant with Abraham, and a pre-history of that remarkable choice running back
to a "beginning" when heaven and earth were created. The
whole tradition expressed and perpetuated a faith which
marked off Israel from all other nations as "the People of God",
bound to a strictly supernatural God whose distinctive demands
and promises were pressed by the prophets upon an audience
all too ready to be as other nations were.

The pattern of gratitude was enriched and deepened, and
this is particularly true of Israel's gratitude to God for *an
originating act of creation*. It is the prophets who had to wrestle
with the disaster of the Exile and the seeming collapse of the
covenanted purpose, Jeremiah and Second Isaiah, who bring
this theme most obviously to the fore. When all the documents
of faith are taken into account—later strands in the Pentateuch,
prophetic writings, wisdom literature and apocalyptic—the
total impression is clear. Israel acknowledged by word and life
a God with power over all things and all circumstances, with an
absolute claim on all things as His creatures, and of a goodness
which merited absolute trust. This pattern of gratitude had
been evoked in history; it was one to be sustained in history;

and the truth of it, which present history could only partly authenticate because of sin's disordering power, would appear in history or beyond history at the consummation. That is the ground of Old Testament faith in God the Creator.

Behind the New Testament confessions of God the Creator, and especially behind those which speak of creation through Christ, there is a grateful acknowledgment, of this same order, that God has disclosed His power over all things and all circumstances, including now the whole gamut of rebellious devices used by creatures estranged into some wrong allegiance; that He has wrought "an act of justification that penetrates back to the very beginning and sets man's life on the basis of God's creative purpose";[1] that He has disclosed an abiding love for what He made by raising from the dead the body of the crucified Saviour "having reconciled to Himself all things, whether on earth or in heaven, making peace by the blood of his Cross".[2]

Belief that all things have their origin in a divine act of creation, done in perfect freedom, perfect wisdom, and perfect love, is thus to be accepted as one moment in a given pattern of gratitude. But the *truth* of this belief is not settled merely by finding that one's life has been set in such a pattern, nor by managing to maintain it knowing all too clearly that the brink of chaos and despair is only just behind one's heels. Does this gratitude reflect and embody the truth? In terms of Biblical logic, the reply to this urgent question is that we must strive for an ever deeper understanding of that which has evoked the grateful faith, but there can be no final assurance until the truth appears at the end of history. On the first point in that reply a Christian will say that what was given in Israel's experience before Christ, like that which is given elsewhere apart from Israel and from Christ, does not provide adequate ground for satisfactory understanding; but the incompleteness of Israel's experience is remedied when the Christ to whom it pointed appeared on the earthly scene. He will also say, taking up the second point, that in this coming of Christ there was a veiled enactment of the consummation, so the truth about divine

---

[1] T. F. Torrance, "The Atonement and the Oneness of the Church," in *Scottish Journal of Theology*, 7/3, p. 262.
[2] Col. 1: 20

creation has been disclosed eschatologically in the form of an open secret.[1]

But Christ came on the earthly scene, not in the role of Creator but in the role of Reconciler. By faith He is worshipped as Lord and as Saviour of the world; the effect of His coming may be described as a "new creation". But by what right is he worshipped as "the beginning of God's creation"[2] where the reference is to Gen. 1 and 2; that is, to the accomplishing long ago of heavens and of an earth made by the word of God (2 Pet. 3: 4)? It has been argued that the Fourth Evangelist (John 1: 3) "turns the idea of a creation which was accomplished once for all at the beginning into that *which to the human mind appears* as a continuous process".[3] But this interpretation, despite the reservations implicit in the italicized words, tends to obscure the real distinction between the divine works of creation and of reconciliation, and I do not think the Fourth Evangelist meant to do so. It is a presupposition of Biblical thinking that there is a line of salvation-history which runs forward to the consummation and also backward to *the* creation of all things—that is, to an event where God established a theatre for the historical enactment of the covenant of grace. That which was done "in the beginning" is no doubt fairly said to have been recapitulated as an act of reconciliation in the midst of time. But there is no confusion in the Christian witness between an act of creation, done once for all, and an act of reconciliation, also done once for all. The two acts have different settings in the dimension of time, both in God's time and in our time. The act of creation brought man into existence as the responsible partner of God at the centre of an ordered world where there is room, both in time and space, for ages of history to unfold and for the Reconciler to appear as man for man. By what right is the Reconciler to be worshipped as co-agent with his Father in that original work of creation?

New Testament scholars have explained the various ways by which Jews and Greeks habitually expressed the relationship between God and the world. The explanations usually involved

---

[1] I take this to be the meaning of "mystery" in Ephesians 1: 9–10.

[2] Rev. 3: 14

[3] Ehrhardt, *op. cit.*, p. 40 (my italics).

a Mediator, characterized as Logos, Wisdom, Son of God, Heavenly Man, active with God in the world's creation and able to intervene as the world's Saviour. When the first Christians found in Jesus a Saviour and Lord, it was an easy and natural step for them to clothe His person in this kind of imagery; and scholars have shown how the language of these explanations is taken into Christian service in passages where the cosmic role of Christ is affirmed. The religious and philosophical allusions which made such passages readily intelligible to the first readers are neither familiar nor convincing to the ordinary intelligent Christian of to-day, and I find it hard to suppose that some schooling in this technical background is either necessary or desirable for present believers, in order to assist their affirmation of Christ's cosmic role. It is important to observe that the texts in question (e.g. Col. 1: 1–16; Heb. 1: 1–2; John 1: 1–3) are not calculated to express a particular cosmogony but to characterize Jesus. Further, it has been well said that it is "exegetically impossible to understand them of an eternal divine Son or Logos *in abstracto*, but solely of him in his unity with the man Jesus".[1] All our thought on these matters must therefore be controlled by what we know of Jesus in His historical work. But then it is extremely difficult to believe that He, the crucified and risen Man, embodies resources through which this universe has been made.[2] It is of no help, however, to imagine those resources under the figure of some divine cosmic magnitude, corresponding to the Logos or Wisdom of ancient religious philosophy, and then try to add this as an invisible factor to Jesus as we know Him. In any case, this is not how the Bible encourages us to think. We shall return to this problem of philosophical categories before long. Meanwhile, let us attempt to make a direct statement of the New Testament affirmation whose logic we have to reproduce in our own

---

[1] H. U. v. Balthasar, *op. cit.*, p. 128.

[2] The difficulties as I see them will be mentioned in the last section of the essay. Having now seen the Isenheim altar in its present setting at the Musée d'Unterlinden in Colmar, I now realize that an artist can do what science and philosophy cannot do for me. The awful figure hanging from the flattened arc of the crossbeam is very man, brought to the nadir of humiliation; but he is the one who came to what was and remains his own possession and the resurrection panel only confirms what is already evident, that he is able to subdue it all unto himself.

responsible faith without leaning on the language and thought-
forms of first-century religious philosophy.

What is it that moves the believer to worship Christ as co-
agent of the creation? The answer, I think, is that Jesus Christ
has brought *man* into existence, historically and securely, as the
responsible partner of God to whom the rest of creation has
been subjected; and he has done so precisely at the point where
man had incurred the doom of annihilation (cf. Heb. 1–2).
This mighty work is attributed to Jesus, the Messiah of Israel,
who brought his own people—and in principle therefore the
rest of the cosmos—to a crisis where God's final judgment was
enacted in a veiled form and the coming dispensation of a new
creation was inaugurated. What issues from this crisis is man,
raised from death for eternal life in a new context of heavens
and earth wherein dwelleth righteousness (2 Pet. 3: 13). Christ
Himself, and those who are "in Christ" as in a "new Adam",
have already entered upon this life, but the appropriate environment is one for which we still wait. The dominion of
Christ, and of man in Christ, is presented to us in and through
this eschatological detail. What it means is that Israel's faith,
Israel's election by God, Israel's covenant-history with God,
and also therefore the original work of creation which is pre-
supposed in that history, are all fully and finally authenticated.

This statement raises two further problems which must also
be deferred for a little while: the problem posed by the anthropocentric character of the whole story, and the problem of
whether or not there are discernible signs in the history of
nature that creation has this Christocentric ordering. Before
passing to the last part of the essay, to which three problems
have now been relegated, there is one further point to be made.

This testimony is taken seriously only in faith, and then it
has to be acknowledged that the agent of the mighty works is
not a man ultimately separate from God, nor a divine magnitude ultimately separable from the man Jesus, but is the second
person of the God who must henceforth be acknowledged as the
Holy Trinity. The dominion and love which are expressed in
the work are the dominion and love of Jesus Christ who is very
man, but they are, identically, the dominion and love of the
Father to whom He explicitly gave perfect obedience, and,

identically, the dominion and love of the Spirit by whose work they are carried into effect and we are persuaded of them. It is this awareness of *God* in Christ which finally sets men free to say that in Jesus Christ they have encountered the Creator of the world. Only the divine architect and builder of history could display such perfect dominion over its disorder; only the archetypal lover of men could bring to our race the assured hope and present anticipation of faithful partnership with God. Looking to Christ, therefore, we should make the grateful confession that the ground of all existence is simply the divine claim and promise which have been made good by His ministry and resurrection and which were *His* claim and promise before ever the world was. This means, however, that some decision has to be taken as to the form in which He acted with God in the beginning. By which of the available titles can this best be expressed? We could claim, I think, the authority even of the Fourth Evangelist for saying: by the title "Son of God", the hypostatic correlate of the title "Father". He is the Son who as such fulfilled the roles ascribed sometimes to Word, Wisdom, Torah; a Son destined by eternal generation to be man for us men. The deed done in time by the incarnate Son is one into which the agent's being was wholly poured before the worlds were made; what is expressed in the history of the Son of Man is the perfect utterance of what He always is as Son of God. There lies the point of the contention that it is Christ's resurrection which is effective, not only in the redemption of mankind, but in the true and abiding creation of the world. But it does not follow, I submit, that creation is to be treated as a seemingly continuous process, nor that it should be amalgamated with conserving and redeeming processes, after the fashion of pagan religions inspired by the cycles of nature.

There are certain obstacles for the modern mind which hamper any full and free expression of faith in the cosmic role of Christ, and we shall glance at three of them by way of conclusion. Faith is not achieved by negotiating these obstacles. Rather is their negotiation one of the delicate and exacting tasks to which the believer must address himself if he is to understand and enjoy that which he believes.

First among these is the fact that we approach Jesus Christ with preconceived ideas of what the creation is, and therefore with preconceived ideas about the resources adequate for its production, and so with preconceived ideas about the character of a possible world-Creator. The present philosophical climate is unusually helpful in this respect, for philosophers are now disposed to utter solemn warnings about the stupidity of metaphysical attempts to measure reality as a whole. Nevertheless, there are factors which militate against Christian belief. Some kind of world-picture is in everyone's mind. Most of it may be the fruit of sheer positivist description, but the elements of description tend to be accompanied by "explanatory notes" of one kind or another. The main trend of the "notes" can usually be labelled either "Idealist" (with an "animist" flavour) or "Naturalist" (with a "materialist" flavour). In the ancient world the "Naturalists" fought a losing battle. The cosmos, as anciently imagined, was one that could be explained, necessarily and absolutely, by postulating the appropriate "ideas" and "souls". The modern picture, on the other hand, finds the fundamental cosmic reality in the multifarious forms of physical "energy" or "action" which are still being tracked down. The "Idealist" tradition has waged a vigorous and fruitful battle to keep "ideas" and "souls" in the picture at the most fundamental level, but the fact remains that if you talk nowadays about the creation of the world, it is no longer possible to brush aside the question of this amazing physical power and the control which lies behind its wonderful deployment. To offer an explanatory note which suggests that it is all a matter of "ideas" entertained by "souls" will hardly do. Therefore we tend to suppose that there is some root of absolute necessity in the ineluctable givenness of physical energy, and to this root, perhaps, can also be traced the ideal principles on which the world seems to be constructed. We hesitate to say that we have found the origin from which the world has come unless what we have found yields to our minds the reason of this absolute necessity. Jesus of Nazareth, even when He is presented in the most careful theological fullness, does not do this.

To this we may reply that what is being sought is the reason of a wholly fictitious absolute necessity. We can do this by

I

calling on the existentialist critique of all notions that this is a stable meaningful world in and for itself. Alternatively, or by way of supplement, we can point to the growing conviction that what is most concrete, and therefore most actual, is not physical energy, nor yet souls with their traditional microcosmic status, but sheer event or eventful history. In this way it may be possible to recover something like Luther's doctrine of creatures as *larvae Dei*:[1] entities intrinsically incomplete in themselves or when taken all together; masks which carry an echo of the one complete Being who is using them but which in themselves conceal Him in all His works and ways; "Dei larvae, allegoriae, quibus rethorice pingit suam theologiam: they are meant, as it were, to contain Christ."[2]

The second obstacle is to be found in the clearly anthropocentric character of Christian doctrine. The first two chapters of Genesis have for their focus God's election of man; the rest of the creation is man's appropriate environment. It was relatively easy to think in this way in the ancient world or in the Middle Ages. It is now very hard to imagine that the history of nature can be explained, even in principle, by reference to God's purpose with man. It savours very strongly of wishful thinking. At the moment we are haunted by the notion that man's knowledge of the hydrogen bomb and man's freedom to use it could destroy the species of which we are members. But there is no reason to imagine that the Creator would thereupon ring down the curtain and banish from the stage of space-time the earth itself, the solar system, the Milky Way and all the concourse of galaxies to which ours belongs. Nevertheless, the Christian doctrine, with its emphasis on Christ not only as the Wisdom of God but also as the Second Adam, calls for an anthropocentric view.

There is a strand of Christian thinking which has shown

---

[1] There is a useful note on this doctrine in P. S. Watson, *Let God Be God*, pp. 76–81. The doctrine is worth mentioning because it serves to give a better indication of what is wanted than does Thomist doctrine, a point which Watson explains. Philosophers and theologians must do a lot of work together if there is to be a new and satisfactory decision as to what we are talking about when we say "creatures". My own view is that among the philosophers it is Whitehead who has most to give.

[2] W.A., XL. 1, 463 and 9 with the German words translated.

some awareness of what is involved. It was represented in the Alexandria of Clement and Origen, among the Cambridge Platonists of the seventeenth century, and now in the work of Charles Raven who finds in Christ the consummation of a principle "which enables both the highest development of the individual parts and their full co-operation in an ordered society" and which "seems to apply on every level from the atom to the saint".[1] For Raven, Christ is "an adequate symbol of the divine", the perfect Son of Man towards whom the creative process consistently points. He is mankind's example and representative, whose office it is to give the Spirit free course and thus "to quicken sensitiveness, heighten vitality, remove callousness, and so enable response to the beauty and meaning and worth of the world".[2] Raven has done his best to justify the belief that heaven and earth exist for the production of human persons in community. He has looked honestly at nature and pointed to the many ways in which it seems to carry the trade mark of Christ—a suffering Christ, let it be remembered—who supremely symbolizes the creative process moved everywhere by love.

It is easy to criticize this story, by questioning its conformity to the Biblical grounds adduced in its support, or by noting to what extent Raven's world turns out to be Western man's dream of Paradise and the porch thereinto. But it cannot be dismissed like that. The history of nature is coming under man's dominion to an increasing degree; it is being increasingly permeated by man's purposes; and the effect is not wholly detrimental. Is not this a token, however ambiguous or proleptic, that it is already permeated by the mind and will which received historical expression in the man Jesus Christ? The mind and will by which mankind tends to permeate the cosmos independently must of course be transformed if they are to become the mind and will of Christ. But signs of this transformation are not altogether lacking in the changing pattern of man's thought and purposes.

The last obstacle to be mentioned is a failure in practice rather than a difficulty in theory, though it will not be overcome by practice without careful theological assistance. It is

[1] *Experience and Interpretation*, p. 145.   [2] *ibid.*, p. 151

unlikely that we shall enjoy a renewed faith in the Christocentric doctrine of creation until the Holy Spirit moves men to a more distinguished practical response of gratitude and obedience in the ordinary business of living. We can look back to the practical piety of Luther's *Catechism* and recognize nostalgically that the pattern and direction of life which it promoted had a distinction which is not there in modern substitutes. We remember the *joie de vivre* of medieval artists and scholars and craftsmen. We find it difficult at present to imagine that this universe has been framed with special reference to God's purpose in Christ with mankind. Such a thesis, which may be defended on a broad view at some risk of special pleading to keep up public morale, is very hard indeed to defend when one descends to details like the domestic cat or the spiral nebula in Andromeda. The medieval Church was singularly ready to keep such eccentric details in the picture; it fitted them into its *Speculum Naturale*, carved them in stone upon its cathedrals, and thus made them media for the worship of Christ. With more reservations, we remember also the confident Christian contributions which have been made to law, politics, philosophy and learning, which in their own way expressed a firm belief in Christ's dominion. Can we look forward to a movement of the Spirit by which some men will be empowered to show in modern terms the symbols of Christ's dominion as Creator of the world? It is for the artist to release the symbols which chiefly move us to gratitude. It is for the technician, the politician, the ordinary worker, the educator, to release the symbols which chiefly point to new obedience. The theologian, as part of his own work, can point to the poverty of our present condition and to the riches by which that poverty ought to be banished. What he can also do, in common with all his brethren of mankind, is to do right, entrust his soul to a faithful Creator, and pray, and prepare if need be to suffer, for new integrity in the humble ways of life.

5

THE SPIRIT OF CHRIST

by G. W. BROMILEY
Rector of St. Thomas' Church, Edinburgh

THE SPIRIT OF CHRIST

by

G. W. BROMILEY

IN the Bible and historical theology there is no Pneumatology apart from Christology. The person and work of the Holy Spirit is known only in relation to the Word made flesh. Certainly, mention is made of the Spirit in the Old Testament, just as there is mention of God apart from Jesus Christ. But the Old Testament does not stand alone. It is preparatory to the coming of Jesus Christ in whom it finds its fulfilment. Its office is to lead to Jesus Christ. The main function of the Holy Spirit in the Old Testament is in relation to the prophetic testimony which points forward to the Incarnate Word. And the Spirit Himself is not definitely known in His person and work, just as God the Father is not definitely known. It is only in the light of fulfilled revelation that we can see the Father and know the Holy Ghost. And that revelation means Jesus Christ.

There is, of course, a temptation to have it otherwise. The refusal of the Eastern Churches to accept the"filioque "clause testifies perhaps to an underlying impulse to separate the Holy Spirit and His work from Jesus Christ, to give to the Holy Spirit an autonomy in revelation and redemption, to achieve a Christianity of the "spirit" without the corresponding embodiment in the "flesh". There are other and more blatant examples of the same tendency. The fanatics of the Reformation period invoked the authority of spiritual visions and revelations even in opposition to the fleshly letter of the Old or New Testament. The Quakers pushed this teaching to its extreme, claiming an experience of the Holy Spirit which could not be made dependent upon the outward forms of Christianity, or in the last resort upon Jesus Christ Himself. But the witness of historical theology and of the Bible and of Jesus Christ is against them. If Jesus Christ is the Word made flesh, it is He who occupies the central place not merely in the things of God but in our knowledge of God Himself. If no man comes to the Father but by Jesus Christ, it is also Jesus Christ who sends that other Comforter who testifies of Jesus Christ and makes possible His abiding presence.

But that means that it is only in relation to Jesus Christ that we can genuinely speak of the Holy Spirit, and know His person and understand something of His work. In a sense this is paradoxical. The Bible makes it plain that we cannot know Jesus Christ except by the Holy Spirit. "No man can say that Jesus is the Lord, but by the Holy Ghost."[1] But the point is that we know Jesus Christ first. It is only afterwards, and in the light of Jesus Christ, that we understand the operation and the person of the Holy Spirit. We cannot begin to speak independently of the Holy Spirit, and we ought not to try. At every point, in relation to the life and ministry of Jesus Christ, in relation to the preaching of Jesus Christ, in relation to the Christian life in Jesus Christ, the Holy Spirit is indissolubly linked with the Incarnation of the Word of God, the divine Son.

We see this first of all in connection with the life and ministry of Jesus, for it is by the working and in the power of the Holy Spirit that the divine revelation and redemption is accomplished.

The way was prepared by the Holy Spirit. It was for this purpose that the Old Testament was given. Conventionally, the Old Testament was divided into three sections, the Law, the Prophets and the Writings.[2] But strictly, all the Old Testament is prophetic of Jesus Christ. This is true not merely of the writings themselves, which in spite of their human character are in a very special sense the work of the Holy Spirit.[3] It is also true of the persons and incidents which make up the content or history of the Old Testament. All these find their true end and fulfilment and meaning in Jesus Christ, who is the sum and centre of all the Scriptures. "They are they which testify of me."[4] The inspiration of the Old Testament was not an inspiration in the void, or for the purpose of conveying inerrant historical information or reliable philosophical truth. It was an inspiration with prophetic importance: a pointing to the last

---

[1] 1 Cor. 12: 3   [2] cf. Luke 24: 44   [3] 2 Tim. 3: 16; 2 Pet. 1: 21
[4] John 5: 39; cf. Luke 24: 27, 44

days when God would speak by His Son.[1] To say that the Old Testament is given by the Holy Spirit is to say already that it is the office of the Holy Spirit to prepare the word and work of the Incarnate Son.

Jesus was conceived by the Holy Spirit.[2] This is the testimony of the Gospels and the historic creeds. On the human side it involves the Virgin Birth. To deny the Virgin Birth is to separate between Jesus Christ and the Holy Spirit. For the Virgin Birth does not stand alone as an isolated and pointless wonder. It is the reverse side of the conception by the Holy Ghost. It establishes the fact that the God-Manhood of Jesus Christ is not merely a superimposed idea, but a fact of history. It brings the Holy Spirit into the closest possible contact with the supreme mystery of the saving act of God: the fact that the Word became flesh.[3] That the Word did become flesh is attested by the fact that Jesus was born of the Virgin Mary. That it is the Word that became flesh is attested by the fact that Jesus was conceived of the Holy Ghost. That He was conceived by the Holy Ghost, and not by the Father or the Logos, reminds us perhaps that the redemptive work of Christ is a work of the whole Trinity. Jesus came from God,[4] but He was sent by the Father,[5] and conceived by the Spirit.[6] It is also a warning that the Holy Spirit does not do His work in some sphere of the spirit isolated from that of the flesh. Even in the Old Testament witness it had been the office of the Spirit to work out that witness in words and deeds and persons and writings. When the fullness of the time came, and God sent forth His Son,[7] the work of the Holy Spirit was a work of incarnation: Mary was overshadowed by the power of the Most Highest and that holy thing which was born of her was the Son of God.[8]

The life and ministry of Jesus were lived out in the power of the Holy Spirit. The divine conception was not an isolated action. It was the beginning of an operation in which the power of the Holy Spirit was fulfilled in the person and words and actions of a human character, Jesus of Nazareth. Of course, in the Synoptic narratives it is not constantly reiterated that Jesus did this or that in the fullness or power of the Spirit. Yet there

---

[1] Heb. 1: 1–2   [2] Matt. 1: 20   [3] John 1: 14   [4] John 3: 13; 16: 27
[5] John 3: 16–17   [6] Luke 1: 35   [7] Gal. 4: 4   [8] Luke 1: 35

is a sufficient number of references to make it plain that from first to last the life, and especially the ministry, of Jesus was under the impulsion and empowering of the Holy Ghost. Even the statement that as a boy Jesus waxed strong in spirit[1] carries a definite suggestion that the Spirit was at work. At the baptism in the river Jordan, which marked the beginning of the ministry of reconciliation, the Holy Spirit descended upon Jesus in power.[2] It was by the Spirit that He was led into the wilderness and strengthened to reject the temptations of the Devil and to see His true Messianic calling.[3] In the synagogue at Nazareth He significantly read from Isaiah: "The Spirit of the Lord is upon me."[4] It was in the Spirit that He taught. The fact that He used a different formula from the prophetic "Thus saith the Lord" did not mean that He spoke with any different authority, but that He was conscious of a unity with the Spirit which the prophets themselves could not claim. It was by the Spirit of God that He worked His miracles, as He definitely claimed when the Pharisees accused Him of devilish power.[5] It was with an insight into the inspired Scriptures of the Old Testament that He accepted the sacrificial vocation of a servant and suffering Messiah[6] which Israel as a whole had rejected. He gave His life a ransom for many in the conscious knowledge that this was the divinely appointed baptism with which He must be baptized,[7] the cup which He must drink.[8] Finally, if it was God who raised Him from the dead, the apostolic testimony is that the divine work of resurrection was accomplished by the life-giving Spirit. Indeed, we might go further, for it is by the Holy Spirit whom He Himself has sent that the Risen and Ascended Jesus is still present to His disciples, not merely as the eternal Logos, but as the One who died and rose again for us.[9]

The close relationship between the Holy Spirit and the historical Jesus gives rise to many independent problems, especially in the Christological sphere. For example, it might be asked why the divine-human Person of Christ was not self-sufficient, apart from the endowment of the Holy Ghost.

---

[1] Luke 2: 40   [2] Mark 1: 10; Luke 4: 1; John 14: 16–18   [3] Mark 1: 12
[4] Luke 4: 18   [5] Matt. 12: 28   [6] cf. Heb. 9: 14   [7] Luke 12: 50
[8] Mark 14: 36   [9] John 14: 16–18

Adoptionist speculations can very easily arise out of the very closeness of the relationship. The difficulties are not insuperable. There is the "essential" answer, that the incarnation does not involve a disruption of the inter-Trinitarian relationship. There is also the "economic" answer, that redemption is a combined operation of the Trinity, and that as the representative and Head of the new people of God, Jesus knows the same work of the Spirit as His people know. But the main point is that the relationship between Christ and the Spirit is there at the very heart of the Christian faith, in the incarnation and the saving word and work of the One who is called the second man, the Lord from heaven.[1] It is in the light of this primary relationship to Christ Himself that the further work of the Holy Spirit must be considered and known.

We see this relatedness further in the present office and work of the Holy Spirit, which is to testify to Jesus Christ, and which itself follows an incarnational pattern.

When we have to do with the work of the Holy Spirit, we deal with the subjective side of the divine revelation and redemption. God has spoken and acted in the historical life and work of Jesus Christ. That speaking and acting was itself in the power of the Spirit. But the objective speech is not completed until it is actually heard. The objective salvation is not fulfilled until men are themselves saved. If there is a speaker and a speech, there must also be a speaking. If there is a saviour and a salvation, there must also be a saving. To put it plainly and simply, the Gospel does not end with the objective and outward fact. There is also the inward and subjective application. It has to be received. It has to be understood. It has to be known. It has to be appropriated. It has to become part of the very life and being of those to whom it comes. The accomplishment of this subjective side of the work of God is the office of the Holy Spirit.

But it is not a purely subjective work. That is to say, the Holy Spirit does not operate merely in the context of the individual life. To say that would be to justify any product of the human mind or experience. Every fancied vision or inspiration or revelation or insight could be claimed as the work of the Holy

[1] I Cor. 15: 47

Spirit, the only test of its genuineness being its subjectivity. To believe that is to destroy necessarily the relationship between the Holy Spirit and the Incarnate Christ. It is also to introduce confusion in place of the One Spirit whom we know in the New Testament. "Try the spirits whether they are of God,"[1] was the apostolic warning. The test by which the true Spirit is known is the relationship to Jesus Christ come in the flesh.[2]

Naturally, there has to be the subjective work of the Spirit. The word of Jesus Christ is a word of truth and power in my life only as I believe it. Jesus Christ is the Son of God and the Saviour in my soul only as I receive Him. This is self-evident. It is also self-evident in the Bible and Christian history that this believing and receiving is not something which man can do of and for himself. "The natural man receiveth not the things of the spirit."[3] "No man can say that Jesus is the Lord, but by the Holy Ghost."[4] But this subjective operation of the Holy Spirit does not stand alone. It is related integrally and necessarily to the objective facts by which God worked out His word and work in the historical life and person of Jesus Christ. It is the office of the Holy Spirit, not to do a religious work in the abstract, but to bear testimony to the concrete work of God in Jesus Christ,[5] and to bring in the individual to an inward acknowledgment of Jesus Christ and an apprehension of His word and work.

This point is illustrated by the prophetic testimony of the Old Testament to which we have already referred. Although the Old Testament brings before us a wide range of historical situations, and a considerable variety of religious insights and emphases, it would be a mistake to understand it either as a series of sporadic and disconnected revelations, or as the record of a religious evolution, for the Old Testament has an inner and vital unity as the preparatory testimony of the Holy Spirit to Jesus Christ.[6] This testimony does not destroy the deep historicity of the Old Testament. It is not esoteric. But it is the fulfilment of the essential office of the Holy Spirit according to the incarnational pattern of the One whom it attests.

If this is true of the prophetic testimony of the Old Testa-

---

[1] 1 John 4: 1   [2] 1 John 4: 2   [3] 1 Cor. 2: 14
[4] 1 Cor. 12: 3   [5] John 16: 13–14   [6] Luke 24: 27

ment, it is no less true of the apostolic witness of the New. Indeed, we are distinctly told in the Johannine discourses that a primary function of the Paraclete is to bear witness to Jesus Christ.[1] This is not an isolated text. The Paraclete was to assist the disciples in recalling all the things which Jesus had said and done.[2] He was to guide the disciples into all truth:[3] not the progressive discoveries of new abstract truths, but the apprehension of the One who is Himself the truth. The Holy Spirit was to take charge of the apostolic mission. The disciples were not to rush into proclamation, but to tarry in Jerusalem until they were endued with power from on high.[4] Even a cursory reading of the Acts of the Apostles irresistibly suggests that the words and works of the apostles were simply an outworking of the testimony of the Holy Spirit to Jesus Christ. At any rate, that is how both Paul and John understood it.[5] The work of the Holy Spirit is to show us that Jesus is the Lord. The Spirit does not speak of Himself. He does not draw attention to His own person and work. He does not give any autonomous or individual revelation. His purpose is always to bear witness to Jesus Christ, to bring the individual hearer to an apprehension of Jesus Christ as Saviour and Lord.

This means that the subjective operation of the Holy Spirit is complemented always by the objective facts of the Gospel. The subjective operation is necessary. Without it the Gospel is to us mere history. Jesus is, shall we say, a great religious teacher. The death and reported resurrection are incidents which call for discussion and explanation as best we can. But the objective facts are also necessary. Without them faith is subject always to the arbitrary pressure of individual preference and speculation. Apart from the subjective work, we cannot say that Jesus is the Lord, or His death a death for sin, or His resurrection the first-fruits of the new creation of God. But if the subjective work is really of the Holy Spirit, it will always be Jesus of Nazareth who is the Lord, and the divine forgiveness and re-creation will be inseparably connected with the historical life and death and resurrection of that man Jesus.

Here again we see that the work of the Holy Spirit conforms

---

[1] John 15: 26   [2] John 14: 26   [3] John 16: 13   [4] Acts 1: 8
[5] cf. 1 Cor. 2: 12–13; 1 John 4: 13–14.

to the pattern of the incarnation of Jesus Christ, which is itself fulfilled in the Holy Spirit. For the true hearing of the Word of God two things are necessary: the inward working and the outward facts. Apart from the outward facts there is no Word of God. The Holy Spirit will not speak unless He bears testimony to Jesus Christ. But apart from the inward working there is no understanding of the facts. It is the Holy Spirit who must bear testimony to Jesus Christ. In a word, in the attesting work of the Spirit we move on the two levels which correspond to the two natures of Jesus Christ Himself, the divine and the human, the eternal and the historical. We must not try to separate the two, for they are the one witness, just as Jesus is the one Christ. Nor must we try to deny either the one side or the other, to find the working of the Spirit in purely subjective inspirations, or to harden the witness into historical or intellectual formulations. Both are necessary to the work of the Spirit, the objective facts in which He Himself has already acted, and the subjective illumination which is the individual apprehension and response.

But if the working of the Holy Spirit conforms to the pattern set at the incarnation, this is no less true of the means which the Holy Spirit employs. The inward illumination which is the completion of revelation does not take place directly. It does not take place in the sphere of pure mind or spirit. It is not a supernatural recollection and understanding of the person and word and works of Jesus Christ. It is itself mediated by the persons and words and works ordained of God and used by the Holy Spirit for that purpose. Just as God by the Holy Spirit revealed Himself and accomplished our redemption in history, in Jesus Christ, so by the Holy Spirit that revelation and redemption is mediated to us in history, in the Christian Church and ministry, in word and sacrament. The Holy Spirit is the supreme and inward witness. But the Holy Spirit does not work alone. He works through the human and historical testimony of persons and words and works.

We have already seen something of this truth in relation to the testimony of the Spirit to Jesus Christ, especially in the Acts of the Apostles, which are just as much the Acts of the Holy Ghost. But it is worth re-emphasizing the point from a slightly different if complementary angle. For the work of wit-

ness Jesus does not simply send the Holy Spirit and leave everything on a spiritual and supernatural level. He also appoints
the twelve, and in a wider and looser sense all His disciples, and
says to them: "Ye shall be witnesses unto me."[1] He also gives
His apostles authority to preach the word,[2] a commission to
administer the sacraments,[3] and power to do confirmatory acts
of healing.[4] This mission is a reflection or repetition of His own
mission, from which it derives its power and to which it bears
testimony. It is a mission in terms of history, of flesh and blood,
of words and acts. Yet it is not apart from, or even complementary to, the witness of the Holy Spirit, just as the person
and work of Jesus Christ was not apart from or complementary
to the work of the Holy Spirit. It is itself the witness of the Holy
Spirit according to its human form and nature. The witness of
the apostles is in human terms, but it does not depend upon
human factors. It is also a witness in divine terms. The apostles
are not great men, but men filled with the Holy Spirit.[5] Their
word is not with human eloquence or wisdom, but in demon-
stration of the spirit and of power.[6] Their actions do not derive
their power from human skill or effectiveness, but from the
Holy Spirit. We again move on that twofold level, where there
is both an external and an internal witness, and yet the two are
one. "For we are his witnesses of these things; and so is also the
Holy Ghost, whom God hath given to them that obey him."[7]

It is worth noting that even the form of this witness corresponds to that to which it bears witness: the person of Jesus
Christ, and the revelation and redemption of God accomplished in Him. It is a witness in the form of body, the body of
Jesus Christ which is the Church and its ministry.[8] The Holy
Spirit bears His testimony in and through those who are believers and disciples of Jesus Christ. This is the truth which
underlies the description of the Church as an extension of the
incarnation. The word extension is a bad one, indeed, the
phrase as it stands might suggest that the Church shares the
essential deity of Christ, or could in some way complete His
work. To that extent it is unsatisfactory. On the other hand, it
does stand for the very real truth that just as the revelation and

---

[1] Acts 1: 8; cf. Isa. 43: 10   [2] Mark 16: 15   [3] Matt. 28: 19; Luke 22: 19
[4] Mark 16: 17   [5] 1 Cor. 1: 26–9   [6] 1 Cor. 2: 4   [7] Acts 5: 32   [8] cf. 1 Cor. 12

redemption of God took place in the body, in the body of Jesus Christ, so the witness to that revelation and redemption takes place in the body, in the body of those who are called into union with Jesus Christ as His people, sharing both the fellowship of His sufferings and the power of His resurrection.[1]

Again, the Holy Spirit bears His testimony in and through the word of the Church: the apostolic preaching, the prophetic and apostolic Scriptures, and the living proclamation of the apostolic Church. Now just as we cannot speak of the Church as an incarnation in the same original and primary sense as we do of the person of Christ, so we cannot speak of the apostolic witness as a revelation in the same way as we do of Jesus and His word. Yet it is also the case that as Jesus spoke by the Spirit, so the apostles and the apostolic Church proclaim the Gospel in the power of the same Spirit. The Holy Spirit does His work of pointing to Jesus Christ by means of the spoken and written word of that people which He indwells as the people of God. It is a concrete, historical witness, and as such, the ministry of reconciliation.

Finally, the Holy Spirit bears His testimony in and through the works of the Church, the divinely appointed actions of the sacraments, the apostolic and other miracles, and the Church's works of mercy and service. It is only mediately and as a testimony that these acts are the redemptive acts of God. To that extent they cannot be compared directly with either the miracles or the death and resurrection of Jesus Christ. But they are still the works of the attesting Spirit, conforming to the incarnational pattern as we have it in the life and activity of Jesus Himself. To that extent, even as human and historical works, with all the limitations and natural insufficiency which that involves, they are an embodiment of the ever new but unchanging witness of the Spirit.

The fact that the testimony of the Spirit takes an objective form in a people and words and actions preserves it from the arbitrariness of subjectivism and individualism. The Holy Spirit does not work by supernatural visions and insights unrelated either to the Gospel itself on the one hand or the present embodiment of the Gospel in the Church and its ministry. The

[1] Phil. 3: 10

Christian cannot get away from Jesus Christ crucified and risen, as though there were an independent kingdom of the Spirit. But he also cannot get away from the concrete attestation of Jesus Christ in Church and Word and Sacrament. This is not a justification of stagnation in the Church. The witness is a living witness, which has to be renewed in every generation. And because the Church is human, and therefore fallible, there are constant tensions, and the Church and its proclamation will need constantly to be recalled to the apostolic testimony. But it will always be a witness in the same divinely appointed forms. A faith which depends upon the private and inward operation of the Spirit, whether in the form of intellectual apprehension, emotional experience, or dreams and visions, will not be the genuine work of the Spirit of God. To put it paradoxically, there is no such thing as a purely spiritual operation of the Spirit.

Yet the operation of the Spirit is spiritual. That is the converse side of the truth which there is perhaps a greater danger of forgetting. The testimony of the Holy Spirit is made in the form of Church and Word and Sacrament, but that does not mean either that the Spirit is dependent upon the human factors, or that the presence of the historical witness is a guarantee of the inward witness of the Spirit. It is not because the Church is a well-organized and successful and powerful body that its witness succeeds in the world. It is not because the minister of the Gospel is a great orator or a man of striking personality that his word is the word of life and power.[1] It is not because the Sacraments are invested with a rich aesthetic or psychological appeal that they serve the attestation of the Spirit. The Holy Spirit does use the Church and the Word and the Sacraments. Therefore the consecration of all legitimate powers and resources is rightly and properly demanded. But the efficacy of the inward witness is not necessarily proportionate to the powers and resources available. If the Spirit uses the things of this world, as He does, He can just as well use the weak and despised things, the things which are not, to confound the wise and mighty.[2] The real power of Church and Word and Sacrament may well be in inverse ratio to their

[1] 1 Cor. 2: 1–4   [2] 1 Cor. 1: 27–28

K

human and historical efficacy. "God's strength is made perfect in weakness."[1]

Again, the mere presence of the human and historical witness is not itself a guarantee of the efficacious witness of the Spirit. Protestantism no less than Roman Catholicism has been tempted in this respect, the one in relation to the Word, the other in relation to Church and Sacraments. It is salutary to remember that even in the case of Jesus Christ, although He was the incarnate Son of God, and filled with the Holy Spirit, not everyone who saw Him recognized Him as the Son of the Most High,[2] not everyone who heard His word acknowledged it to be the Word of God, not everyone who watched His miracles accepted them as acts of God.[3] In a word, the presence of Jesus Christ and His Word and works did not guarantee a response of faith and discipleship and the reception of His saving benefits. The same is true in relation to the Word and Church and Sacraments which are the human, historical witness to Jesus Christ. It is not merely that they are affected by human sin, although this can be an additional stumbling-block. But the very fact that they are human and historical means that they are necessarily equivocal. Many people may read the written word or hear the word of preaching, and not have that inward attestation of the Spirit which means that they read and hear it as the word of God. Many people may see the Church and its activities and assess it simply as another religious organization with a greater or lesser attractiveness or value. Many people may receive the Sacraments and know little or nothing of their true meaning and power. It is not merely a question of the correctness or regularity of the external form. It is not merely a question of the righteousness or sinfulness of those who are the human ministers. It goes deeper than that. The whole treasure of the Gospel is contained in earthen vessels.[4] Inevitably, there will be those who see only the earthen vessels. Apart from the inward attestation of the Spirit, which is sovereign, and cannot therefore be controlled by human factors, it is all that they can see. The mere fact that we can give the world the witness of a sound Gospel or a regular

[1] 2 Cor. 12: 9   [2] Matt. 16: 13 f.; Luke 4: 22
[3] Luke 11: 15   [4] 2 Cor. 4: 7

Church and ministry or a rightly administered Sacrament does not mean that we can give the world the witness of the Holy Spirit.

Yet as Jesus Christ was one Person, even in His deity and humanity, so there is a unity of the external and the internal witness. Jesus did not cease to be the Son of God, filled with the Holy Ghost, just because certain people thought that He was John the Baptist or Jeremiah or one of the prophets.[1] The witness of Peter did not cease to be the witness of the Holy Spirit just because the rulers and high priests refused to receive it. Where the Church is really the Church of Jesus Christ, where the word of the Church is the apostolic word, where the Sacraments are administered in obedience to the dominical command, we cannot separate between the outward and the inward witness, or suspend their unity only upon their efficacy. The ultimate and insoluble mystery of the Holy Spirit is the mystery of His work, not in those who bear witness, but in those who see and hear. The wind bloweth where it listeth . . . so is everyone that *is born* of the Spirit.[2] In practice, of course, this is the decisive point. That is perhaps why it is the very thing which we can neither explain nor control.[3] The Spirit Himself remains the internal Master. But it does not mean that the relationship between the inward and outward witness is arbitrary or sporadic. It is not mechanical. It cannot be taken for granted. It is not even a guarantee of automatic efficacy. But on the other hand it is a real relationship. The sovereignty of the Spirit is not a sovereignty of accident or caprice. It is the witness of this people, this Word, these Sacraments, which is the witness of the Holy Spirit, and which will be used by the Holy Spirit to accomplish His inward work.

We see the relatedness finally in the being and life of the people of God, for as the aim of His witness, and the means to it, the Holy Spirit reproduces in Christians and the Christian Church the sonship and ministry of Jesus Christ.

The Holy Spirit has no end or purpose which is independent of the revelation and redemption accomplished in Jesus. Witness is made to Jesus Himself in order that Christians may themselves enter into that which has been done for them by

---

[1] Matt. 16: 14   [2] John 3: 8   [3] 1 Pet. 2: 9

their representative and substitute, and that in so doing they may themselves be witnesses. The saving action of God has one goal: that fallen men and women may be redeemed in Jesus Christ, and that they may show forth the praises of the one who has redeemed them.[1] The Holy Spirit was Himself active, as we have seen, in the life and ministry by which this redemption was accomplished. His present office is to bear witness to it in order that it may be apprehended and appropriated by an entry into the representative work of Christ.

It must be emphasized that this operation of the Holy Spirit in believers and the Church is not an autonomous work. Christians are not redeemed because of the subjective fact that the Holy Spirit works in them in the same way and according to the same pattern as He worked in Jesus Christ. The Holy Spirit does the subjective work only on the basis that it is, not merely a repetition of, but a definite entry into, an identification with the work which He has already done in Jesus Christ. Even as Christians who have known the inward working of the Spirit, the people of God cannot stand alone. They can stand only in Jesus Christ. The work of the Holy Spirit is a work which involves identification with Christ. The work has already been done for us. For that very reason it can and must be done in us. The Reformers grasped this point when they refused to allow that even the subjective work of the Holy Spirit in the Christian, even faith, even the new life which springs from faith, is itself a ground of justification. The only ground of justification is the representative work of Jesus Christ to which the Holy Spirit points us and with which it is His purpose and action to identify us.

But it is in fact the purpose and action of the Holy Spirit to identify the people of God with their Saviour and Head. That is why Christians can be and are in fact called to be the embodiment of the witness of the Holy Spirit to Jesus Christ. The Christian life is a life in the Spirit. The fullness of it has already been achieved for us by Jesus Christ Himself. But in the Holy Spirit we ourselves enter into it, in response to and in fulfilment of the attestation of the Spirit. We can see this broadly at four points and in four respects.

[1] I Pet. 2: 9

First, we enter in the Spirit into the birth of Jesus Christ, and therefore into His divine Sonship. As Jesus Himself was conceived by the Holy Ghost, Christians are born again by the Holy Ghost.[1] They belong to this world by a natural birth, but they also belong to the new world of the family and people of God by a spiritual birth. They are not the sons of God in their own right. They cannot be born of the Spirit autonomously. It is only in the One who was conceived by the Holy Ghost that this is possible.[2] But in that One it is possible. In that One believers acquire the same incarnational duality as Jesus Christ Himself. They live. But the life which they now live in the flesh, they live by the faith of the Son of God who loved them and gave Himself for them.[3] Their life is a human life, a life in history. But their true life is a divine life, a life in the Holy Spirit. That is why in a dependent and secondary sense the people of God are in their very life and being an embodied witness to the Incarnate Son and Saviour.

Second, we enter in the Holy Spirit into the word and works of Jesus Christ, and therefore into His revelation and redemption. We enter into His word. Receiving a new life by the Spirit of God, a life in Christ, we are granted to have the mind of Jesus Christ, as expressed in His word.[4] "Let the Word of Christ dwell in you richly,"[5] is the exhortation of the apostle. The rich indwelling of the word of Christ by the Holy Spirit has its counterpart in the spoken word of the Christian. His speech is with grace, seasoned with salt.[6] He speaks in psalms and hymns and spiritual songs.[7] He delights to testify to Jesus Christ. He does not accept the standards and interests of the sinful world, but those of the heavenly kingdom of which he is a member by the Holy Ghost. But he also enters into the works of Jesus Christ. Not all Christians, very few indeed, can perform miracles of healing as Jesus and the apostles did. But all Christians, in the Holy Spirit, can reflect in their life and ministry and service the love of God shed abroad in their hearts.[8] They can love, not in word only, but in deed and in truth.[9]

It is to be noted that the entry is into both the word and the

---

[1] John 1: 12–13; John 3: 3 f. [2] cf. John 1: 12 [3] Gal. 2: 20
[4] Phil. 2: 5 [5] Col. 3: 16 [6] Col. 4: 6 [7] Eph. 5: 19
[8] Rom. 5: 5; cf. Rom. 8: 1 f.; Gal. 5: 16 f. [9] 1 John 3: 18

works of Jesus Christ. It is not a vague humanitarian philanthropy divorced from the actual message of Christ. But it is also not a secret inward experience, or an appreciation of sound doctrine, divorced from the practical expression in every order of life. In the Church itself humanitarianism is not enough, but neither is piety or sound doctrine which is not concretely expressed in terms of human life. Again, it is not a withdrawal from the world. There is no question of a life in the Spirit, which replaces entirely the ordinary relationships of life. Jesus Christ Himself was not of the world,[1] but He was certainly in it.[2] He taught and ministered, not in an utopian seclusion, but in the context of the Palestinian situation to which He belonged. The "communities" are right in their insight that life in the Spirit involves a total reconstruction of life, but they are wrong in supposing that this is to be worked out in a world-renouncing withdrawal.

Yet, thirdly, we do enter in the Holy Spirit into the death of Jesus Christ, and therefore into His victory over sin.[3] We do not die to the world, or the body, as such. That is why the world-renouncing aspect of the Gospel and the Christian life is not in any real contradiction with the world-accepting. We die to the body of sin, the sinful world.[4] The crux of the matter is to be found, perhaps, in Paul's use of the word flesh, in which the genuine antithesis is not between body and spirit, but between the "old" man and the "new".[5] Just as the death to sin was an integral part of the incarnation of Jesus Christ, so the dying and reckoning ourselves dead to sin[6] belongs necessarily to our entry in the Holy Spirit into that which Jesus Christ has done for us. This putting off of the old man may often mean physical suffering and even martyrdom.[7] It will always mean literal death in some form. Such are the conditions of sinful life. But the choice even in martyrdom is not between the spiritual and the physical as such. It is between the redeemed world, to which the Christian belongs in Jesus Christ, and the fallen and sinful and perishing world which has already been judged in Jesus Christ. It is by virtue of this entry into the passion and death of Jesus Christ that Christians bear what is perhaps their

---

[1] John 3: 31   [2] John 1: 10, 14   [3] Rom. 6: 3 f.; 8: 1 f.   [4] Rom. 6: 11 f.
[5] Col. 3: 9 f.   [6] Rom. 6: 11; 8: 9–10   [7] cf. John 15: 20; 16: 33

most striking and effective witness in the world, and participate in a derivative sense in the divine ministry of reconciliation.[1] But, of course, this ministry is not an independent possibility, nor does it have independent value either for ourselves or others. We can die to sin only because Jesus Christ Himself has "borne our sin in his own body on the tree".[2] We can participate in the ministry of reconciliation only because our entry into that death is a witness in the Holy Spirit to the one atoning death of Jesus Christ Himself.

Finally, we enter in the Holy Spirit into the resurrection and ascension of Jesus Christ, and therefore into His resurrected and glorified humanity. In a sense, Christians are already raised with Jesus Christ,[3] for Jesus Christ died and rose again representatively. His death was His people's death, His resurrection His people's resurrection. The whole point of faith is to know that in Jesus Christ God has already acted for us.[4] The victory has already been won. The eschatological intervention of God has taken place. For that reason new life in the Spirit is eternal life,[5] the earnest or even the first-fruits of the resurrection.[6] But although the resurrection has already taken place for us, and in that sense we too are resurrected, and our life is hid with Christ in God,[7] it is the work of the Holy Spirit literally to fulfil that resurrection by the quickening of our mortal bodies. That is the final hope of the people of God, that as they are born and live and die with Jesus Christ, so they will also be raised with Him. It is not merely a question of immortality. The Holy Spirit did not raise Jesus Christ Himself to a purely spiritual life. It is a question of resurrection. Nor is it a matter of divinization. The witness of Scripture is surely that the Risen and Ascended Christ maintains His glorified humanity, and therefore that the people which in Him are partakers of the divine nature[8] will participate in the resurrection and glorification of the Incarnate Son, their representative and Lord and Head. Perhaps it is the true offence of the resurrection of the body that it testifies to a genuine, although not a sinful and corruptible humanity, even in the eternal life which we are to

---

[1] 2 Cor. 5: 18   [2] 1 Pet. 2: 24   [3] Rom. 6: 11; Gal. 2: 20
[4] Rom. 8: 29–30, 34; 1 Cor. 15   [5] John 3: 1–16; Rom. 8: 1 f.
[6] 1 Cor. 15: 20   [7] Col. 3: 1–3   [8] 2 Pet. 1: 4

enjoy with God. The incarnation of Jesus Christ in the Holy Spirit is worked out in Christians in this world as they enter into His life and death for them. It is fulfilled to all eternity as by the Holy Spirit they enter into His resurrection and glorification, and therefore into His lordship and glory as both Son of God and Son of Man.

6

THE PRIESTHOOD OF JESUS

by J. B. TORRANCE

Minister of Invergowrie Parish Church, Dundee

THE PRIESTHOOD OF JESUS

A Study in the Doctrine of the Atonement

by

J. B. TORRANCE

THE story is told of an old lady who went to her minister, a well-known evangelical minister, and asked him: "Tell me, sir, when were you converted?" The minister, knowing well that she was interested in the details of his Christian experience, replied: "Madam, I was converted nineteen hundred years ago when Jesus Christ died on a cross for my sins and rose again." He was concerned to point away from himself and his own faith to Jesus Christ. The decisive event for him was not primarily anything in his own experience, important as that may be, but that Jesus "suffered under Pontius Pilate, was crucified, dead, buried . . . , the third day He rose again from the dead, He ascended into heaven". It was as though he said: "When Christ died long ago, I died, and when Christ rose again from the dead in the garden of Joseph of Arimathea, I rose again, and when Christ ascended into heaven, I ascended in Him, and now my life is hid with Christ in God." That is the true testimony of faith. In the words of the Apostle: "We thus judge that if one died for all, then all died."

John Calvin, in his Commentary on John's Gospel (ch. 10, v. 8 f.), asks what is in effect the same question: "When does a person begin to belong to the flock of the Son of God?" In reply he says:

> According to the election of God we are already sheep *in His heart* before we were born, but we begin to be sheep *in ourselves* by the calling by which He gathers us into His fold. . . . We are already God's sheep, before we are aware that He is our Shepherd. In like manner it is elsewhere said that we were enemies when He loved us and for this reason Paul tells us that we were known by

God, before we knew Him. . . . For the secret purpose of God, by which men were ordained to life, is at length manifested in His own time by the calling—the effectual calling—when he regenerates by His Spirit to be His sons those who formerly were begotten of flesh and blood.

For Calvin three answers can be given to the question. First, I have been a member of Christ's flock from all eternity in the heart of the Father. Secondly, I became a member of Christ's flock when Christ the Son lived, died and rose again. Thirdly, I became a member of Christ's flock when the Holy Spirit sealed in my faith and experience, what had been planned from all eternity in the heart of the Father and what was finished and completed once and for all in Jesus Christ. There are three "moments" but only one act of salvation, just as we believe that there are three Persons in the Godhead, but only one God. We may never divorce any one from the other two. So when Christ sent His disciples to preach the Gospel, He commissioned them to baptize "in the name of the Father and of the Son and of the Holy Spirit". Of these three "moments", the second is the decisive one of the Gospel. *Christus pro nobis* is prior to *Christus in nobis*.

Behind the reply of the minister to the woman's question, there lies an understanding of the New Testament doctrine of the atonement and, more particularly, an understanding of the atonement in terms of our Lord's High Priesthood. Our concern in this discussion is to show that few things are more urgently required in theology to-day than just such an understanding. The whole doctrine of the Person and Work of Christ needs to be radically re-examined in terms of the Biblical testimony to the priesthood of Jesus.

The early Church, in her Christological controversies, was concerned supremely to defend a doctrine of the Person of Christ which would do full justice to His perfect humanity and perfect deity, and safeguard it against an undue emphasis on our Lord's deity on the one hand (Docetism) and against an undue emphasis on His humanity on the other (Ebionitism). Her views received clearest expression in the Chalcedonian formula of the hypostatic union of God and man in Christ, with the use of the four adverbs, *inconfuse, inseparabiliter, immutabiliter, indivise*. Few statements have proved more important or more normative in the thinking of the Church than this. But at once two things must be said.

1. However adequate we may think the Chalcedonian formula about the mystery of Christ's Person may be (and we believe it is), its weakness is that it is too static and abstract. It is an understanding of the doctrine of the Person of Christ too divorced from a New Testament understanding of the historic life and work of Christ in terms of His birth, death and resurrection. A Biblical doctrine of Christ which seeks to be true to the New Testament witness must always think of our Lord in terms of His mission to this sinful world, His identification with sinners, not only by His Incarnation and incorporation into our body of flesh and sin, but also by His life, His baptism in the waters of Jordan, His sympathy, His obedience, His suffering and baptism of blood on the Cross. It is not enough to say "God was in Christ" without in the same breath saying "reconciling the world unto Himself", and reconciliation is not complete simply in virtue of the Incarnation, but is brought to its *telos* by our Lord's life of obedience, His death and resurrection. In the words of the Epistle to the Hebrews: "Though He were a Son, yet learned He obedience by the things which He suffered; and being made perfect ($\tau \epsilon \lambda \epsilon \iota \omega \theta \epsilon \iota \varsigma$) He became the author of eternal salvation." "For it became Him in bringing many sons unto glory, to make perfect ($\tau \epsilon \lambda \epsilon \iota \hat{\omega} \sigma a \iota$) the Captain of their salvation through suffering." An adequate doctrine of the Person of Christ must always be worked out in terms of Christ's work as Saviour, and His work as Saviour must be thought of in terms of His person as the God-man. In other words, the doctrine of reconciliation is not something added to the doctrine of the hypostatic union of God and man in Christ as a separate article of faith, but is rather the doctrine of the hypostatic union understood in terms of expiation and atonement. For this same reason the very distinction between person *and* work of Christ can be a misleading one.

2. The Chalcedonian formula was further defined by the early Church in terms of the two conceptions of *anhypostasia* and *enhypostasia*. Against an undue emphasis on the humanity of Jesus the doctrine of *anhypostasia* asserted that apart from the

event of the Incarnation the human nature of Christ had no independent *per se* subsistence. Apart from the hypostatic union we can think of no humanity of Jesus. On the other hand, against any attempt to think too exclusively in terms of our Lord's deity, the doctrine of *enhypostasia* asserted that, nevertheless, in the Incarnation, the humanity of Jesus was given a real concrete subsistence within the hypostatic union. The flesh is enhypostatic in the Word. *Anhypostasia* and *enhypostasia* are twin conceptions which must always be held together.

Now this distinction is of extreme importance when we come to-day to consider the doctrine of atonement, because here we find, broadly speaking, two kinds of doctrine. On the one hand we find a rather Pelagian emphasis on the humanity of Jesus, where stress is laid on Jesus as man placating God by human sacrifice, a doctrine where Jesus as man becomes the subject and God the object of the work of propitiation. On the other hand, in reaction to this kind of doctrine, we find views of the atonement where the work of reconciliation is treated as a pure act of God carried out, as it were, over the head of man, where injustice is done to the real humanity of Jesus. This kind of view readily quotes the words: "*God* was in Christ reconciling the world unto Himself." It rightly stresses that God is the Subject of the whole work of atonement, but it stresses it to the point where we lose sight of the work of Jesus as man, as Himself the ἱλασμός. A true Biblical doctrine of atonement will seek at once to recognize that God is always the Subject of His own work of reconciliation and, yet at the same time, while avoiding the pitfalls of semi-Pelagianism, will do justice to the fact that within God's work of reconciliation it is Jesus Christ Himself who reconciles us. There are not two actions but one. Atonement is the work of the God-man. The twin conceptions of *anhypostasia* and *enhypostasia* serve to safeguard us from these two extremes. For this reason, as it has been pointed out, it is significant that when the New Testament speaks of Christ's work of propitiation the middle voice is used: ἱλάσκεσθαι.

A clear example of a one-sided emphasis of this kind comes in Gustav Aulén's influential book, *Christus Victor*. In reaction to a semi-Pelagian view where the emphasis is placed too exclusively on the work of Jesus as man, Aulén argues for what he calls a "classic" or "dramatic" doctrine of the Atonement.

> Its central theme is the idea of the Atonement as divine conflict and victory; Christ—*Christus Victor*—fights against and triumphs over the evil powers of the world, the "tyrants" under which mankind is held in bondage and suffering, and, in Him, God reconciles the world to Himself.[1]

This, he tells us, is the teaching of the New Testament and was the view of the early Church. From this standpoint he vigorously attacks what he calls the "Latin" view or "objective" view, where the main thought is that of satisfaction made by Jesus as man to God for the sins of the world—a view which he maintains had its origins in Tertullian and Cyprian, and finds clearest expression in Anselm's *Cur Deus Homo*.

> The most marked difference between the "dramatic" type and the so-called "objective" type lies in the fact that it (the "dramatic" view) represents the work of Atonement or reconciliation as from first to last a work of God Himself, a *continuous* Divine work; while according to the other view, the act of atonement has indeed its origin in God's will, but is, in its carrying-out, an offering made to God by Christ as man and on man's behalf, and may therefore be called a discontinuous Divine work.

The value of Aulén's book is that it recalls us to an important aspect of the teaching of the New Testament, that the background of the Cross is the world of evil powers and principalities which hold men down in bondage to fear and death, and this has been too often neglected in theories of the Atonement. But its weakness is that it gives such an emphasis to the fact that God is from first to last the Subject of Atonement, that no adequate place is given to the fact that in the New Testament within the one work of God in reconciliation, it is Jesus Christ incorporate in human flesh who, by His life of obedience to the Father and His death in our place, makes propitiation for our sins. For Aulén the humanity of Jesus is simply instrumental in God's work.

> The redemptive work is accomplished *by* the Logos *through* the Manhood as His instrument; for it could be accomplished by no power but that of God Himself.[2]

[1] *Christus Victor*, pp. 20 ff.   [2] *ibid.*, p. 50

But this is inadequate. The humanity of Jesus, as Calvin used to say, is not merely the instrument of God's salvation, but the "material cause" of it.[1] Aulén is so concerned to show that the "objective" view has its origin in Latin views of penance, merit and satisfaction, that he overlooks all that the New Testament has to say about the priesthood of Jesus and His propitiatory sacrifice for our sins. In other words, this is a doctrine of Atonement which, while seeking to do justice to the *anhypostasia* of Christology, fails to do justice to *enhypostasia*. The opposite extreme which Aulén seeks to avoid at all costs is an overemphasis of *enhypostasia* and the humanity of Jesus which fails to do justice to *anhypostasia*, that God was in Christ. Here again we can see how these twin conceptions must be held together.

The result of a view like that of Aulén is that, whereas he gives a clear presentation of the Kingship of Christ in His victory over the *power* of sin, by doing injustice to the Priesthood of Christ, there is no real answer to the deeper problem of *guilt* and of *past* sin. No doctrine of the Atonement can be regarded as adequate or true to the New Testament which does not give an answer to this problem. Atonement brings to the sinner not only deliverance from the power of sin but peace of conscience, with the assurance that his past is forgiven. The death of Jesus in the apostolic testimony is presented in these terms: "... being justified freely by His grace through the redemption (ἀπολύτρωσις) that is in Christ Jesus: whom God hath set forth to be a propitiation (ἱλαστήριον) through faith in His blood, to declare His righteousness for the remission of sins that are *past*, through the forbearance of God" (Rom. 3: 23–25). After reading Aulén we are left thinking of Anselm's words *nondum considerasti quanti ponderis sit peccatum*.

It is clear that what is required is a new understanding of the sacrificial work of Christ which seeks to disentangle a Biblical understanding of the priesthood of Jesus from a medieval semi-Pelagian doctrine of merit, whereby man can make atonement and satisfaction for his sins, or in any way manipulate or placate God by works of penance or supererogation. The propitiatory sacrifice of Jesus in the New Testament is throughout

---

[1] *Instit.* III. xi. 7; III. xiv. 17; III. xiv. 21, etc., also *Comm. on Ephesians*, ch. I.

a work of God's grace, though wrought out among men and on behalf of men in the humanity of Jesus.

All our knowledge of God is analogical in character and nowhere is this more clear than in considering the doctrine of the Atonement. The clear recognition of this fact puts us at once on our guard, for several reasons.

(a) No analogy should be pressed to the point of univocity. When we use analogies of ransom, sacrifice, victory, mercy-seat, deliverance, reconciliation, redemption, etc., although they are God-given Biblical analogies and are perfectly adequate for their purpose, none of them must be pressed to extreme, as, for example, the early Church sometimes pressed the analogy of ransom. In recognizing that these Biblical concepts are analogies, we recognize that there comes a point where we suspend our judgment. As on the Old Testament Day of Atonement the real act was done within the veil, so at the Cross the innermost mystery remains a mystery, more to be adored than expressed.

(b) In so far as no one analogy expresses the whole truth, our correct procedure must be that of comparing analogy with analogy, Scripture with Scripture, until we reach a deeper understanding. God in His self-revelation has seen good to compare Himself to creaturely realities and give us in Holy Scripture human comparisons and analogies to His divine nature. For this reason the only road to knowledge of God is that of comparing comparison with comparison. It is the procedure demanded by the nature of revelation, and to come to the truth we must be true to the nature of the given. Hence in our doctrine of the Atonement it is a mistake to take one analogy and make that the sole one for understanding the work of Christ. The weakness of Aulén's view, as we shall see, is that he takes the analogies of kingship and victory and develops them at the expense of the analogies of priesthood and sacrifice. Likewise the analogy of priesthood must not be pressed at the expense of the analogy of Christ's kingship.

(c) As the analogies of Scripture are God-given, we must seek so far as possible to listen to what God has to say there about the work of atonement, rather than come to Scripture with extra-Biblical analogies and read these into our understanding of the death of Christ. However useful for didactic purposes non-Biblical analogies may be, for dogmatic purposes all such analogies must be subordinate to and corrected by the God-given analogies of Scripture. Particularly in seeking to understand the judicial aspect of Christ's work on the Cross, we must be on our guard lest forensic analogies from medieval penal codes, or notions of merit drawn from the penitential systems of the Latin Church, falsify our Biblical perspective and lead us to seeing in Scripture what is not there.

(d) In approaching the mystery of the Cross we must recognize that so far from fitting the death of Christ into our categories, we ourselves by *metanoia* must become conformable to His death by the renewing of our mind. The death of Christ cuts across all our categories as well as our pride and sets our lives, as well as our thinking, on a new basis. We can only listen to what Christ has to say on the Cross by receiving the divine forgiveness. Here, as always in theology, the only road to "the truth as it is in Jesus" is the road of "living the truth in love" (ἀληθεύοντες ἐν ἀγάπῃ), Eph. 4: 15–21. For this reason, strictly speaking, we can have no *theory* of the Atonement. We cannot think our way synthetically into a knowledge of God and His ways, but can only listen in humility to what He says to us in Christ. Revelation brings with it its own norms of interpretation and all we can do is to seek within the context of a life of faith and continual *metanoia* to think analytically. No wonder Anselm spoke of theology as *fides quaerens intellectum* and wrote it in the form of dialogue and prayer.

We have thus seen two things. First, the Chalcedonian doctrine of the hypostatic union needs to be worked out dynamically in terms of the life, death and resurrection of Jesus Christ, if we are to have a truly Biblical Christology. Secondly, our understanding of the Person and Work of Christ must be analogical in character and grounded in the God-given analogies of Scripture. Both these things lie behind the Reformed attempt to understand the Person and Work of Christ in terms of the threefold office (*triplex munus*) of Prophet, Priest and King. It was a brilliant step forward to work out the Chalcedonian Christology in terms of Biblical exegesis and not in terms of the metaphysical categories of medieval scholasticism.

That is the genius of John Calvin's *Institutes*, and especially of
Book Two where he deals with Christology and Soteriology. It
can only be regarded as a retrograde step when later Protestant
theologies began to solidify the more plastic Biblical thought of
Luther and Calvin by casting it into a scholastic mould by the
resuscitation of Aristotelian categories and by writing *Loci
Communes*.

When we consider the work of Christ in terms of the Biblical
analogies of Prophet, Priest and King, we can recognize at once
that no one of these analogies must be taken at the expense of
the other two. For example, if we think of Christ solely in terms
of His prophetic office and not also in terms of His priesthood
and kingship, we shall see Jesus only as the Bearer of a Divine
Word to man. We shall see the parable of the Prodigal Son as
the whole Gospel, and seek to demythologize if not excise all
that is said about Christ's death as a propitiation for our sins.
This was the road taken by Bultmann in his early book, *Jesus
the Word*, where he sought one-sidedly to reconstruct "Jesus"
from His sayings. The result is that a story like that of the healing of the paralytic (Mark 2: 1–12) is regarded as the conflation
of an authentic word of Jesus (a word of Divine forgiveness)
and a legend of healing. But this, as K. L. Schmidt showed long
ago, destroys the indissoluble unity of word and deed which
always characterizes the Gospel tradition.[1] Again, if we seek to
construct a soteriology solely in terms of the analogy of Christ's
kingship at the expense of His priesthood, as we have seen,
we emerge with a view like that of Aulén's *Christus Victor*,
which, while rightly emphasizing Christ's work of delivering us
from death and the power of evil, has little if anything to say
about the pardon of past sin or the Christology of the Epistle to
the Hebrews. Finally, any view which operates solely with
Christ's priesthood, and not also in terms of His prophetic
office and kingship over the Church, will almost certainly
present us with a Pelagian view of Jesus as Representative Man
making atonement for man's sins from man's side, and a doctrine of the Church as the extension of the Incarnation where,
in the continuing priesthood of the Church, man seeks to mani-

[1] In the article "Jesus Christ", in *Religion in Geschichte u. Gegenwart* (2); cf. K.
Barth, *Doctrine of the Word of God*, *Dogmatics* I/1, p. 459.

pulate the Divine Will and merit grace by sacramental acts and works of supererogation. In the Old Testament we see the beginnings of this tendency in the conflict between the prophet and the priest. When the priest concentrated purely on the liturgical aspects of his work in sacrifice and neglected his prime function as a mediator and teacher of God's Word to Israel, his very liturgical acts lost their true characteristic as an act of obedience and witness to God's sovereign grace, and were falsely regarded as having a meritorious efficacy in themselves. The prophets arose (many out of the priesthood itself) to summon the priests and people back to a life and worship of obedience to God's Word.

But if the Chalcedonian doctrine of the hypostatic union must be worked out Biblically in terms of Christ's work as Prophet, Priest and King, so, conversely, Christ's work as Prophet, Priest and King must be understood in terms of the hypostatic union of God and man in Christ.

When we think of the prophetic ministry of Jesus, we think of Jesus as the Word made flesh. We think of Him as God Himself in our midst, for God was in Christ revealing Himself to the world; and yet at the same time we think of Him as Man, as Jesus of Nazareth, a prophet mighty in deed and word. We think, on the one hand, of the testimony of Hebrews that "God who . . . spake in times past unto the fathers by the prophets, hath in these last days spoken unto us by His Son"; and we think, on the other hand, of the testimony of Peter and Stephen in the book of Acts, who quote of Jesus the words of Moses in Deut. 18: 15: "The Lord thy God will raise up unto thee a Prophet from the midst of thee, of thy brethren, like unto me; unto Him ye shall hearken." When Jesus says to the paralytic in Mark 2, "thy sins be forgiven thee", He does not merely speak about God's forgiveness of sins, but He Himself as the Son of Man forgives sins, and men are astonished at His doctrine, for He speaks as one having authority (ἐξουσία) and not as the scribes. Were it not that God was in Christ (*anhypostasia*), His words would indeed have been blasphemy, and yet it was the very voice of Jesus of Nazareth, the Son of Man (*enhypostasia*) with power on earth to forgive sins, that spoke. Here again we must think of the twin concepts of *anhypostasia* and *enhypostasia* in relation to the prophetic ministry of Christ. The hypostatic union of God and man in Christ means that Jesus is at once God's Word to man, and at the same time the Man of faith, "the Amen, the faithful and true Witness" to His Father, the Servant of the Lord who witnesses a good confession before Pontius Pilate.

Likewise when we think of the kingly ministry of Christ, we recognize that the coming of the Kingdom in Christ is the coming of God Himself to rule His people. God was in Christ driving out the evil spirits, destroying death and the powers of evil, delivering men from the Devil and restoring order to His world. With kingly authority Jesus says: "If I with the finger of God cast out devils, no doubt the Kingdom of God is come upon you", and the apostles quoted of Him the words of the second Psalm in acclaiming Him as the Messianic King. Jesus is *Christus Victor*. But the coming of the Kingdom is not only the coming of the King. It is the coming of One who, born of a woman and made under the law, is the only perfect loyal citizen in His Father's Kingdom. He alone as Man among men, on behalf of men, succeeds where Adam failed. He offers for us to God a life of perfect obedience, He treads the wine-press of God's wrath alone for us, He rises as the first-born from the dead and is the first of the New Creation (the καινὴ κτίσις). A doctrine of realized eschatology means not only that the coming of the Kingdom was the coming of God in Christ to rule the world; but it means also that in the coming of the Kingdom there comes One who, in His obedience to His Father's Will, realized for us once and for all in His own body of flesh all God's purposes of judgment and grace toward man. He has become our wisdom, our righteousness, our redemption. Paul is thinking of the work of Jesus as man when he writes to the Corinthians: "But of Him are ye in Christ Jesus, who of God is made unto us wisdom, and righteousness, and sanctification and redemption." The Kingdom of God as God's will for man has been realized for us intensively in the humanity of Jesus, and what has been realized intensively for us *in Christ* must be worked out extensively *in us* in the world, by the Holy Spirit, through the mission of the Church. Through the preaching of the Gospel we are called to become now in ourselves what we already are in Christ. This is the Gospel of the Kingdom that the Church is commissioned to preach to every creature. Only then will the end come, "when He shall have delivered up the Kingdom to God, even the Father; when He shall have put down all rule and all authority and power. For He must reign till He hath put all enemies under His feet" (1 Cor. 15: 24–25). What has been realized for us intensively in Christ, will one day be revealed extensively in a new heaven and a new earth. The doctrine of the hypostatic union of God and man in Christ, understood in terms of Christ's kingship, means that the coming of the Kingdom is the coming at once of the *regnare* and of the *regnum*. But this can only be more fully understood when we consider what the New Testament has to say about the priesthood of Jesus.

When we come to consider the Priesthood of Jesus, we find that the writer of the Epistle to the Hebrews is concerned to maintain two things. On the one hand, Jesus as High Priest is the Son of God. Only as the Son of God could He be the Author of eternal salvation and offer a perfect sacrifice for sins. Apart from His divine Sonship, His priesthood has no independent status or function. "So also Christ glorified not Himself to be made an High Priest; but He that said unto Him, Thou art my Son, to-day have I begotten Thee. . . . Thou art a Priest for ever after the order of Melchisedek" (Heb. 5: 5). His divine Sonship at once makes His priesthood belong to a different order from the Aaronic, and gives His ministry a finality it could never otherwise have. Unlike the Aaronic priests, He does not merely symbolize or bear priestly witness to something else that God does. He is God Himself come down as Priest to share our humanity. Yet on the other hand, as High Priest, Jesus is Man. We cannot think of our Lord's priesthood save in terms of His humanity. "Verily . . . He took on Him the seed of Abraham. Wherefore in all things it behoved Him to be made like unto His brethren, that He might be a merciful and faithful High Priest in things pertaining to God, to make propitiation (R.V.; ($\lambda\dot{\alpha}\sigma\kappa\epsilon\sigma\theta\alpha\iota$) for the sins of the people" (Heb. 2: 16–17). "For every High Priest taken from among men is ordained for men in things pertaining to God, that he may offer both gifts and sacrifices for sins" (Heb. 5: 1). From this point of view God is the object of the priest's activity.

There are thus two aspects of our Lord's High Priesthood. As Son of God, He represents God to man, and as Man, He represents man to God. The writer to the Hebrews dwells on both these aspects in chapter three. "Wherefore, holy brethren, . . . consider the Apostle and High Priest of our profession, Christ Jesus, who was faithful to Him that appointed Him." On the one hand, Jesus is the Apostle or *Sāliah* of God, mediating God's Word to men. So, as Professor W. Manson has pointed out, in the Old Testament, on the Day of Atonement, the High Priest was regarded as the *Sāliah* of God and not of men.[1] But on the other hand, as High Priest, He leads us back to God. In the words of Bengel: "As Apostle, Jesus pleads the cause of God with us, as High Priest, He pleads our cause with God."[2] But these two aspects of our Lord's priestly ministry may never be separated. They are one work. In both He does for us what we could never do for ourselves. As Apostle He proclaims that the Kingdom of God is at hand ($\dot{\epsilon}\gamma\gamma\upsilon\varsigma$) and brings it near to men, and as our High Priest He enters for us into the Holy of Holies that we might draw nigh ($\dot{\epsilon}\gamma\gamma\iota\zeta\epsilon\iota\nu$) to God through Him.

Both aspects correspond to the twofold task of the Priest in the Old Testament, to teach God's Law to the people and to bear witness by liturgical acts of obedience to God's holiness and grace revealed in His Law. He proclaimed God's judgments and God's mercy by word of mouth and bore witness to them in action by symbolically sacrificing a lamb or other animal victim. But in the New Testament in Christ we have the substance which was foreshadowed by the Old Covenant. Jesus *is* God's Word of judgment and mercy to man and His sacrificial work on the Cross is not simply a symbolic witness to God's judgment and mercy, but *is* God's judgment and mercy in action to save the world. Here the Priest and the Victim, the Priest and Suffering Servant are one, for Jesus is led as a Lamb to the slaughter to be wounded for our transgressions and bruised for our iniquities that we might be healed. The doctrine of the hypostatic union of God and man in Christ, understood

[1] *The Epistle to the Hebrews*, p. 54.
[2] Quoted by A. B. Davidson in his *Hebrews*, p. 82.

in terms of our Lord's Priesthood, means that Jesus is at once the Apostle and High Priest of our profession, at once the Son of God and the Suffering Servant, at once our Faithful High Priest and the Lamb of God, at once the Judge of all the earth and the Man who was judged for us.

But again we must think in terms of the twin conceptions of *anhypostasia* and *enhypostasia*. The doctrine of *anhypostasia* safeguards the fact that the Priesthood and Sacrifice of Jesus are the work of God Himself. God is the Subject of the atoning sacrifice, and not man. It is God who provides the Lamb and makes propitiation for our sins in Christ and who Himself bears our sins by taking the judgment on our sins to Himself. Apart from the Incarnation and the hypostatic union, there could be no priesthood of Jesus and no atoning sacrifice for our sins. The doctrine of *anhypostasia* rules out any Pelagian thought of Jesus as Representative Man propitiating God from the side of man by a meritorious act of human sacrifice as well as any thought of an efficacious sacrificial mass. It safeguards the teaching of the New Testament that Jesus as our Representative is also our Substitute (ἀντίλυτρον ὑπὲρ πάντων). He is the one who is sent by God to do for us what we could never do for ourselves. On the other hand, the doctrine of *enhypostasia* safeguards the fact that in the *assumptio carnis* the priesthood and sacrifice of Jesus are truly human, that within the hypostatic union the sacrifice of Christ is not only God's own act of sacrifice, but is a sacrifice offered to God on behalf of men by Jesus as man. It asserts, what is asserted so forcefully in the Epistle to the Hebrews, that "we have not an High Priest who cannot be touched with the feeling of our infirmities; but was in all points tempted like as we are, yet without sin" (4: 15). If Jesus were not very man He would not be able to "have compassion on the ignorant and on them that are out of the way" (5: 2). He would not be our elder brother. But as very man He was judged in our flesh and as man He has once and for all offered to God a human obedience, a human response, a human witness, and as man He is our surety at the right hand of God.

The significance of this emerges when we again consider the views of Aulén. Aulén, in his concern to reject any "Latin" view that would maintain that the atoning sacrifice of Christ is to be conceived solely as a sacrifice offered to God by man, seeks to show that the priesthood of Jesus is to be understood solely as a work of God in relation to men and not conversely. He writes: "the sacrifice of Christ is primarily and above all a heavenly and 'eternal' sacrifice; on this ground it supersedes the old sacrificial system. The heavenly High Priest, as R. Gyllenberg writes, 'represents the heavenly world in relation to men, not men in relation to heaven; and in His work He represents God towards men, not men towards God'."[1] This, as throughout Aulén's work, is a view which defends the *anhypostasia* of Christology at the expense of *enhypostasia*. But both must be taken together if we are to be true to the New Testament witness. The act of God in Christ for us, and the act of man in Christ for us are inseparable. Together they teach the substitutionary character of Christ's atonement. *Anhypostasia* emphasizes that God substitutes Himself for us. *Enhypostasia* emphasizes that the man Jesus is substituted for us. This is the doctrine of "the wondrous exchange" (*mirifica commutatio*) taught by the Reformers.[2] "He hath made Him to be sin for us, who knew no sin; that we might be made the righteousness of God in Him" (2 Cor. 5: 21).

In the Old Testament, God's covenant relation to Israel and Israel's covenant relation to God were mediated through the priesthood. The priesthood was understood as only functioning within the covenant and God's saving relation with His people. The Law of the Covenant and the divine oracles were brought to the people by the priest and the priest, again, led the people in their worship of God. Their worship and liturgy were conceived as acts of obedience to the divine ordinance of grace and not as having meritorious efficacy in themselves. In leading Israel's worship the High Priest was the Representative of the people. This was symbolized by the fact that he bore the names of the twelve tribes inscribed on his breastplate and in the onyx stones on his shoulders. All that he did, he did in virtue of his solidarity with Israel. The significance of this comes out most clearly on the Day of Atonement when the High Priest takes the blood of the sacrificial victim and enters within the veil into the Holy of Holies and sprinkles the blood on the mercy seat.

[1] *op. cit.*, pp. 93 ff.   [2] Calvin's *Institutes*, IV, xvii, 2.

There he intercedes with God for the people, and then returns to the people from God to pronounce the Aaronic blessing of peace. Two statements can be made about that action. (1) When the High Priest enters into the Holy Place, in virtue of his solidarity with the people, all Israel might be said to enter the sanctuary *in the person of the High Priest*. (2) When the High Priest passes within the veil with the blood of the atoning sacrifice, God accepts all Israel *in the person of the High Priest*. That twofold statement brings out the cardinal teaching of the Old Testament that the priest was the mediator of the covenant, and that God's saving relation with His people was mediated at the hands of a priest by means of a propitiatory sacrifice. The High Priest realized *in his own person* on behalf of Israel God's covenant communion with His people.

This is of extreme importance when we come to consider the work of Christ in the New Testament as the Mediator of the New Covenant. Jesus stands in solidarity with us. In His High Priestly prayer in John, chapter 17, He says: "For their sakes I sanctify myself, that they also might be sanctified through the truth." In chapters 18 and 19 our High Priest is Himself sacrificed on the Cross as the Lamb of God who takes away the sin of the world. In chapter 20 He says to Mary: "Touch me not, for I am not yet ascended to my Father" (into the Holy of Holies). In the same chapter He comes back from His Father to the disciples and says: "Peace be unto you", and breathes on them the Holy Spirit. This is the teaching elaborated so clearly in the Epistle to the Hebrews, and which lies behind the Pauline doctrines of "in Christ" and of Christ's solidarity with us as our Mediator. On the ground of His solidarity with us, we can again make two statements: (1) When Christ suffered, died, was buried, rose again from the dead and ascended into Heaven for us, nineteen hundred years ago, *we* suffered, died, were buried, rose again and ascended into Heaven *in Him*. We have entered into the presence of God in the Person of our High Priest on the ground of His atoning sacrifice. (2) When Christ was judged for our sins on the Cross, when He rose again for our justification and ascended to the right hand of the Father, *God* accepted us *in Him*. We are accepted in the Beloved, in the Person of our High Priest. These two statements, taken together, present the New Testament teaching that all God's covenant relations to us, in forgiveness, in reconciliation, in justification and sanctification, are mediated to us in and through the person of Christ. So Calvin writes:

> As Christ has entered into heaven, so faith ought to be directed there also; for we are hence taught that faith should look nowhere else. And doubtless it is vain for men to seek God in His own majesty, for it is too far removed from them; but Christ stretches forth His hand to us, that He may lead us to heaven. And this was shadowed forth formerly under the Law; for the High Priest entered the Holy of Holies, not in His own name only, but also in that of the people, in as much as he had in a manner the twelve tribes on his breast and on his shoulders; for, as a memorial for them, twelve stones were wrought on the breast plate, and on the two onyx stones on his shoulders were engraved their names, so that *in the person of one man all entered into the sanctuary together.* Rightly then does the Apostle speak when he says that our High Priest has entered into heaven; for He has entered not only for Himself, but also for us.[1]

This notion of solidarity is integral to any true doctrine of the Atonement, and can only be seen aright when we think of Atonement in terms of our Lord's Priesthood. Where a Biblical penal doctrine of Atonement is worked out solely in terms of analogies derived from the law court, and divorced from the Biblical analogy of priesthood, we have a doctrine of substitution which teaches that, because the Innocent One dies in stead of the guilty, the guilty escapes "scot free". The sins of the guilty are transferred to the Innocent One in virtue of a legal transaction. But the weakness of this is that the only relation between the guilty party and the One who is judged in his stead is one of legal contract. The Biblical doctrine is not so much that I escape "scot free" as that *I as a sinner have been judged in the Person of Christ my High Priest.* Forgiveness means that all my past sins have been truly dealt with, and only that fact brings peace and assurance. Our relation to Christ as Substitute must be understood at once in terms of God's free act of grace, and in terms of our God-given solidarity with Jesus.

[1] *Commentary on Hebrews*, 6: 19.

When the doctrine of Atonement is understood in terms of priesthood, we see that we stand related to the Death of Jesus in two ways: ontologically and pneumatologically. Ontologically, all men are related to Christ in terms of Christ's solidarity with them: "We thus judge that if Christ died for all, then all died" (2 Cor. 5: 14). But that by itself would lead to universalism, and obscure the New Testament teaching about faith and decision. On the grounds of our ontological relation to Christ, our Second Adam, we are called through the Holy Spirit into union with Him. Without Pentecost and without the sealing of the Holy Spirit in faith, we cannot regard ourselves as members of Christ's Body and partakers of His blessings. That is the meaning of the much debated statement in Calvin's *Institutes*, Book 3, chapter 1, where he says "that until our minds are intent on the Spirit, Christ is in a manner unemployed, because we view Him coldly without us, and so at a distance from us". It does not mean that there is *no* relation with Christ apart from the decision of faith. Calvin is asserting rather that the ontological relation which we already have with Christ in virtue of His High Priesthood (expounded in Book 2) must have its counterpart in the pneumatological relation (expounded in Book 3), described in the New Testament as the sealing of the Holy Spirit. The High Priest must breathe His Spirit on us.

It could likewise be shown that the New Testament doctrine of justification and imputation must be understood in these terms. The righteousness which is imputed to us by faith is no legal fiction. It is the righteousness of Jesus Christ who in our name and in our stead has offered to God a perfect obedience and said "Amen" to the divine judgment on our sin. He is our righteousness and we are accepted in Him. The Pauline phrase δικαιοσύνη θεοῦ must be thought of in terms of the hypostatic union, as a divine righteousness (*anhypostasia*) and yet as a valid human righteousness (*enhypostasia*), as Calvin argued with Osiander at the time of the Reformation. As a validly human righteousness it is imputed to us by grace in virtue of our two-fold relation to our High Priest in solidarity and faith union. The Pauline doctrine of Atonement understood in terms of justification and expiation must be regarded as complementary to the teaching of Hebrews about our Lord's High Priesthood.

There are many other advantages in thinking out the Christian doctrine of Atonement in terms of our Lord's Priesthood which lie outwith the scope of this discussion. Not only does it point a way to an understanding of the propitiatory sacrifice of Christ which avoids any semi-Pelagian doctrine of human merit and preserves the Biblical doctrines of grace and solidarity, but also it avoids the unfortunate separation between the Person and Work of Christ, by relating the Death of Christ integrally to His Life of obedience, His Resurrection and Ascension to glory. It relates Christ's work on the Cross to the doctrine of the Church as the Body of Christ of which He is the Head, and it preserves the eschatological perspective of faith by directing it to the New Humanity, to where Christ sits at the right hand of God in the Heavenly sanctuary, ever living to make intercession for us.

7

THE WORD AND THE GOSPEL

by T. H. L. PARKER
Rector of Little Ponton with Stroxton

7

THE WORD AND THE GOSPEL

by

T. H. L. PARKER

The Preaching of the Word of God is itself the Word of God

IN all the many books that have been written on preaching, how many do more than insist that the subject matter of the sermon shall be in accord with the Scriptures, that the preacher shall "preach Christ", that he shall preach directly and simply, aiming at the blessing of his congregation, that he shall be a man of faith and a student of the Bible? This sort of thing has been said again and again, even *ad nauseam*, said with the emphasis now on one aspect, now on another, said with orthodox or liberal intention, said with the chilling boredom of platitude or with the depth and fervour of deep conviction. But however highly we esteem preaching, and however powerfully we may say these things, we have not begun to come to grips with it until we have tried to understand its nature; and we shall only arrive at its nature by way of understanding why the term "the Word of God" is applied to it—as it is, not only in the Lutheran and Reformed Churches, but also in the Church of England,[1] and even in the Church of Rome. Therefore, leaving aside the eulogy and rhapsody so common in writings on the subject, this present essay aims simply at being an investigation into the meaning and significance of the statement standing at its head, perhaps first used by Bullinger and then fixed in its classic form in the Second Helvetic Confession: *Praedicatio verbi Dei est verbum Dei.*[2]

---

[1] See, e.g., Article xix; or the Ordinal; or the Collect for St. Bartholomew's Day. Hooker's strong words must be regarded as a private opinion and un-Anglican at that: "We therefore have no *word of God* but the Scripture. Apostolic sermons were unto such as heard them his word, even as properly as to us their writings are. Howbeit not so our own sermons." (*Ecc. Pol. V*, xxi. 2.)

[2] *Confess. Helv. post.* 1562, art. 1, 2.

I

Before we can ask in what sense preaching is the Word of
God, we must define our terms. By *preaching* we mean any verbal
declaration of the Gospel. Therefore, we shall use *preaching* and
Gospel interchangeably, as referring to the one action of the
Church in bearing witness to Jesus Christ. Moreover, to save
wordiness in a short essay, we shall use *Gospel* to refer to the
witness of the Church from the day of Pentecost onwards. As
far as bearing witness is concerned, the same thing must be said
of both Scriptural and post-Scriptural preaching, with the one
difference—very important in itself, certainly, but not concerning us here—that the one is the original and normative testimony of eye-witnesses, while the other depends upon it in regard
to that quality. What the New Testament is primarily and
radically, the post-Scriptural preaching of the Church is secondarily and dependently: but both, as the witness of the one
Church to the one Word of God in the power of the one Holy
Ghost, are to be called the Gospel. By *the Word of God* we do not
intend any one part or activity of the Word of God, any one
manifestation of the πολυμερῶς καὶ πολυτρόπως of Heb. 1: 1,
but that one Word of God which was "in the beginning with
God and was God", which was spoken "at sundry times and in
divers manners unto the fathers by the prophets", and whose
glory the Church has seen because He was made flesh. It is the
existence of Jesus Christ as witnessed to in the New Testament
that we have in mind when we use the expression *the Word of
God*. To be yet more precise, the existence of Jesus Christ as
witnessed to in the prologue of St. John's Gospel, though not
that interpreted in isolation from the rest of the New Testament.

In the beginning was the Word, and the Word was with God, and
the Word was God. The same was in the beginning with God. All
things were made by him, and without him was not anything
made that was made. In him was life, and the life was the light of
men. And the light shineth in darkness, and the darkness compre-
hended it not. . . . That was the true light, which lighteth every
man that cometh into the world. He was in the world, and the
world was made by him, and the world knew him not. He came
unto his own, and his own received him not. But as many as

received him, to them gave he power to become the sons of God, even to them that believe on his Name: which were born, not of blood, nor of the will of the flesh, nor of the will of man, but of God. And the Word was made flesh, and dwelt among us (and we beheld his glory, the glory as of the only begotten of the Father) full of grace and truth.

Here we are told that it is of the nature of God that He "speaks". "Speech" is not accidental but substantial to Him, and eternity is marked, not by "fearful silence" but by the Word which in and from the beginning was with God. God's Word was not called into being by a desire or a necessity to address or commune with His creation, whether angelic or human. For when God alone was, the Word was with God and the Word was God.

But the Word spoken by God is to be viewed strictly in relation to the Divine speaker; it must not be considered linguistically. That is to say, we are not to apply some concept of human language to this Word and therefore predicate of God that He speaks in such or such a way. Since He is spoken by God, the Word perfectly partakes of the nature and being of God: "and the Word was God". To say of God that He "speaks" is to employ a figure which certainly represents truly the activity of God so designated, but which will be misrepresented if it is interpreted in terms of human linguistic categories. Language is indeed to be predicated of God: but God speaks in His own way, and not in a human way; He speaks His own Word, and not a human word. "If, then, we attribute the spoken word to God, it will not be thought to derive its subsistence from the impulse of the speaker, and like our speech to pass into non-existence. But just as our nature, by being perishable, has a speech which is perishable, so the incorruptible and eternal nature has a speech which is eternal and substantial."[1] The force of this distinction between the Divine and human language is to be found in the absolute difference (apart from the Word made flesh) between God and man in general—cf., for example, Isa. 55: 8–9; Eccles. 5: 2.

On the other hand, the propriety of this anthropomorphism

[1] Gregory of Nyssa: *Address on Relig. Instruction* (quoted from *Christology of the Later Fathers*, ed. E. R. Hardy, pp. 270–1).

must be emphasized. When Professor Tillich draws attention to
the danger of interpreting "Word of God" in terms of human
words,[1] he is doing us a valuable service. But we part company
from him when, in place of human words, he in fact substitutes
something equally human, but far less concrete—self-manifestation or self-expression: "The many different meanings of
the term 'Word' are all united in one meaning, namely, 'God
manifest'—manifest in himself, in creation, in the history of
revelation, in the final revelation, in the Bible, in the words of
the Church and her members. 'God manifest'—the mystery of
the divine abyss expressing itself through the divine Logos—
this is the meaning of the symbol, the 'Word of God'."[2] Now,
what is "self-manifestation" or "self-expression" but at best a
generalization, at worst an abstraction? But "word" is particular
and concrete. Before we discard this anthropomorphism we
shall do well to note that it is deeply and extensively rooted in
the Scriptures and is a part—or rather a source—of a wider
group of concepts which will die of starvation if "the Word" is
emptied of its content as language.

The fact that God speaks His own Word in His own way
constitutes the miracle of the Incarnation at the end of the
prologue, just as it constitutes the mystery of the Godhead at
the beginning and the miracle of creation in the middle. If we
are to vary the image of language, it must be in the same
direction as the change that the prologue makes: "The Word
was made flesh, and dwelt among us." This does not mean that
the concept "flesh" now replaces "Word", but rather that the
two are interdependent. God speaks His own Word in His own
way, and this way now is "flesh". We are not substituting another category for that of language, but saying that this other
category is God's language to man. The existence of the man
Jesus of Nazareth is God's language. Existence means both the
fact that Jesus of Nazareth existed and also the form and manner of His existence. It would be a travesty of Christology to
think of the nativity or the conception of Jesus as God speaking
His Word into the world, and then that Word as it were
travelling to its allotted end as sound waves move from their

[1] *Systematic Theology*, I, pp. 174 ff.
[2] *op. cit.*, p. 177. cf. *The Protestant Era*, p. 210.

point of origin outwards. Not only was the humanity of Jesus in itself mediatorial, but so also were the form and manner of His existence—indeed, His humanity cannot be separated from its form and manner; without them it is an empty shell, or rather nothing at all. The form of His existence was that of a servant; the manner of His existence was humiliation. His life was characterized by encounter with temptation and by patient acceptance of suffering—both constituting obedience to the will of His Father. But in direct connection with this, and not at all in contradiction to it, stand His teaching, His miracles and the resurrection, where His glory does not merely shine through rents in the cloaking veil of His humanity but illuminates and authenticates it as the humanity of the Word of God. This existence of Jesus Christ is God's speech to men.

We should not allow the undeniable awkwardness and, indeed, incongruity, formed by the juxtaposition of the two distinct concepts of language and corporeality, to hide from us their relationship in this context. The "flesh" of Jesus is not a life lived in disobedience to or neglect of God; it is not only a life completely and perfectly offered up in sacrifice to God; it is primarily a life sent and ordained by God. It is God who speaks this Word. And this means that the Word spoken is the eternal counsel or wisdom of God effected by God, the everlasting determination of God realized by God. This determination is expressed in John 1: 4 as "life", comprehending the "all things were made by him" of the previous verse and the reconciliation of men to God of v. 12 f. The Word of God which is the "flesh" of Jesus Christ is not merely meaningful speech, not only the declaration of God's purpose or of the realization of that purpose, but is itself the effecting of His counsel. By this Word-made-flesh we are in very fact translated out of darkness into the kingdom of God, and life and immortality are in very truth brought to light. We might express it by saying that this Word is to be thought of with its Hebrew associations in the first place, with its Greek only secondarily. It is the powerful activity and effectiveness informing the Old Testament concept of language which is primary in the Word-made-flesh.

To summarize: The central meaning of "the Word of God" is the existence of Jesus Christ, and this existence is God's own activity of bringing into being His new creation. When we say "The preaching of the Word of God is itself the Word of God," this is what we mean by "the Word of God".

II

But it is clear that very much more needs to be said if the statement is to be reverent and obedient thinking and not blasphemous nonsense. How can it be said that preaching is the Word of God in the above sense? What is the relationship between the Word and the Gospel? The fact of a relationship is so patent in the New Testament that we need not argue the case.[1] Its nature is not so straightforward. We cannot be content with regarding preaching in a simple and direct way as the human declaration of God's work in Christ, the narrating and explaining of that reconciling activity. This would empty preaching of its character as the Word of God and leave it a man's word about God. Nor is the relationship that between a biography and its subject. As we read a biography we may feel that the subject of it has come alive and is a living presence to us. That this is an illusion, however, depending largely upon the skill of the author and the imagination of the reader, becomes clear when we compare biography with fiction. The great fictitious characters enjoy a "reality" only equalled by the subjects of the great biographies. An imaginary reality, no doubt—that is, a fiction deriving its reality from imagination in writer and reader. But can we say that men of history have any other reality for us? At the best, they live again only in the sense that their ideas or achievements become a living issue to another age. The biographer is a resurrection man, and it must be said of his subject, "He, being dead, yet speaketh." But in the Gospel this must be radically altered: "He, being alive, now speaketh." The Gospel is more than eloquent biography.

The way in which we shall try to understand this relationship between the Word and the Gospel is by the application to it of the meaning of the Incarnation. I am not aware whether this line has been taken in the past in regard to preaching; but

---

[1] *Vide* E. C. Hoskyns: "In the synoptic gospels and in the Acts of the Apostles the *Word*, with or without an explanatory genitive, is a synonym for the *Gospel*." (*The Fourth Gospel*, 2nd edn., p. 159.)

certainly the doctrines of the Eucharist and of the two Natures of Christ have from early times been applied to one another. And what has been done in the case of the Sacrament of the Gospel may surely also be attempted for the Gospel itself.

Jesus Christ is God-Man. Both divine and human natures are to be ascribed to Him without reservation: completely God and completely man. But "although he be God and man, yet he is not two, but one Christ". It is this union of the divine and human that is the heart of the matter for us at the moment. And when we ask: "In what way one?" we may listen to the answer given us by that Creed so sadly out of favour for many years past, the *Quicunque vult*: "One; not by conversion of the Godhead into flesh, but by taking of the manhood into God; one altogether; not by confusion of substance, but by unity of person." In the Person of Jesus Christ there is neither transubstantiation nor mixing. The Godhead was not changed into manhood, nor the manhood into Godhead. Then there would remain indeed but one nature, yet not the nature of the God-Man. Nor were the divine and human natures mixed and mingled in Him, so that some third being, neither God nor man, was produced.

The positive assertions are less easily understood: "One . . . by taking of the manhood into God; one altogether . . . by unity of person." We shall do well at this point to remember John Owen's warning on the medieval schoolmen: "Endeavouring to render all things plain unto reason, they have expressed many things unsound as unto faith, and fallen into manifold contradictions among themselves." This we must say, however: In the Incarnation we are confronted with the act of God's sovereign freedom. The Son of God *took* and *assumed* human nature. There was nothing in humanity to force Him to take it, nor did human nature there reach a peak where its union with the divine became possible, perhaps even inevitable. To say this would be to obscure or minimize the miracle of the Incarnation, the incredible condescension expressed in Phil. 2: 5 ff.: "Who, being in the form of God, thought it not robbery to be on an equality with God, but made himself of no reputation, and took upon him the form of a servant. . . ." The Word of God freely and graciously assumed human nature and made it one with Himself, Himself one with it. Here is no ascent of man, but the descent of the Word, no human self-elevation, but the ineffable condescension of the Godhead. The Word of God took manhood into Himself, and, preserving intact both His divine and human natures, was the one Jesus Christ.

Now, that which is hypostatically true of the Word made flesh, is sacramentally true of the Word-made-flesh in the Gospel. To call the Gospel "the Word of God" is not to alter the meaning of this expression, as if it meant one thing when applied to the Incarnate Word and another when applied to the Gospel. The Word of God which is the substance of the Gospel is the Incarnate Word. In the Gospel the Word made flesh Himself comes and meets with His people, not in the immediacy of His flesh but through the human words, which, taken up by the Holy Spirit, become one with the eternal Word made flesh. What Lancelot Andrewes wrote of the sacramental union in the Eucharist is true also of this: "the gathering or vintage of these two in the Blessed Eucharist is, as I may say, a kind of hypostatical union of the sign and the thing signified, so united together, as are the two Natures of Christ."[1] And Calvin seems to come close to the matter when he says that "the death of Christ is the substance of the Gospel (*mors Christi, doctrinae est hypostasis*)."[2] By the power of the Spirit the Gospel transcends its nature as religious history and becomes, in its mystical union with the Word made flesh, the vehicle of the redeeming work of God—nay, more, itself partakes in this redeeming work. We must undoubtedly view this from the Godward side, as the divine assumption of humanity. The words of the Gospel do not stand on any human peak which is on a level with the divine, not even as the top rung of a ladder reaching up into union with the divine Word. They are and they remain man's words, the account of man's witness to the divine miracle of the Word made flesh. If the preacher or his words are deified, or if the preacher imagines he can in some way unite his words with the Word, he is destroying his Gospel by reversing the order of the divine economy. "Say not in thine heart, Who shall ascend into

---

[1] Sixteenth Sermon on the Nativity, *Works*, vol. I, p. 281 (Lib. Ang. Cath. Theol.).

[2] *Comm. in Isaiam*, 53: 11.

heaven? That is, to bring Christ down from above."[1] The words of the preacher become the vehicle of God's redeeming work by assumption. The Word, as He took flesh to Himself once for all, graciously takes to Himself the Gospel, making it the medium of His self-revelation.

We may with perfect propriety also apply the negating clauses of the *Quicunque vult* to this relationship: "not by conversion of the Godhead into flesh . . . not by confusion of substance". The Gospel is the Word of God, not because the Word is changed into man's words, nor because man's words are changed into the Word, nor because the Word and the man's words are in some way mixed to become one. In the Gospel God's Word retains His divine Nature and man's words their human nature. If mere remembrance is ruled out on the one extreme, so is transubstantiation on the other. Both conversion and confusion leave us without a mediatorial quality in the Gospel by destroying the one or the other nature. And it is of the very essence of the Gospel, as of the Word made flesh who is its substance, that it is mediatorial. In it God in Christ reveals Himself to us as our Redeemer. If the divine Nature in the Gospel is destroyed, it is not God Himself revealing Himself to us. If the human nature, then the revelation is not on our level and therefore fails to be revelation. But by the action of the Holy Spirit, these two, retaining their distinct natures, become sacramentally one, and hence the Gospel becomes one with its substance, the preaching of the Word of God one with the Word of God.[2]

---

[1] Rom. 10: 6.

[2] We may here take up a point of Lancelot Andrewes. When he has said that preaching is a kind of incarnation ("we also are after our manner *verbum carnem facere*, to incarnate the word". We have a word . . . which is a type or abstract of the very Word, or wisdom of God; and that is the word which is preached unto us" *op. cit.*, I, p. 99), he goes on, somewhat inconsistently, to speak of preaching as the Word and the Eucharist as the flesh: "The word we hear is the abstract of *Verbum*; the Sacrament is the antetype of *caro*, His flesh" (*op. cit.*, p. 100). Undoubtedly, Word and Sacrament are bound together, but not by this duality; rather because in each is the same Word made flesh. In this essay I have kept strictly to my subject, preaching, and have not related it to the sacraments. That relationship would certainly need to be treated in a more extended work. But the fact that I have not done so here should not be taken as an indication of exalting preaching above the sacraments.

III

We may now go on to consider the significance of *Praedicatio verbi Dei est verbum Dei.*

If this is true in the sense that we have given above, it follows that in the Gospel Jesus Christ meets with us. In and through the words of a man we are confronted by God's saving activity in the Word made flesh. Let us remember again that God does not speak many words of different meaning but that one Word which in the beginning was in His bosom and which in time was made flesh. It is this last that is decisive. There is no question here of a sort of sequence of "Words of God", each the manifestation of the eternal Word: (1) the Word of creation, (2) the Word of the law and the prophets, (3) the Word made flesh, (4) the Word of the Gospel. It is not as if the Word which was once made flesh is now made Gospel, for He did not take flesh as an episode, laying it aside when it had served its purpose, but He rose again and ascended into Heaven with that same body that He took of the Virgin now changed into His glorious body. Never now is He to be separated from His "flesh". Hence, the Word which is the substance of the Gospel is the Word made flesh. It is the Jesus Christ of the Gospels who meets us in the preaching of the Word: He Himself, in His humility and His glory, in His hiddenness and His revelation, as Servant and as Lord, as numbered with the transgressors and as of one Godhead with the Father and the Holy Spirit, "the glory equal, the majesty co-eternal". It is Jesus Christ as the Mediator between God and man who is present in the Gospel.

The Acts of the Apostles has a special significance in this respect. In it we are shown the Church preaching the Gospel and engaging in the activities correlative to that preaching. But inasmuch as the author regards this as the second part of a larger work, dealing, as a whole, with the ministry of Christ, the Church's work must be viewed in the strictest relationship with that ministry. We should apply this more stringently than most commentators seem to do. Either, like Rackham, they regard the work of the Church as the work of Christ—"the work of the Church now to be described is still the work of the Lord,

although He has now been *taken up* into heaven"[1]—or the work
of Christ, like R. J. Knowling, as "a *beginning*, a prelude to the
glory and mighty working to be revealed and perfected in the
ascended Lord".[2] Against the latter we must assert uncompromisingly the completeness and perfection of Christ's work
in the days of His flesh. Nothing whatsoever remained to be
done— τετέλεσται. On the other hand, Rackham is not
sufficiently precise. The Church's work is (in so far as this is
really the case) the work of the Lord, not merely because He is
yet at work in a general way, but because He continues His
ministry in the ministry of the Church. His ministry is no mere
past event, to which each successive generation must painfully
grope back in memory or imagination, nor is its contemporane-
ity with succeeding generations to be explained metaphysically.
Rather, we must say that it is fulfilled in the preaching of the
Gospel by the power of the Holy Spirit. It is not easy, as writers
on the Eucharist have learned long since, to find one word that
shall do justice to the reality of this divine event without violat-
ing the once-for-all nature of the Incarnation. When we say
"fulfilled" we wish to avoid such a repetition as shall make
Christ "often suffer" while asserting such a reality as is not to
be divorced from the Incarnation. On the one hand, "they had
fulfilled all that was written of him",[3] and on the other, St. Paul
considered that the purpose of his ministry was "to fulfil the
word of God".[4] In this sense also we are told in Acts that "the
word of God increased".[5] We shall go astray here if we think
of this reality (in analogy to the sacrifice of the Mass) made
contemporaneous by repetition. Similarly, we must leave aside
the idea of an extension of the Incarnation. But neither is the
Gospel "memorialist", the mere recollection of the saving
events and thus a *signum nudum*. Against the former we assert
the uniqueness of the Incarnation; against the latter, the unity
of the Word made flesh with the Word of the Gospel.

The activity of the Word-made-flesh in the Gospel is that
which He fulfilled on earth—the ministry of reconciliation.
"But all things are of God, who reconciled us to himself

---

[1] R. B. Rackham, *The Acts of the Apostles* (Westminster Comm.), p. 4.
[2] R. J. Knowling, *The Acts* (Expos. Grk. Test.), p. 51.
[3] Acts 13: 29   [4] Col. 1: 25   [5] Acts 6: 7

through Christ, and gave unto us the ministry of reconciliation; to wit, that God was in Christ, reconciling the world unto himself, not imputing their trespasses unto them, and hath committed unto us the word of reconciliation."[1] God's gracious work of reconciliation through His Son, which took place once for all and which was, as the Prayer of Consecration in the Book of Common Prayer puts it, "full, perfect and sufficient", is fulfilled in the "word of reconciliation", the proclamation of which constitutes the "ministry of reconciliation". And this ministry of the Word becomes the ministry of reconciliation fulfilled by Christ when it is taken up and used by the Holy Spirit. Therefore, in the Gospel we do not merely hear a man's account of the divine activity in the Incarnate Word, but the Incarnate Word Himself meets us in His reconciling ministry. The Gospel is the very place of judgment and forgiveness; where they are not merely declared but effected. Christ's crucifixion and resurrection are "placarded" before our eyes,[2] not only as a past event, but, in the power of the Holy Spirit, as a present event.

We may look at the Gospel in another way, as the tent of meeting.[3] The Incarnate Word, as the fulfilment of the tabernacle in the wilderness, was the meeting place between God and man: "the Word was made flesh, and *tabernacled* among us, and we beheld his glory." This tabernacle is the transcendent fellowship given through reconciliation. In His Son God has made Himself known to His people as their God and revealed to them that they are His people. In the Incarnate Word believers "saw", not simply the Man Jesus, not even simply the Word of God, but in Him also the Father.[4] In the face of Christ shines the glory of God.[5] But St. Paul says this last in the context of the ministry of the Word of God, using the same language of the Gospel as He does of Christ. Of Christ he says: "God . . . hath shined in our hearts, to give the light of the knowledge of the glory of God in the face of Jesus Christ"; and

---

[1] 2 Cor. 5: 18–19
[2] Gal. 3: 1
[3] This concept is surely closer to Scripture than the continental idea of a point of contact, which flourished between the wars.
[4] John 14: 9
[5] 2 Cor. 4: 6; cf. John 1: 4–5

of the Gospel: "lest the light of the glorious Gospel of Christ, who is the image of God, should shine unto them."[1] The Gospel is the tent of meeting with God—with the Father in His Son through the power of the Holy Spirit.

As the meeting place with God, the place of reconciliation and atonement, the Gospel is, since God is one, the meeting place with God in His completeness—with our Creator and Redeemer, with Him who was, and is, and is to come. Here our Creator makes Himself known to us as our Creator and thus makes us known to ourselves as His creation. And conversely, the one who meets with us here is no strange God, reaping where He did not sow, but the one from whom we come, to whom we belong and who in creation has bound Himself to us. The Word in the Gospel comes unto His own. Again, He who meets with us is the one who was made flesh, suffered, died, rose again, ascended to the right hand of His Father, has all power in heaven and on earth and fulfils His high priestly office of mediatory intercession within the holiest place. And finally, since it is the whole and indivisible Christ who comes in His Gospel, He who shall come again now meets with us. That which shall be is, in the unity of Christ, present in the Gospel. The *eschatos* Himself is the Word of the Gospel, and in Him the *eschaton* is spiritually present already. The sacramental nature of this presence must not be allowed to detract from its reality.

We have drawn out the main consequences of the statement *Praedicatio verbi Dei est verbum Dei*. In conclusion, we must remember to ask ourselves whether we have been theorizing in a void or whether these consequences have anything to do with the life of the Church and of the world. In all that we have said, let us substitute the word "sermon" for "preaching" or "Gospel", bearing in mind an ordinary Sunday sermon, perhaps in some big city church with a large congregation, perhaps in a quiet little country church with its "faithful few". After the third hymn the vicar preaches his sermon. To men, women and children—his friends, neighbours or acquaintances—a man speaks. But God is in heaven; they are all upon earth. Dare we make the assertion in concrete that we have made more

[1] 2 Cor. 4: 4

abstractly? "The Word of God which is the substance of the sermon is the incarnate Word. In the sermon the Word made flesh Himself comes and meets with His people" (p. 184). "The sermon is the very place of judgment and forgiveness; where they are not merely declared but effected" (p. 188). "The sermon is the tent of meeting with God—with the Father in His Son through the power of the Holy Spirit" (p. 189).[1]

We must, of course, at once make the provisos: *if* the sermon is genuinely the Gospel; and, according to God's gracious promise. Not just a sermon that takes any non-Biblical subject or treats any Biblical subject in a way foreign to the witness of the Bible; but the sermon which declares the Gospel about Jesus Christ according to the witness of the Bible. And not on the basis of an automatic conjuring up of Christ's presence (as if He were the djin who must perforce come at Aladdin's summons), but according to His sovereignty, in which He has freely bound Himself to His Gospel and His Church.

But when we have made these provisos, and never forgetting them or drifting away from them, then in fear and trembling we not only may say of the sermon what was said of the Gospel, but we even must say it and dare not say anything less. On our side, we must always realize that all that can be said about our sermons is that they are earthen vessels. And yet, because the excellency of the power is of God, within the earthen vessels may be a treasure—the light of the knowledge of the glory of God in the face of Jesus Christ. That this may be so, the preacher will pray, and work, and pray.

---

[1] By focusing on the sermon, I do not intend to exclude other forms which the Word of God may freely take to Himself. The proclamation of Christ may take place under more than one form. But the sermon in the Church and to the world occupies a primary place in the Church's activity. It is, or should be, the occasion when the Church customarily proclaims the Biblical message.

8

A CHRISTOLOGICAL VIEW
OF THE SACRAMENTS

by J. K. S. REID
Professor of Theology, University of Leeds

8

A CHRISTOLOGICAL VIEW OF THE SACRAMENTS

by

J. K. S. REID

How is a theology, a piety or an ecclesiology to become Christo-centric [asks Karl Barth] unless it is so by nature? Even the efforts, the unhealthy zeal and the historical and systematic methods which they have recently used to achieve it, demonstrate clearly and distinctly that they were not naturally and could not become Christocentric.[1]

IT may be that any collection of Christological essays is implicated in this judgment and even condemned by it. Yet it is perhaps to do the truth which it expresses the greatest honour and to pay it the best kind of attention, if, instead of allowing it to frighten one off from writing Christologically, one put the lesson conveyed into practice. This would mean declining to do one's thinking and then at the last moment to give the construction Christological slant, or, otherwise said, declining to construct the position of other materials and then simply to finish it off by putting on a top dressing of a Christological kind. It would mean precisely accepting the condition that the Christological character must be radical, or else the thinking will not be really Christological at all. It is this condition that is willingly accepted in what follows.

In the case of the sacraments, it is in fact easier to comply with the condition than in other matters, though the danger mentioned reappears at another point in a rather different form. It has not proved difficult to adhere faithfully, at least at the outset and for much of the time, to the rubric that the sacraments are to be interpreted Christologically. This is to be understood partly from the difference between rite and sacrament. I take it that a rite is an action regarded as religiously valuable in whose performance human agents play the domin-

[1] *Kirchliche Dogmatik* I/2, 385.

ant role; and that, in contrast to this, in a sacrament the value arising from or adhering to the action is attributable to divine power lying outside the action performed by the human agents involved. In this sense, sacrament is something that belongs at least more evidently to Christianity than to other religions, for which the characteristic action takes the form of rite.[1] Hence where sacraments are spoken of at all, there has been little temptation to detach them from their supernatural basis in divine action. And since for Christian theology the clue to this supernatural action is found in the incarnation, fully Christological character has been more easily maintained in the case of the sacraments than elsewhere. Moreover, by the historical link with our Lord in the days of His flesh and the connection with specific dominical commands (though of course both have been questioned), the sacraments have regularly been attached to the person of our Lord with an unusual closeness and strength which it has been difficult to ignore.

This receives expression in the familiar title applied by Christian communions influenced by the Reformation to one of the sacraments: the Holy Communion is frequently called the Lord's Supper; and this is supported by other phrases such as the Lord's Table and the Cup of the Lord. Nor are these mere names; they really signify what is thought and held about the Holy Communion. It is His supper that is celebrated, His table to which men are invited, and, if there is one truth about the Holy Communion that may be held to be admitted by all communions and all forms of sacramental doctrine, it is that the real president of the feast, the real host of the supper, and also the real agent in all that is done or effected is our Lord Himself.[2] So far as it goes, this is the best of guarantees that the doctrine of the sacraments will start off by being "by nature Christocentric", as Barth demands, and it will therefore not be

[1] Contrast A. E. Taylor, *The Faith of a Moralist*, Vol. II, Chapter VII: sacrament is "so widely diffused a characteristic of actual religions that it must be regarded as typical": "many other religions possess sacraments". But cf. the art. "Sacraments" in Hastings' *Encyclopaedia of Religion and Ethics*.

[2] cf. Y. Brilioth, *Eucharistic Faith and Practice Evangelical and Catholic*, p. 283: "The true celebrant is not the human priest, but Christ the great High-priest, in the midst of His disciples." Brilioth goes on to quote from the Mozarabic Liturgy the beautiful: "Adeste, adeste, bone Pontifex, in medio nostri, sicut fuisti in medio discipulorum tuorum."

necessary to make heroic efforts at too late a point in the course of the argument to Christologize what is said.

In fact, as has been suggested, the danger that affects sacramental doctrine comes from another quarter and assumes another form. It is rather that this apparently secure Christological standpoint be given away and the position surrendered when the attempt is later made to define the matter with greater accuracy. Thus, not for the first time, a point judged to be secure may be endangered or lost by later concentration on details and refinements upon which in the last resort its security did not primarily or even secondarily depend.

There can be little doubt about the place at which this danger is chiefly incurred. As the Holy Communion is really the Lord's Supper, so the sacraments are primarily the dominical sacraments. But they do not remain only the Lord's. "This is" is immediately followed in the account of St. Luke (22: 19) and St. Paul (1 Cor. 11: 23) by "this do". By magisterial command, it is enjoined or conceded that men should have a part to play. This is no more than to say that it is really a sacrament and not something else that is being instituted.[1] But this being the case, a sacrament is immediately exposed to hazards peculiarly or in a peculiar degree its own. Sacrament, though it is and remains the Lord's own, is really sacrament and so is also our doing. This is a point at which the divine and the human, God and man, human and superhuman action, come into such close contact that their relations, so often at other points better left indefinite, must be defined. This is the field in which investigation is to take place—a field in which it is difficult to move with certainty, but from which it is impossible to keep out —for it is here that sacramental doctrinal expressions jeopardize the magisterial dominion of Christ over His sacraments and surrender the Christological character which is the presupposition from which the start was made.

Something positive must first be said about the sacramental position, before the characteristic ways in which it has too often been betrayed are mentioned. We are not left to our own resources and without guide for understanding of this position.

[1] cf. Y. Brilioth, *op. cit.*, p. 284: The Eucharist "is not only an action external to ourselves: . . . we are also dedicated to participate".

The incarnation is the rule for its understanding. By this is not meant any incarnational principle, some natural fittingness on the basis of which it might have been expected that the divine and the human should come together. What is meant is both more and less than this. It is simply the fact of the incarnation, that "the Word became flesh" and God man. This is something less than a principle in the sense that it cannot be credited with universal validity or the other fine attributes ascribable to general principles. But it is also more, in the sense that at least it really did happen as a quite real event. As such it yields, not indeed a general principle, but rather a clue to God's beha-viour and a pattern of His conduct towards men which is in-contestable and therefore reliable.[1] It is in virtue of this factual exemplar that Christianity more than any other religion ought to lay emphasis upon the material and bodily in the service which man renders to God, both in his worship and his work. In both we are enjoined to "present your bodies a living sacri-fice, holy and acceptable unto God" (Rom. 12: 1). This is the ground for that total commitment to God in activity which is the hall-mark of the Christian life. It is also the ground for the appropriate use of material things in worship and the proper bodily disposition of the worshipper (of which the "Catholic" has on the whole a strong, if sometimes perverted, sense, and the "Protestant" perhaps too much suspicion).[2] The same pat-tern is observable, not only where God alone is at work in the incarnation and where man chiefly is at work in service, but also precisely at the point where, as already said, God acts and man too acts, in the sacraments.

As the I of the Son of God took human nature, in order to com-

---

[1] So Martindale (*The Teaching of the Catholic Church*, Vol. II, 738, 737): "the method of our salvation was an incarnational one, where the Spirit operates in and by means of the flesh". "God will not save human nature apart from human nature. The material side of the transaction might have been minimized. God might have saved us by a prayer, a hope, by just one act of love. He might have re-mained invisible to eye, inaudible to ear. But He did not. He took our human nature—the whole of it." In the sacraments, this incarnational method is said to be worked out in detail.

[2] cf. T. F. Torrance, "Royal Priesthood", *Scottish Journal of Theology Occasional Paper*, No. 3, 19. cf. also John 4: 23 f., where it is enjoined that worship be "in the Spirit", and quite indirectly that we should bring with us a "spiritual disposition" or anything of the kind to our worship.

plete in it the work of salvation, and on the completion of the earthly life to bring to the Father an eternal offering of praise, so Christ took certain objects—of course otherwise than the Logos took human nature . . . in order to make present in them for the duration of the time of this world the work of salvation effected for all time in His human nature.[1]

It is true of the sacraments, as of the incarnation, that "the Son of man must be delivered into the hands of sinful men" (Luke 24: 7). And in both cases, the "must" is not an external necessity, but identical with the divine volition which is "not willing that any should perish, but that all should come to salvation" (2 Pet. 3: 9). In the one case it is the Word that is determinative, and in the other it is the institutional word of command. The dominical word is the basis of the Christological character of the sacraments: This do, and: Go and teach, baptizing, these commands resting, as they do respectively, on the indicatives of the old covenant precedent of circumcision and the new covenant: This is. Whatever alienates or infringes Christ's dominical magisterium is a departure from the Christological understanding of the sacraments; and on the other hand, any formulation that preserves this magisterium intact safeguards, so far at least, their Christological character.

If this is the formal standard by which a genuinely Christological understanding of the sacraments is to be judged, the material standard consists in the way in which the "real presence" is defined, in which He is conceived as coming to His own Supper who is Lord of the table. It cannot be said that this is the only point at which a doctrine of the sacraments may be defective; but it is certainly a point, not only of cardinal importance, but one where the right way is most frequently lost. It is right to lay emphasis on the fact that it is a sacramental presence, and not some other kind of presence which we might think of or even prefer. Though we cannot but bring with us categories of thought derived from elsewhere, we must finally let ourselves be taught by this fact. It is fundamentally unprofitable, and at the worst misleading, therefore, to raise the question whether the relation of presence to what is actually done is best represented in terms of Platonism or in terms of

[1] M. Schmaus, *Katholische Dogmatik*, IV/1, 59 f.

Aristotelianism; whether, that is, the presence is to be regarded as the extension of the supersensuous into the sensuous, or as a bare copy of an original.[1] Here it is to the incarnation that we must look if there is to be any proper guidance for our thought. Chalcedon was warding off errors when it declared that in Christ there are two natures which are to be neither confused nor separated. In sacramental doctrine, there are also two things to be considered: there are the visible reals, and there is the real presence; there is what men do and there is what God in and by that doing Himself does. The basic pattern of error in sacramental doctrine is that the antinomy is resolved by the surrender of either the "unconfused" or the "unseparated". Confusion of the two is exemplified by the Roman doctrine of transubstantiation, in which the elements are substantially identified with the real presence, while separation of the two is exemplified by the Zwinglian doctrine of bare signs, in which the elements have not a real but only a symbolic relation to what is signified, only pointing to the presence as something apart from themselves.[2] Either course involves the denial of what is specifically and *sui generis* sacramental; and both implicitly affirm that what is sacramental can really be reduced without remainder to terms other than sacramental. On the contrary, it has to be maintained that this is Christ's sacrament and that in sovereign grace and in virtue of His pledged word He is sacramentally present where it is celebrated. He bestows His presence with magisterial freedom, delimited but not really

---

[1] M. Schmaus (*op. cit.*, 7, 55) propounds the two options, himself preferring the first (which is thought out in accordance with the Platonic theory of forms) to the second (which is based on the sequence of cause and effect). But the real question is: must or indeed can either be chosen as really adequate? If Christ is the pattern of God's action, it cannot be surprising that Plato and Aristotle should fail to anticipate what is there revealed; and on the other hand, it cannot be surprising that the attempt to render what was there done in categories formed *ante eventum* should leave something unexpressed and inexpressible.

[2] There is a parallel to be found in the case of the doctrine of Holy Scripture. There may be either a transubstantiation of Scripture so that it becomes identical with the Word of God itself, or, on the other hand, a separation of Scripture from the Word of God so that the Bible becomes a mere historical record. Both equally deny the dynamic relation in which the Word of God stands to the words of Scripture. See the Report of the Special Commission on Baptism presented to the General Assembly of the Church of Scotland, *Reports 1955*, 563; and my Kerr Lectures.

bound, by His own spoken institutional word. The Christological character of the sacraments consists formally in Christ's
own appointment of the elements with His word of promise
attaching to them, and materially in Christ's giving Himself to
His people when in compliance with His institution they do as
He says.

If this means anything, it means that the Church has its Lord
and Master from time to time given to it in the sacraments, as
really as nineteen and a half centuries ago Judaism and the
Roman Empire had Christ born to it. As then His presence was
apprehensible in the flesh, so now His presence is apprehensible
in the elements. The Word that was with God from the beginning became; and the Word that became by His promised
word becomes. Christ inserts Himself into the life of the Church
as the Logos inserted Himself into the life of the world. In both
cases the certainty we have is a real certainty because it reposes
elsewhere than on ourselves and our experience,[1] and in the last
resort on Christ Himself, on what He was and is and what He
said and says. The incarnational certainty of His presence rests
on a historical fact to whose significance we are awakened to
apprehension through His Spirit. The sacramental certainty of
His presence rests on nothing which we either must or could
bring or do or provide, but on the dominical word transmitted
through the Church's proclamation and practice "from the
beginning". It is because it is a matter removed from the realm
in which we can or need do much, or rather the complementary
fact that it remains in the realm in which He only can do what
is needful, that we have the greatest certainty in the sacraments.
Their virtue is *ex opere operato*, because in the first and the last
stages they are His work and convey His virtue. At the same
time, precisely here where nothing is required of us, all that is
necessary is evoked from us. The sacrament has this done upon
it as the participant, with the Virgin Mary, says: *Ecce ancilla
domini*. Shifting a little the centre of gravity of the analogy, the
Church exercises no more authority over the sacraments than

[1] Contrast Martindale in *The Teaching of the Catholic Church*, Vol. II, p. 749:
"It was because the sacraments give grace that men saw, and insisted on the fact
that they were instituted by Christ; it was not because they were instituted by
Christ that men concluded they gave grace." This evidently prepares a position
from which it is possible to vindicate the non-dominical "sacraments".

does Joseph over the Virgin Birth.[1] Similarly as the Church has
no authority (and hence abundant assurance) in the matter of
the sacraments, so it has no jurisdiction over the period of their
validity. This is bounded by the eschaton itself, or rather by
the Eschatos Himself. He who initiates is also He who will bring
to a finish and an end. There is now the period between the
Cross and the Parousia. For the Cross He came, and at the
Parousia He will come again. There it was in the flesh, and
then it will be in glory; and in the meantime His presence with
His Church is granted sacramentally. This is not to say that it
is only in the sacraments that His presence is bestowed.[2] What
is rather meant is that His abiding presence is to be construed
as essentially sacramental. In other words, just as the incarnation itself is not a mere improvisation or expedient to be
dropped when it has achieved its end, but a genuine insight into
the essential Logos, so the sacraments are not simply transient
manifestations that leave the essence of that which is manifested fundamentally unrevealed. The fact is rather that while
the Church lives looking back to the Cross and forward to
glory, it is meanwhile sustained and nourished by the sacramental presence of Christ, who thus makes Himself available to
His people in a mode as nearly eschatological as can temporally
be. In this twilit period where the aeons overlap and while men
who in Christ belong to the new age have still to contend with
the dying tenacity of the old upon them, they meantime taste
sacramentally the glory to come and are fortified by it. But that
this is possible at the present moment is by means of an anticipation of that which will be by Him who only can so bring it
about, Him that is to come, just as the miracles[3] are anticipa-

---

[1] This is owed to T. F. Torrance in the essay "Eschatology and the Eucharist",
Inter-Communion 338, the volume prepared by the Theological Commission for
presentation to the Faith and Order Conference at Lund, 1952.

[2] It is not clear whether M. Schmaus (*op. cit.*, 34) agrees with this or not. He
affirms (rightly) that proclamation of the Christian Gospel is more than mere
speaking about Christ or the expression of mere human opinions, but a real witness
to and by the Holy Ghost and hence *wirksam* and *heilschaffend*. He adds that preaching of Christ is only *wirksam* and *heilschaffend* when it represents the sacraments
(which is only true if it be carefully interpreted).

[3] For a more detailed account of the analogy here suggested, see T. F. Torrance,
"Royal Priesthood", *Scottish Journal of Theology Occasional Paper*, No. 3., 47 f., where
in the case of the paralytic the time-lag between the forgiveness of sins and the
healing is paralleled with the time between the times in which the Church lives.

tions on the part of Him that was.[1] The power and the glory
will be seen to be His. The sacraments are and remain His.

As said already, the form which infidelity to Christological
representation of the sacraments most frequently takes is basic-
cally an infringement of this sovereign prerogative and jurisdiction of Christ over the material things and visible actions
appointed for sacramental use. Philosophically this infidelity
consists in the attempt to bring sacramental action under
rubrics and categories that empirically have their origin elsewhere and logically have application that is universal. Theologically it consists in a refusal to reckon with and steadily to
apply the significance of sacrament. Religiously it consists in a
failure to take the two factors, the element and the Lord of the
elements, together with the relation in which by His appointment they stand, seriously enough, and to attempt to repose the
trust we have upon an "other foundation than that is laid",
which is the dominical word of appointment. Here without
doubt a number of motives work together in a complex in which
it is difficult or impossible to make distinctions and separations.
There is curiosity: the analytic mind of Western Christendom,
in contrast to the more synthetic spirit of the Eastern Christians, appears to have deemed it necessary to attempt to locate
the point or moment or action in which that takes place which
Christ alone effects.[2] Or again there is anxiety in which, rather
than face the present action of Christ Himself, the agency at
work is located elsewhere than in Him alone, and found in a
sacrificial priesthood[3] or the sanctity of the consecrated ele-

---

[1] The very recent resurgence of interest in so-called "divine healing" raises the
question of the nature of the anticipation that is legitimately to be expected, and
whether the promised sacramental expectation is not the only right anticipation
and the expectation of healing a premature anticipation of what really belongs to
the last things and not to the present things.

[2] This is not quite the distinction which Y. Brilioth (*op. cit.*, 54, 69, 285) makes.
According to him, there is a Synoptic view which holds to the personal presence of
the Saviour once incarnate, of which the incident on the road to Emmaus is the
type; and there is the Johannine view, which conceives of the Saviour as mystically
present, and of this "I am the bread of life" is the type. In fact, both representations can be employed in the interests of Western analysis, and the mystical union
of Christ with His people comes to be regarded as guaranteed by the elements
themselves, which become the means whereby He abides with them.

[3] So T. F. Torrance, "Royal Priesthood", *Scottish Journal of Theology Occasional
Paper*, No. 3, 5: "the sacrificial priesthood as attempted escape from encounter
with the living God".

ments. Or again and closely allied to this, there is pride, by which the mystery is extracted from the hands of Christ and located at a more accessible and humanly manageable point, and, so that a measure of human control can seem to be exercised, the mystery is domesticated. These motives lead to an understanding of the sacraments which alienates from Christ the dominion over the sacraments which is rightly His. Their virtue is localized instead in something else in which, even if not in its own right at least by a right supposed to be conceded by Him, they take over an efficacy which is really His alone. Here latent deism is really at work. But the same latent deism can operate in a different direction and to a different or even opposite conclusion. It may lead not only to confusion of appointed element and Lord, but to their separation. The elements and the liturgy are then regarded as having symbolical significance only, and they point to their Lord but may not be said in any real sense to convey Him. In both cases the significance of sacrament has been surrendered: there is a virtual denial that "This is" really means what it says, and sacrament is a conception which occupies no territory of its own.

It is then by the displacement and obtrusion of one or more of the things that together constitute a sacrament that the Lordship of Christ over His institution, and hence the Christological character of the sacraments, are infringed or impaired. The history of sacramental doctrine shows how easily and how variously this may happen. Three ways may be regarded as typical. These may be respectively called naturalization, spiritualization, and transubstantiation.

Naturalization takes place when the "fittingness" of the elements and the appropriateness of the sign to what is signified is emphasized. Encouragement is given to this tendency by the distinction suggested by the familiar formula which dates back to St. Augustine, that a sacrament is "the outward and visible sign of an inward and spiritual grace". Then it is easy to represent water as effecting cleansing and the water of Baptism effecting a spiritual cleansing, and to represent bread and wine as imparting nourishment and refreshment and the bread and wine of the Eucharist as imparting spiritual nourishment and refreshment. The elements in both cases are thus held to have a certain appropriateness in their respective spheres.[1]

At least two things are obscured by this emphasis, and only by their being restored to their proper place is the Christological character of the sacraments preserved. No doubt there is in some sense a "fittingness", and it can hardly be conceived that our Lord would select something that ordinarily signified the opposite of cleansing or of nourishment to be the sacramental elements. But the virtue attaching to the sacraments is by no means to be located here. It is wrong to bypass the Lord of the sacraments and His appointment of the elements, and to locate their virtue in some kind of natural appropriateness. This is to lose sight of the fact that it is in virtue of the appointment and the promise that the elements have anything to do with efficacy at all. After all, what is conveyed in the sacraments is not primarily cleansing or nourishment, but the Lord of the sacraments Himself cleansing and nourishing His children. The naturalization of the virtue of the sacraments is to be repudiated in honour of Him who retains in His hands the effective virtue. Moreover, and as a corollary of this, the virtue of ordinary water or bread and the virtue of sacramental water and bread are strictly incommensurable. The effectiveness of the first is the result of causal sequence; the effectiveness of the second is the result of the operation of Christ Himself working according to a pledged word of appointment and promise. The water and the bread might by themselves be bare signs; they become sacramentally efficacious signs in virtue of the use made of them by the Lord of the sacraments to convey Himself.

Spiritualization takes place when too great emphasis is laid on the subjective or receptive side. When faith is so obtruded as

---

[1] A notable example of this may be quoted. In the *Draft Catechism with Notes*, issued in 1955 by the General Assembly of the Church of Scotland for experimental use in presbyteries, there occurs the following explanation of the sacraments: "Water is commonly used for drinking and for washing. Few people, however, realize that few things are more important in this world than water. Scientists tell us that life in any form did not appear on this planet until the elements of oxygen and hydrogen had combined to form water (H_2O)." And so on. The note continues: "It is surely most fitting, then, that water should be the symbol of spiritual cleansing, restoration and renewal." This is almost to suggest that the "spiritual gifts" conveyed by the water of Baptism are simply natural properties which few people happen to realize.

to constitute the condition of the efficacy of the sacraments, damage is done to their Christological character. This is the objection so often made by Romans against the Reformed view of the sacraments, and especially the Lutheran form of it, and it must be admitted that the use made of the principle of *sola fide* has frequently given excuse if not justification for the charge.[1] The same charge is with justice levelled against what M. Schmaus (*loc. cit.*) calls the "intentionalists" who, he avers, hold that what sacraments do is to evoke the disposition in participants which has saving efficacy. Nothing can very well be said to exculpate the intentionalists. But Luther and Reformed theology at their best are quite clear that the agent in sacraments is not faith directly. On the contrary, faith itself is that which is evoked in us by Him who Himself, condescending to our weakness, as Calvin has it, further gives Himself in the sacramental signs. The greatest of care has to be taken (as is not always done) to maintain precisely this. Whenever faith is elevated into a *conditio sine qua non* of the efficacy of the sacraments, then that again is taken out of the hands of Christ which rightly belongs only there.

The place that faith and other subjective factors may rightly take is defined by two things. The sacraments are objectively instituted. Our Lord said: "This is", not: This by your faith may be. It is He and not our faith that is efficacious in the sacraments. Whatever subordinate part faith must play, it is not something in the nature of an efficient cause which we have to bring with us. At no point is it truer than here that "Nothing in my hand I bring". He who effectively works the thing, effectively provides the condition for its reception. The other consideration supports this. In the incarnation Christ commits Himself to material things. By the same token, in the sacraments He gives Himself again and again to His people. It is certainly here that the efficacy of the sacraments reposes.

The real error in transubstantiation is of course not that it proposes a miraculous event. What could be more "miraculous" than the Logos becoming flesh or Christ's bestowing His presence in the material elements of the sacraments? It rather

---

[1] See, e.g., M. Schmaus (*op. cit.*, 33), who says that for the Reformers the sacraments do not justify, but faith in the sacraments.

consists in the evacuation of the sacraments of all specifically sacramental meaning. This results from a rationalization of the sacramental mystery, and results in depriving Christ of the gracious activity by which He makes sacraments convey Himself. The exclusion of Christ from that which is His and the sphere in which He operates is exemplified by Martindale (*The Teaching of the Catholic Church*, 763), who declares that what he elects to call "the Catholic tradition" is that "the sacraments are efficacious in themselves".[1] Anglo-Catholicism is not far behind, as Brilioth points out, when it declares that there is a distinction between the divine presence and the sacramental gift, so that the elements themselves acquire a significance (*op. cit.*, 217, quoting Waggett in *The Holy Eucharist*, 1906). As Brilioth rightly comments, this "opens the door to the degradation of the sacrament". The degradation consists in depriving Christ of His activity, and in alienating from Him the efficacy which is His in order to invest the elements with it. The parallel between this and certain forms of fundamentalist biblicism has already been noted.

Two fundamental errors are here involved. The first is that, instead of the entirely free and living activity of the Lord of the sacraments, resting upon the word to which He will not prove unfaithful, we are offered a rite permanently endowed with efficacy. The Christological character of the sacraments then consists, not in their Lord's infallible fidelity in operation, but in a virtue conceded to the elements themselves. The permanent and stable factor which the sacraments incontestably possess is conceived as a property in them and not as the word of Christ Himself, freely given and faithfully discharged. A further error is bound up with this. So long as it is Christ who is recognized as both agent and gift, the sacraments possess an inalienable personal quality: it is the Word who is given in

---

[1] Roman Catholicism, many-sided as always, is sometimes less blunt; cf. de la Taille (*The Mystery of Faith*, bk. II, The Sacrifice of the Church, ch. 23), where, relating the eucharistic sacrifice of Christ to that of ourselves, he admits that "due allowance for the difference of the time of offering and of the persons offering the sacrifice" has to be made, and declares that "our sacrifices and that of Christ do not exist as members of one and the same genus . . . they are only in the same order by way of analogy". In this admitted discrepancy between the twos acrifices, room could be found for a true doctrine.

them, with all that this implies, and it is communion that is enjoyed by the participants. So soon as transubstantiation is accepted, and the elements themselves endowed with the sacramental efficacy, the personal character of the sacraments is lost. The participant is no longer personally confronted with the Word, but only with a property supposed to be conceded to the elements by the Word. Thus communion on the part of the participants is no longer regarded as essential, and the spectacle of the mass is established.[1]

It is not pretended that most or even many of the problems of sacramental doctrine have here been solved. The intention has been to drive a straight furrow through an immensely complex subject, in the belief that if this guiding line is held straight and true other matters will fall into their proper place and perspective. It is, in other words, the Christological character of the sacraments that has at all costs to be conserved, and it is by this standard and on this presupposition and not otherwise or earlier that the many residual problems can alone find right solution. Hugh of St. Victor is right when he says: "A sacrament is a corporal or material element, set forth exteriorily to the senses, which by its similarity portrays, and by its institution means, and by blessing contains, some invisible and spiritual grace"— if only the last phrase be interpreted properly, as nothing else or other than the presence of the Lord of the sacraments. So K. E. Kirk (quoted Brilioth, *op. cit.*, 220) speaks eirenically when, deprecating the raising of the question whether the real presence is "in the service" or "in the elements" and especially the use of the word "in" in this connection, he goes on to say: "if controversy forces us to choose between the two alternatives suggested, it is surely no more than reasonable to suggest that

---

[1] Two notes may be subjoined. On the one hand, the same considerations seem capable of being urged against the practice of reservation. Appropriate respect should, of course, be accorded to the elements in virtue of their being "taken" and consecrated, especially in the disposal of any residue. But the reverence is false which deliberately holds them in suspense from a celebration. On the other hand, it has to be admitted that the factor of communion in the Eucharist may and often does lead to a false individualism, unless due emphasis is laid upon the accompanying "communion with all the faithful in heaven and on earth, both visible and invisible", which is at least encouraged where the custom is to have infrequent but well-attended celebrations, and to have the elements passed from one communicant to another.

the 'visible focus' (if we may use the expression) of the presence of Christ in the Eucharist must be that for which and around which the congregation is gathered, rather than the gathering together of the congregation." And it is further satisfactory to be able to quote a Roman Catholic theologian (M. Schmaus, *op. cit.*, 64, 72) to a similar effect: when emphasizing that "Christ is the dispenser of the sacraments", he goes on to say that "the sacrament, like the virtue of the passion of Christ, is instrument and means of the gracious will of God. . . . In the celebration of the sacrament God remains the Lord of Grace. The celebrant has no dominion over God, but God exercises His gracious lordship over men through the sacrament in exalted freedom, bound only by Himself in His love and His faithfulness."

9

CHRIST, THE CHURCH HIS BODY, AND ITS MEMBERS

Professor of Practical Theology, Christ's College, Aberdeen

o

9

CHRIST, THE CHURCH HIS BODY, AND ITS MEMBERS

by

DAVID CAIRNS

O NE of the most hopeful signs in recent theology has been
the growth of an eirenical spirit among the writers of the
different Confessions. A notable contribution here has
been the book of the Roman Catholic von Balthasar on Karl
Barth's theology, a book which no Protestant can read without
admiration at the sheer labour entailed in studying the many
works of Barth. Those best entitled to judge, say that there has
not only been labour here, but insight. A further example of
this admirable spirit is Oscar Cullmann, who has been able to
enter into profitable discussion with Daniélou and other Roman
theologians.

The writer of this essay would wish to imitate these scholars
in spirit, though he cannot emulate them in learning. It is
necessary to remember that across the frontiers of the Confessions there is a common loyalty to Christ, and we should try
to grasp what Christians separated from us feel to be of the
highest importance in the positions they maintain. Such an
effort of sympathy will at the least help to ensure that the out-
standing differences between us are real differences, and this in
itself is great gain. As Barth has said in his *Dogmatik*, we must
not abuse our fellow-Christians; it might be that in our criti-
cisms of them we were unconsciously opposing ourselves to
Christ Himself. At the most we may address to them a serious
question, which as fellow-Christians we feel at liberty, and,
indeed, obliged to put.

But there is another service which we can do each other
across the denominational, and even across the confessional
frontiers. We can do our best to clear up our partners' misunderstanding of our own teaching. Much of our mutual
misunderstanding arises from the obscurity of theological

writing, and much from the long separate growth of our traditions without the aid to mutual understanding which friendly
free discussion might have given to us. It may be that also on
both sides we are faced with the problem of involuntary yet
wilful misunderstanding of each other. These terms are used
advisedly. For there are so many loyalties, so many prejudices
at stake, that there may be a natural fear on both sides, lest in
the end on some important point, both Roman Catholic and
Protestant may be found to agree much more closely than
either had thought. We should ask ourselves very seriously
whether we are being quite honest when we find ourselves
saying or writing: "What theologians over the fence are saying
seems indeed near to our view, but if you will look closely, you
will see that it is worlds apart."

It would indeed be foolish and conceited to think that in a
few years we could bridge over clefts formed at the Reformation. But if we do our best to clear away misunderstandings,
we may be able to prepare the way for the work of the Holy
Spirit, who will guide us into a better appreciation of each
others' views, and finally lead us into unity.

In this paper I wish to discuss shortly the views of Emile
Mersch and Eric Mascall on the subjects of Christian sanctification and the relation of the Church to its Head, and in
particular to point out their failure fully to understand Protestant teaching on the former theme. I shall do this by giving
first the teaching of Protestantism on sanctification according
to Mersch and Mascall, and contrasting it with the actual
teaching of Luther and Calvin.

In his important book, *Christ, the Christian and the Church*, Dr.
Mascall says very suggestively that the conception which a man
forms of the nature of the Church is determined by his view of
the relation of the Christian to Christ.[1] This way of putting it
may strike those who come from the Reformed tradition as too
individualist. For in the works of Calvin, at least, the relation
of the Christian to Christ and to the Church are never set
against each other, so that the one is prior to the other. For him
the Church is nothing less than corporate communion with
the Lord. Nevertheless, there is a deep truth in Mascall's con-

[1] p. 112

tention; the nature of justification will be one, whether it is
exhibited in the case of the Church or of the individual member; and the impartation of the life of God in Christ will be
understood similarly whether it be the Christian member or the
Body of Christ that is being considered. Consequently, after a
study and defence of the Reformed teaching on the justification
and sanctification of the believer, I shall try to vindicate its
logical coherence with the Reformed (and I believe Scriptural)
teaching on the Church and its relation to its Head.

In his great book, *The Whole Christ*, in the chapter on "The
Dignity of the Members of Christ", Mersch discusses the
Protestant movement, which he claims arose from the metaphysical poverty of the age which preceded it. In the golden age
of scholasticism, he says, God was described as Pure Being. The
transcendence of God was well understood, but so also was the
participation of all created beings in His Being. When this
metaphysical insight was lost, owing to the growth of nominal-
ism, it became inevitable that God and the creature should be
considered as extremes within Being, and the sole relation
between them on this presupposition could only be that of the
distance that separated them. Hence there grew up a dualism
and a pessimism about man; the finite-infinite dualism having
added to it a moral and theological one. To our insignificance
we have added our sin. If men are so despicable, both by
nature and through sin, how can they become just and holy?
"By extrinsic imputation", said the Protestants. "At best they
can be mere receptacles of goodness. . . . At all events they
cannot be collaborators in the work; they cannot be truly
united with the gift, blended with it, transformed into it."[1]
What can incorporation in Christ the Son of God mean on
such a view? It can mean nothing else, say the Protestants, than
the entry into us of the very life of the Saviour, over and above
our own sinful life.

On occasion the Protestants have been known to speak with
vigour and insistence of this entrance of the life of the divine
Head into us, the members. . . . The impression they give is quite
false, however; Christian faith is one indivisible whole. In rejecting one part of it, they have deprived themselves of all, and the

[1] p. 503

incorporation in Christ which they prize so highly becomes a nonentity.

For this life they speak of does not vivify, it remains external to us.

> The body is dead; it lies in closest proximity to the Living One, but it is a corpse, nonetheless. . . . One cannot help wondering whether this flow of energy is so powerful after all, since it does not produce any activity; and whether the humanity of Christ can still be called Life, if it cannot truly vivify us.[1]

Now let us consider Eric Mascall's view, expressed in the chapter "Incorporation into Christ" in the above-mentioned book, *Christ, the Christian and the Church*. Here it is stated that Protestantism has been reluctant "to admit that grace can produce a real supernaturalization of the soul in its ontological depths".[2]

> This does not mean [Mascall continues] that the Reformers do not expect to see acts of supernatural virtue in the justified man, quite the contrary. But because they do not believe in a real communication of the life of God to the human soul, they are unable to see the man himself as the subject of these acts. The sole subject, in any real sense, is God, although the merits of the acts are attributed to the man by imputation. The supernatural and the natural in the justification are thus like two parallel streams with no real connection; the former, which is wholly good, is God's operation; the latter, which is wholly bad, is man's.[3]

It is hard to avoid the conclusion that the outlines of this picture were unconsciously dictated by the desire to produce a contrast with what Dr. Mascall goes on to describe as "The Catholic Doctrine".

> There is thus a sharp contrast [he says] with the Catholic doctrine, for in this latter, a man's good acts, while they are to be attributed entirely to God as primary cause, are none the less to be attributed to man as their secondary and freely acting secondary cause, whose real efficacy is not destroyed, but is mysteriously and subtly reinforced and confirmed by the overarching influence of supernatural grace.[4]

---

[1] p. 504. The same criticism of Luther is made by Congar in his *Divided Christendom* on p. 42 and p. 259. It is my thesis that this is completely in error, the Luther here criticized is a man of straw.

[2] p. 80.   [3] p. 81.   [4] p. 81.

It must be conceded that, in this passage, Dr. Mascall is clearly at several points trying to do justice to the views of the Reformers, but the main point which we must investigate is the justice of his claim that the Reformers do not believe in a real communication of the life of God to the human soul. This, it will be remembered, is the burden of Mersch's argument too. It is one of the ironies of theology that by the Romanists, Dr. Mascall as an Anglican is subject to precisely the same criticism as Mersch makes of the Protestant Churches: "Rejecting one part of Christian truth, they have rejected all, and the incorporation in Christ they prize so highly becomes a nonentity."[1]

Let us now very briefly examine Luther's own teaching, to see whether it justifies the strictures of Mersch and Mascall. Luther teaches that it is faith alone, without works, which apprehends the grace of God in Christ, but faith is never without works. If works do not follow, there is no faith. Good works follow faith as the shadow follows the body (on Isaiah 52: 7). In a sermon on 1 John 5: 4 and following: "This is the victory that overcometh the world, even our faith", Luther says:

> This John says, to show us truly what real faith, of which the Scripture speaks, means and is. For there is much else which the world calls faith (Jews, Turks and Papists); but this is the true victorious faith which believes that Jesus is God's Son. And that is an invincible power created by the Holy Spirit in the hearts of Christians. Therefore such faith is not a cold, idle, unfruitful and ineffective idea . . . but a living active power, such that where it is, there fruit, victory and conquest must follow, or if they do not, then faith and the new birth is not there.

One more quotation from many may be permissible. It comes from Luther's famous preface to his Commentary on Romans.

> Faith is a living creative active mighty thing, so that it is impossible for it to cease doing good works. Nor does it ask if good works are to be done, but before one asks, it has done them, and is always at work. Faith is a living well-considered confidence in God's grace, so certain that it could die a thousand times in that conviction. Such confidence and knowledge of divine grace make a man happy and bold and joyful towards God and all creatures. And so the man becomes without compulsion willing and glad to

---

[1] *The Whole Christ*, p. 504.

do good to everyone, to serve everyone, to suffer all things in love and praise to God who hath shown him such grace. So that it is impossible to sever works from faith, yes, just as impossible as to sever burning and shining from fire.

These quotations are typical of many, and surely they render quite superfluous Dr. Mascall's question: "Does justification and regeneration of the sinner (on the Reformed view) bring about a real change in him?" Could that change be more vividly or poignantly expressed than here?

We must now inquire briefly what is the nature of the relationship to Christ which the believer has through Word and Sacrament in the thought of Luther. It will be enough to cite one famous passage, taken from a sermon on John 15: 5: "I am the Vine, ye are the branches." Luther says:

This then is the way of it. When I am baptized, or converted by the Gospel, the Holy Spirit is there and takes me like a piece of clay, and makes out of me a new creature, that now has other senses, heart and thoughts, a true knowledge of God, and a thorough, heartfelt trust in His grace. In fine, foundation and ground of my heart is renewed and changed, so that I become a wholly new growth, planted into the vine Christ, and growing out of Him, and now I am like Him and His kind, so that both He and I are of one nature and being, and I bear fruits in and through Him which are not mine, but those of the Vine. And so Christ and the Christians become one cake and one body.

In the light of a statement like this, which is typical of Luther, it is hard to see what, except prejudice, can have been behind Father Mersch's statement that "while on occasion Protestants have been known to speak with vigour and insistence of this entrance of the life of the Divine Head into us, the members, the impression they give is quite false. Christian faith is one indivisible whole. In rejecting one part of it, they have deprived themselves of all, and the incorporation in Christ which they prize so highly becomes a nonentity."[1]

If that fine Christian and theologian were still alive, we might ask him, as Karl Barth suggests Christians may do across the confessional boundaries: "Would it not be better to face the facts unflinchingly, and frame our theories in accord with them,

---

[1] *op. cit.*, p. 504.

instead of starting with *a priori* prejudices? If our doctrine of the Church cannot allow that Christ's incorporating grace is given to those with whom we are not in communion, and yet the facts manifestly show that it is, then would it not be better to acknowledge these facts, however inconvenient for us, than to close our eyes to them?"

Such then is Luther's teaching about the way in which the life of Christ passes into believers. It is also, however, important to say, that while for Luther regeneration marks a real renewal of the believer's nature, there remains an element of sin against which he must continue to struggle. It would surely be illogical for believers in the institution of the Confessional to refuse their assent to such a thoroughly Christian doctrine. Even a St. Paul knew of the real danger that he might become a castaway. But if it is agreed ground that in the Christian life there remain elements of sin, then it is hardly fair, as Dr. Mascall appears to do, to use statements in the Reformers' writing which refer to this continuing sin in human nature, as a basis for the inference that in Reformed doctrine the supernatural and natural are considered to run on like two parallel streams in the believer's life without any real connection between them; the former, which is wholly good, being God's, and the latter, which is wholly bad, being man's.[1]

We must now go on to consider Calvin's teaching on the relation of the Christian to Christ. This teaching may very easily be misconstrued by the reader, particularly if he be a Romanist or Anglo-Catholic, and thus accustomed to a different terminology. For Calvin, the Gospel is summed up under two main heads: repentance and justification. Both of these mean something different for Calvin than for a reader with the above-named background.

Misunderstanding with regard to Calvin's teaching on repentance is particularly easy. It means for him a great deal more than might be expected. It means the whole turning of a man's life away from sin and towards God, a process, therefore, which explicitly includes regeneration, a process which continues throughout a Christian's whole life, and is only possible through the power of the indwelling Holy Spirit. Calvin says:

[1] *op. cit.*, p. 81.

"In the conversion of the life to God, we require a transformation not only in external works, but in the soul itself, which is
able only after it has put off its old habits to bring forth fruits
conformable to its renovation."[1]

By His action "the Holy Spirit instils His holiness into our
souls, so inspiring them with new thoughts and affections that
they may justly be regarded as new".[2] This mortification and
new nature we obtain by union with Christ. If we have true
fellowship in His death, our old self is crucified by His power,
and the body of sin becomes dead, so that the corruption of our
nature is never again in full vigour. "In one word, then, by
repentance I understand regeneration, the only aim of which is
to form in us anew the image of God."[3]

The residue of sin, however, remains, to humble us under a
consciousness of our infirmity, but the corruption of our nature
is being healed, though our warfare continues till death.

On the theme of justification the difference between the
Reformers and the Romanists is more familiar ground. It is
Calvin's main thesis here, which he is ready to defend against
all comers, that justification in the New Testament means in
the New Testament not a making righteous, but an acquittal.
And here we may claim that the trend of modern Biblical
scholarship has been to support him. Justification, especially
for St. Paul, is the acquittal or forgiveness of the sinner by God,
or God's reconciliation with him, for Christ's sake, and the
righteousness thereby conferred on him is not his own, but
Christ's.

Romanist and Anglo-Catholic writers have attacked this
view, much as did Osiander in Reformation times, on the
grounds that surely God's grace has the power, not merely to
forgive sinners, but to make them really righteous. They ask
whether God's work is not caricatured if it be limited to the
giving of an imputed righteousness, which has, to put it mildly,
something of the character of a fiction.

But to argue thus is to miss the whole point of the Reformed
teaching, and to forget that for both Luther and Calvin, justification is not the sum of salvation. In Calvin, God's work of
salvation includes not only justification or acquittal, but also

---

[1] *Inst.* III, iii, 6.   [2] *Inst.* III, iii, 8.   [3] *Inst.* III, iii, 9.

repentance or regeneration. Where justification is present, regeneration is also present. But Calvin insists with great pertinacity that while the two can never be separated in fact, they can and must be separated in thought. And this is no mere hairsplitting. Let the critics try patiently to understand why Calvin's emphasis here is so persistent and passionate.

There can be no doubt at all that this passion comes from the knowledge that repentance and regeneration are never in this life complete and perfect. Therefore any righteousness of our own, even if it be subsequent to regeneration, can never give us an assurance of salvation secure enough to be a foundation for the Christian life. In his long and somewhat obscure discussion of Osiander's views (which are in many ways akin to those of Mersch and Mascall), Calvin is especially emphatic on this point. He says that Osiander's teaching "undermines our assurance of salvation, and, by hurrying us into the clouds, tries to prevent us from embracing the gift of expiation in faith, and invoking God with quiet minds."[1]

It may of course be that Romanists and some Anglo-Catholics do not wish men to have a fixed assurance of salvation, on the grounds that this tends to an independence of the Church unfitting for a Christian. Any such independence would indeed be worthy of rebuke, but it would be hard to maintain that the Christian has no grounds for the belief that he has peace with God through Jesus Christ (Rom. 5: 1). And in return we might ask our Roman brethren the question whether a reliance in part on infused merit given through the sacraments would not have a worse effect than reliance on acquittal for Christ's sake.

Reflecting on these and other similar differences between us and Rome, one may ask whether there is not some hope in the fact that even where we are in detail opposed to each other, it is often because we are contending for the same values, in this case the intimate and vital union of the believer with his Lord?

Let us sum up Calvin's teaching. He holds that there is a real union of the Christian with Christ, which is received by faith. He is not able to explain it, but who will blame him for this failure? He says:

[1] *Inst.* III, xi, 2.

Therefore to that union of the head and members the residence of Christ in our hearts, in fine, the mystical union, we assign the highest rank; Christ, when He becomes ours, making us partners with Him in the gifts with which He was endued. Hence we do not view Him as at a distance and without us, but as we have put Him on, and been engrafted into His Body, He deigns to make us one with Himself, and therefore we glory in having a fellowship of righteousness with him.[1]

The effects of this union are twofold, corresponding to justification and regeneration. They allow us to have Christ's righteousness imputed to us, securing our acquittal before God. This is the work of justification. And they enable us to die with Christ, and to rise again with Him in newness of life. This is the work of repentance and regeneration, which continues in the believer all his life long.

Those who wish to study more closely Calvin's teaching on this union with Christ by faith should examine what he says in Book IV of the *Institutes* about the Sacrament, which still represents the teaching of the Reformed Church, though time, and perhaps grace, have taught us to speak less boisterously than he does of Christians who think otherwise. In that context of union with Christ, Calvin speaks finely of

this mystery which I feel, and therefore freely confess that I am unable to comprehend with my mind, so far am I from wishing anyone to measure its sublimity by my feeble capacity. . . .For whenever this subject is considered, after I have done my utmost, I feel that I have spoken far beneath its dignity. And though the mind is more powerful in thought than the tongue in expression, it too is overcome by the magnitude of the subject. All then that remains is to break forth in admiration of the mystery which it is plain that the mind is inadequate to apprehend, or the tongue to express.[2]

If the line of reasoning developed above is valid, there is not, after all, so great a difference between "Catholic" writers and the Reformers on the question of a true impartation of new life by God to the believer. Consequently, there is not here likely to be the basis for a corresponding difference in the respective doctrines of the Church. The Reformed teaching of Luther and

[1] *Inst.* III, xi, 10.   [2] *Inst.* IV, xvii, 7.

Calvin is inexpressibly richer than its critics have been willing to admit.

But if here there is a much smaller difference than has been imagined, there are, on the other hand, real and very grave differences between the Reformers and Rome in teaching about the Christian man and the Christian Church. I refer to what we Protestants believe to be the grave error of the Romanists on the subject of justification. There is, as we have seen, no vital difference on the subject of the impartation of new life to the believer. Protestants as well as Romanists agree that God's grace is not only able to declare man acquitted, but to render him really and essentially righteous. But Protestantism *is* in serious conflict with what the Romans go on to assert, namely that such righteousness can become essentially meritorious, so that God is bound to give salvation as a reward earned to the sanctified—in the Roman sense of the word, justified—man.

Here we must put another serious question to our Roman brethren. It is this: "Does not this view imply that the saved and regenerate man now wishes to repeat the fundamental sin of all legal morality, the wish to be something in himself apart from God and from Christ—even if he safeguards himself by acknowledging that he is what he is as a result of infused grace?" Attempts to disclaim this, and to say that we give God the glory, are almost inevitably tinged with insincerity. It is precisely in defence of that close union with Christ which the Romanists aver to be their interest, that the Reformed thinkers are eager to deny the erection of a doctrine of merit in the Christian life upon the basis of a conception of infused righteousness. It is true that the Reformers further deny that any infusion or gift of grace could be such as to provide a basis for a doctrine of super-erogatory works or of the meritorious standing of the Christian before God on the ground of such an infusion. But they believe that in acknowledging that in this life we continue always to be wholly dependent on justification understood in the Pauline and Protestant sense of the word, we are really standing nearer to God and to Christ than if we are basing ourselves in whole or in part on the merit of our own achievements, even though these be considered to be the result of infused grace.

Before going on to ask what character a doctrine of the

Church in harmony with this teaching about the Christian man would possess, I wish again to state that this line of thought does not imply the priority of the individual Christian to the Church in any way. But it is reasonable to suppose that the thought of the New Testament, here as elsewhere, will be generally of one piece, and it is clear that any conclusions reached by us through inference from the doctrine of the Christian man will have to meet the test of agreement with actual New Testament teaching about the Church. In this essay there is not space to undertake such a confirmatory enquiry.

Taking then a line from the Reformed doctrine about the Christian man, his justification and sanctification, we shall conclude that the Church must not be considered in any way separate from its Lord, but always thought of as in closest union with Him. This union will be such as to preserve its essential and continual dependence on Him through justification by faith. We shall not ascribe to the Church any treasury of merit, though we shall hold that it has the authority and the obligation to plead by its prayers with Him on behalf of men. We shall value the Church's tradition as of great authority, because divine guidance has been promised to it, and we cannot believe that its story has been one long succession of errors. But we shall note that the promise of guidance to the Church is not a promise of infallibility.

We shall subordinate later tradition to that original tradition which is preserved in the Scriptures; not because the Scripture writers were sinless or infallible, but because theirs is the original witness to the Lord, and we believe that it is through His Word that He guides the Church, reforms it and justifies it from day to day. To rank later tradition as of equal authority with the earlier is to call in question the once-for-allness of Christ's Incarnation, and to question His power to rule the Church through His Word, and to endanger silencing His voice through the voice of the Church, which, however well-intentioned, cannot be simply identified with His.

We shall be exceedingly suspicious of phrases which suggest that the unity between Christ and the Church is such, that the Church can be described as a continuation of the Incarnation. That it is the Body of Christ, St. Paul frequently asserts, but nowhere that it is the continuation of the Incarnation. If the Church, like the Christians of whom it is composed, be continually in need of the divine forgiveness given in Christ, then it cannot be the prolongation of the Incarnation of the Sinless One, however intimate its union with Him may be.

At the present moment a discussion is being carried on about the use of the various figures in the New Testament which describe the Church. What is their status? Are they metaphors, or analogies, and what is the legitimate use for us to make of them?

In his very suggestive and forceful book, *The Body of Christ*, Dr. Ernest Best concludes that this term is a metaphor employed, among others, by St. Paul to describe the relationship of the members of the Church to Christ and to each other. He argues that it must not be used in other, wider, contexts, such as the description of the relation of the Church to the world.

There are more problems than one involved here. Some will feel inclined to question the validity of the judgment which holds that Paul used the term only in such a restricted way. They will claim that he used it also to describe the function of the Church towards the world. For the building up of the Body is surely only the reverse side of the mission of the Church to the world.

But there is a further question which must be raised about the legitimacy of widening the application of the phrase beyond its original contexts in St. Paul's writings, and it is this question which is relevant to our present theme.

In dealing with the scriptural use of figures of speech, we may define metaphor as the use of a figure to illustrate one resemblance only, as, for example, when the psalmist calls God his rock, indicating thereby only one quality of resemblance, and saying that God is His steadfast defence. At the other end of the scale there might be an analogy so close that every characteristic essential to the figure chosen would have a characteristic corresponding to it in the entity which it was chosen to illustrate. It would appear that the description of the Church as a prolongation of the Incarnation is a conclusion drawn from the confident belief that there is a very exact detailed analogy between a human body and the body of Christ. Since a human body is the incarnation of a human spirit, the Church which is the Body of Christ must be the incarnation of His spirit, and as His Body of flesh was the Incarnation of His spirit, the Church must be the prolongation of the Incarnation.

But we may raise the question whether between metaphor as defined above and the confident and detailed use of analogy as illustrated above, there may not lie an intermediate region, where there is a relation between figure and reality closer than in cases of metaphor, yet not so close as in analogies of the type given. In judging what extension of the original use of a figure in Scripture is legitimate we must find a criterion. We might go rather further than Dr. Best (who will not allow any use of the figure beyond the context in which the original Scripture writer uses it), provided that we call a halt before we find ourselves led to conclusions which are called in question by the manifest drift of Scripture itself.

It would seem that this kind of cautious advance is what Karl Barth makes in his *Dogmatik*,[1] where he indicates various meanings of the New Testament term *soma*, and says that all these we must hold in our minds when we think of the Church as Christ's Body. But Barth is equally clear that there can be no co-ordination between Christ and the Church such as is indicated in Pius XII's Encyclical, *Mystici Corporis*, where the Church's Infallibility and Impeccability are uncompromisingly proclaimed.[2]

This is not the place where a long study of the various phrases used by St. Paul to describe the Church and its relation to its Head can be undertaken. That has been done by Dr. Best in the volume mentioned above. As he points out, the assertion that the expression "Body of Christ" is to be taken realistically and ontologically must not be too far pressed, for the use of the phrase by St. Paul himself is subject to development and modification as different aspects of the subject of discourse require emphasis. Further, the too realistic treatment of the figure "Body of Christ" would lead to the neglect and disparagement of the other figures used by St. Paul in the course of his thought about the Church.

Protestant thought will further be chary about any too *sim-*

pliste equation of the work or mission of the Church with the mission and work of Christ Himself. It is clear that considerable Bible study must yet be done in this field. But we must note that the mission of Christ is to point men to Himself and to save the world, while the Church's mission is not to save the world in the same sense, but by its word and witness to point the world to the Saviour. The saying of Christ "As the Father hath sent me, even so send I you" (John 20: 21) does not imply an identity of mission between the Lord and the Church.

Is there not some analogy of the relationship between Christ's mission and the Church's mission in the relationship between the Divine Word and the human word in the proclamation of the Gospel? Is there not a further indication of it in the relationship between the bread and wine in the Sacrament and the Body and Blood of Christ? In both cases that which is human is used by men in the hope and with the promise that God's action will supervene upon human action, taking it up into itself, yet without destroying its human character. There is thus an indirect but real identity between God's act and our acts, which we cannot control but which we may hope for, and indeed expect, since it is promised to us in the Church. Our words and our acts are ours, and are obedient and free, but it is only when they become God's that they are saving acts and words.

Were the Church literally a continuation of the Incarnation, then its actions would automatically and inevitably be the actions of Christ; a position so absurd that no one would think of maintaining it. Further, since the Church has many members, all of them living more or less in the world, and in varying degrees of conformity with the will of Christ, we have an impossible question to face if we are asked what is the criterion by which we judge actions to be the actions of the Church. We certainly cannot claim that all the actions of all its members are the actions of the Church, nor would anyone claim that when we speak in such a context of the actions of the Church we mean only such actions as would be deemed by law to be the official actions of the Church. The Roman Church, which goes further in the direction of asserting a direct identity of Christ with the Church than does any other Communion, does

P

not do more than claim that the *ex cathedra* decisions of the Pope in matters of faith and morals are as the decisions of Christ Himself.

And yet in spite of these difficulties, we must agree that in the Church there is an organic unity and mutual influence of persons, not without taint of sin and error, yet under the guidance of the Spirit. And this enables us to say: "This and that the Church has done in the world, or done for me."

It is this Church which is more than the sum of its individual members, whose actions can and do become, in spite of imperfection, the acts of Christ to men, in so far as it is faithful, lives in the grace and forgiveness of God, and prays and hopes for the blessing of its Head. It is this Church which lives by faith, and is acquitted and justified by God for Christ's sake, and regenerated, though not yet perfectly, by its union with its Head. It is this Church which is the Bride of Christ, the Temple of Christ, and the Body of Christ.

IO

CHRISTOLOGY, THE HOLY SPIRIT AND THE ECUMENICAL MOVEMENT

by D. T. JENKINS

Professor of Ecumenical Theology, University of Chicago;
Minister of King's Weigh House, London

10

CHRISTOLOGY, THE HOLY SPIRIT AND THE ECUMENICAL MOVEMENT

by

DANIEL JENKINS

THOSE who have taken part in the discussion of the doctrine of the Church which has been promoted by the Faith and Order department of the World Council of Churches have come increasingly to see that questions of Christology are bound up with those which deal with the unity and disunity of the Churches. The Lund Conference of 1952 affirmed: "We believe in Jesus Christ our Lord, who loved the Church and gave Himself for it, and has brought the Church into an abiding union with Himself. Because we believe in Jesus Christ, we believe also in the Church as the Body of Christ." Those who made that statement did so because they recognized that their attitude to Jesus Christ should be determinative of their attitude to the Church. All who gathered together at Lund believed in the truth of the familiar words, *Ubi Christus, ibi ecclesia*. It was that common conviction which drew them together. At the same time, to the extent that they took it seriously, they had to acknowledge that it concealed differences as well as affirmed agreements between them, for it was manifest that they still remained divided in their understanding of the Church's nature and its limits. That this should be so makes the subject a peculiarly appropriate one for ecumenical discussion.

At first glance, Christology would appear to be much more obviously a source of agreement rather than of disagreement among the member churches of the World Council. The basis of membership is an affirmation of faith "in Jesus Christ as God and Saviour". The use of the word "God" rather than the more customary "Lord" in this context has seemed to some of the more Liberal Churches, both within and outside the World

Council, to be an almost truculent assertion of Chalcedonian orthodoxy. Whether that is true or not, it certainly makes clear the intention of its framers to find their unity in a commonly-held conviction about the person and work of Jesus Christ similar to that held by most Churches throughout the ages.

When the recent history of Protestant thought is borne in mind, this fact becomes noteworthy. A generation ago, many Protestant Churches would not have joined in an affirmation of this kind with anything like the readiness they showed at Amsterdam. In the larger setting of Christian history, however, it is hardly so surprising. No theological doctrines have been worked over more carefully, in nearly all traditions, than those of the person and the work of Christ, with the possible exception of the related doctrine of the Trinity. Nowhere has the main path of orthodox belief been more clearly marked out and no-where have the pitfalls been more clearly fenced around. Once its member Churches re-established their grip on classical Chris-tian faith—and this has happened to most of those Churches which seemed to be in danger of losing it a generation ago—it would be hard for the World Council to do other than affirm its uncompromising Christological orthodoxy. It is true that some of the member Churches remain unwilling to impose the definitions of the ecumenical councils as binding tests upon their members, but all have been glad to confess their unity in belief in Jesus Christ as God and Saviour.

Because this is so, it might seem reasonable to conclude that the strategy of those most anxious to restore the broken unity of Christendom should be to concentrate on celebrating and maintaining this agreement. Theological hair-splitting has been a fruitful enough source of trouble throughout the Church's history. Why create more trouble by implying that a widely acknowledged unity may be more apparent than real? A responsible theologian will have enough sense of the hazards and temptations of his calling to treat these objections seriously. They should at least prompt him to bring out and to cherish the considerable amount of agreement which does exist among the Churches on this matter. But the ecumenical theologian's position is not that of a man who is trying to patch up a structure which is only partially damaged while its foundations remain quite sound. It is more like that of a doctor who is trying to track down the seat of infection in a living organism, which may be very far from the places where the trouble manifests itself. Christians are divided over the doctrine of the Church. The Church is the Body of Christ. Is it not reasonable, therefore, to suspect either that the agreements between Churches concerning Jesus Christ are not as real as they appear to be or that their significance is not properly grasped? This is a place where it is of peculiar importance to follow the method for ecumenical discussion suggested by Karl Barth, to seek the agreements in our differences and the differences in our agreements.

The most considerable attempt yet made to do this in relation to Christology is that of Professor T. F. Torrance of Edinburgh in his Albrecht Stumpf memorial lecture on "The Atonement and the Oneness of the Church", which was published in the *Scottish Journal of Theology* for September 1954. To attempt to summarize its closely-reasoned argument would be impossible, but it is necessary to note some of its main points, because they try to throw light on existing divisions among the Churches through a fresh interpretation of Christological statements which are accepted by all bodies represented in the World Council, Protestant and Catholic.

Professor Torrance welcomes the procedure of the Faith and Order department in starting from the oneness of Christ so as to reach a new understanding of the unity of the Church in Christ. The doctrine of the Church must be stated in terms of the analogy of Christ and in this lecture he tries to do this with special reference to the atonement.

The discussion opens with a statement about the hypostatic union of the Godhead and manhood in Christ. He fully accepts all that Chalcedon and the Tome of Leo have to say about the mystery of the God-man in Christ but regrets that they should have made their definitions without reference to the mission of Jesus. Theology needs to restate the hypostatic union in terms of the cross and resurrection. To try to restate it in terms of a speculative sophiology, after the manner of some modern Orthodox theologians, is to be misled. The dynamic character of the union, which was implied but not brought out in the original definition, must be made clear with reference to the work of Christ. This is of the first importance to the Church because it is in the relation between Christ's person and His work that the Church finds the meaning of its existence as the one Body of the one Lord. Christ identified Himself as the One with the Many of mankind in order to give Himself for them. After Pentecost, the Church was sent out as the Many to represent the One who was the Saviour of all. This work of representation the Church does in Christ's way, by *anhypostasia*, by self-denial and crucifixion, and by *enhypostasia*, by incorporation and resurrection. The twofold way in which the Godhead is represented in the manhood of Christ thus has its analogy in the life of the Church; an analogy which can be further traced in Baptism and Holy Communion.

In the same way, the terms *inconfuse* and *inseparabiliter*, which were applied to the two natures of Christ, can also be applied analogically to the relation between Christ and the Church. In relation to the Eucharist, for example, the *inconfuse* would negate a doctrine of transubstantiation, and the *inseparabiliter* a doctrine which dissociates the elements from the Body and Blood of Christ. This can be further extended to show how the *inconfuse* negates a docetic conception of the Church, as though it had been transubstantiated into something beyond history, and the *inseparabiliter* negates a conception which divorced the Church from ontological union with Christ.

A similar analogy can be made in relation to the saving work of Christ with reference to the doctrine of the Spirit. There is no cleavage between the eschatological and the ontological status of the present existence of the Church because there is no division in the hypostatic union of Christ.

In the concluding section, some of the implications of this discussion are drawn out for the matters which unite and divide the Churches at the present time. It must be insisted both that the Church really represents Christ and yet that it does so in such a way that Christ's distinction from it is also asserted. The Church is Christ's vicar "not by substituting itself in the place of Christ but by letting Christ stand as substitute in place of the Church". The Church is the suffering servant and authority is transmitted to her in the way appropriate to the suffering servant. Succession is to be understood in the same way, being both asserted and set aside by Christ in the Spirit. Above all, this conditions our understanding of the sacraments. The Eucharist is the renewal of the Church's original unity given to it in the first place through the death and re-birth of Baptism. Its meaning is that the Church cannot conserve its wholeness by looking chiefly to itself and by trying at all costs to maintain intact its own partial and limited traditions but that it can do so only by spending itself freely and offering its body in sacrifice, like a true suffering servant. It recovers its wholeness by putting on Christ anew in the Eucharist, which is the appointed means by which the atonement given by Christ in Baptism is constantly renewed in the life of the Church. Since the road to unity lies through this atonement, by which we are reconciled to Christ and to one another, the Eucharist must be understood as a means for promoting the unity of the Church and not merely as a gift to be enjoyed in common by Churches when they have achieved re-union by other means.

It follows from this, and here perhaps is the most controversial part of the argument, that nothing could be more destructive of the life of the Church than to erect barriers to intercommunion between divided Christians. Such action implies nothing less than an attempt to limit the range of the atoning and reconciling work of Christ, and to draw man-made limits to the expansion of the new humanity through the power of the Gospel. The conclusion of the matter is that a true understanding of the atoning and incorporating work of Christ, interpreted in terms of the hypostatic union of His person, should lead us to see that the road to unity is through intercommunion, so that all who are baptized should have free access to the appointed means for healing their divisions, the Eucharist.

This sketchy outline does little justice, of course, to the subtlety and power of Professor Torrance's argument, but perhaps it does serve the purpose of showing how he succeeds in demonstrating that the discussion of fundamental Christological issues can throw light on current ecumenical problems. He will not carry everyone with him, especially on the vexed question of intercommunion. In particular, his argument would have been greatly strengthened if he could have gone some way to meet the difficulties of those, both Catholic and Protestant, who might grant him his main point and who might yet be concerned lest free intercommunion between divided Churches perpetuate division by allowing them to meet together at a common table without giving concrete expression to a common spiritual responsibility. Nevertheless, the lecture does succeed in defining most clearly the attitude with which all churchmen should approach the question of their unity in Christ. It is all the more effective because it takes care to argue so firmly with reference to a Christological orthodoxy to whose acceptance nearly all Churches are committed. This is truly ecumenical theology.

Professor Torrance's argument requires little qualification but it may, perhaps, benefit from further extension. He is surely right in his insistence that the hypostatic union in Christ must be interpreted in the light of His mission and he has shown what this would mean with reference to the work of Christ itself. The full implications of that cannot be drawn out, however, unless the argument is carried a stage further and the matter discussed also with reference to the work of the Holy Spirit. It was Pentecost which founded the Church as a distinctive community and Pentecost did not come till after the Ascension. There is certainly an analogical relation between Christ and the Church but that relation stands in danger of being misunderstood unless it is clearly recognized that Christ is now known by the Church only in the Holy Spirit. It is not merely the fact that Christ who was God humbled Himself to become man and rose again from the dead which should control our understanding of the present form and order of the Church. It is also the fact that the same Christ has ascended up on high and dwells on the right hand of the Father and has released the gifts of His Spirit over His people. The marks of the presence of Christ in the Church are now those of the Spirit.

This needs emphasis because it is constantly in danger of being overlooked in ecumenical discussion. It is true that the Lund Conference on Faith and Order duly noted that the doctrine of the Church needs to be stated in close relation both to the doctrine of Christ and to that of the Spirit. Yet it is not an accident that the doctrine of the Holy Spirit has for so long been the poor relation of Faith and Order discussion. It has been comparatively neglected in theological discussion throughout the ages. That Catholicism has shown something less than enthusiasm in trying to relate the work of the Holy Spirit to that of Christ, especially as it affects the form and order of the Church, is obvious. Even the Churches of the Reformation have failed to give it the prominence which it deserves. We may accept the contention of Professor Regin Prenter, in his book, *Spiritus Creator*,[1] that the doctrine of the Holy Spirit was of central importance and was treated with great originality in Luther's thought and yet have to note that he asserts that Lutheranism has not followed Luther in this respect. It was only isolated theologians here and there, like the Independent John Owen, who dealt thoroughly with the Holy Spirit in relation to the Church, apart from the "spiritualizing" sects, who lacked a strong theological or ecclesiological interest, until the Liberals began to do so in their own way in the nineteenth century. It has been one of Karl Barth's great services to the Church that he has reminded us again of the importance of the doctrine of the Spirit to the Church's understanding of itself. This will not prevent the strong pressure of traditional interests from unconsciously directing ecumenical discussion away from this aspect of the relation of Christ to the Church unless a deliberate effort is made to face it.

There are three reasons why such an effort is likely to prove useful. First, it is likely to make it easier for Churches to "discern the Lord's body" in their own midst, in other Churches and in the world around them to-day. Churches of various denominations often find themselves in difficulties because of the inadequacy of the categories they possess for determining where the limits of those bodies which they will recognize as being with themselves part of the true Church are to be found. The reason for this may be that they look at the matter in the wrong way and assume that the initiative in Church formation rests chiefly in their own hands. They forget that, since the Ascension and Pentecost, the influence of Christ is universalized.

[1] Translated by John M. Jensen, Muhlenberg Press, Philadelphia, 1953.

He is no longer limited to a particular time and a particular place, as He was in the days of His flesh. To speak without qualification of the Church as the extension of the Incarnation is seriously misleading, although it is proper to draw an analogy between the mind which was in the Incarnate Son and that which should be in the fellowship of the Church. His Spirit can move freely through the whole universe and He is able to call whom He will into communion with Himself. A Church which understands both the humiliation and the exaltation of Christ will be most careful to recognize, in the most practical way, that in the matter of Church formation it is the servant and not the Master.

Such a Church will not see its task as trying to domesticate the Holy Spirit, so that it will only operate conveniently in a well-defined sphere under careful clerical control, but to discern the spirits, whether they be of Christ. When it discovers that they are, it should demonstrate the catholicity of its order by the ease and the rapidity with which it finds it possible to enter into communion with those who are so obviously possessed of the Holy Spirit, that they may obey Christ by living together as His People. History shows abundantly that when Churches fail to act in this way, the Spirit quickly confounds their pretensions by raising up sons to Abraham and brethren of Christ in the most unexpected places. Christ is determined to rule in His own House and to make freely available the benefits of His atoning work, in despite of His family as well as through its instrumentality.

All Churches will, of course, be quick to point out that this is not the whole story. In practice, if not always in doctrine, most Protestant Churches will be as emphatic as Catholic in this respect. There must be a concern for historical continuity in the Church's life, and the Bible insists on the importance of such a concern. That is true; but it is a continuity in the Spirit, and the Spirit refuses to give absolute authority to any institutional attempt to express that continuity, even though those attempts may themselves be made at the Spirit's behest. The test of a good organ of continuity is partly whether it succeeds in maintaining living contact with the Christian past, but also whether it succeeds in making it easy for a Church to gather into order with itself those who demonstrate that they have been called by the Spirit through bringing forth its fruit. It may be observed, in view of the claims made for it, that few organs of continuity fail the second of these tests more conspicuously than the "historic Episcopate", especially in its Anglican form.

The Church "guards the deposit" best by putting out its talents boldly to usury in the commerce of the world. If it tries to bury them in the ground, it is in danger of rejection, even though they be genuine currency. For such a Church ceases to live by faith, which alone justifies Churches as well as individuals in God's sight; otherwise the old Israel would never have been rejected, and faith vindicates itself by trustful ventures into the unknown. The Spirit is the Lord, the giver of life, and Scripture and Christian experience teach that the way to life, for Churches as for individuals, is through running the real risk of death. Churches should, therefore, always be partly "in process of formation" and suspicious about their health if they have no problems of order and mutual recognition to face. Such a situation would be a sure indication that they were becoming conformed to this world which passeth away.

This is closely related to the second point. To see the work of the Spirit in relation to that of Jesus Christ will teach Churches a fresh conception of the nature of Church order itself. The function of Church order is to ensure both that the Church retains continuity of life with the historical Christ, and in so doing that she is kept moving forward to meet her coming Lord. It is true that the Spirit dwells within the Church but it does so as the Lord of the Church, who is for ever calling the Church to move on and not to make any of the temporary resting-places which she loves to adorn and make comfortable in this world her permanent home. The Spirit dwells within the Church but always as the earnest of her inheritance, which encourages her to hasten forward to seek it in its fullness.

The deficiencies of most classical forms of Church order are quickly exposed when they are looked at from this point of view. That a proper conservatism on the historical level has its place in the organization of the life of God's people is undeniable, although it must be carefully distinguished from the Spirit-guided backward look to the living facts of our redemption.

Such conservatism is part of our obedience to the Commandment to honour our father and mother. But few Churches are in danger of forgetting this, although they may all be highly selective in their choice of fathers and mothers. They are in much greater danger of exaggerating it, indeed to such an extent as to raise the question as to whether it does not often become the characteristically ecclesiastical form of secularism. Professor H. A. Hodges, in his recent book on Anglicanism and Orthodoxy, speaks of a certain docility as being characteristic of the genuinely Catholic temper, as he sees it strikingly exemplified among the Churches of the Orthodox East. He contrasts it favourably with the aggressive, forward-looking attitude of the West, especially as found in Protestantism, and to which he ascribes some of the responsibility for the rise of modern secularist humanism. It is true that all attitudes hold within them the possibilities of corruption and that those inherent in the corruption of this have been amply demonstrated in the modern world. At the same time, Professor Hodges appears surprisingly complacent in the presence of the dangers inherent in the attitude of docility, although Christian history, not least in the Orthodox East itself, is full of testimonies to their reality. It could be maintained that many of the calamities which have befallen Church and society in East and West in modern times have been due to the failure of Churches to prevent demonic influences from taking over the control of the new scientific and cultural forces because of their own excessive attachment to irrelevant aspects of the past.

The purpose of Church order is not to encourage Christ's people to stand gazing into the heavens in the hope that they can retain their vision of their departing Lord, but to ensure that the Church is in the right place to receive orders for present action from their living Lord in the Spirit. The preaching of the Word, the celebration of the sacraments and the responsible assembly of the Church in which her members seek together to follow the Spirit's guidance, are means by which the Church is constantly recalled to her living Lord who guides her forward to new ventures of faith. Church order, like Christology, needs to be interpreted in dynamic fashion with reference to the mission of the Church, and therefore in an eschatological setting. Unless that is done, Churches will continue to believe complacently that they automatically possess Christ in sufficiency and that there is no need for them to press onward, forgetting those things which are behind, to the goal of their high calling in Him. The ecumenical movement will make progress only in so far as this happens, because, without this eschatological reference, Churches will distort their order into a means by which they turn their earthly tabernacles into permanent homes and shut out the disturbing influence of the Holy Spirit from their midst.

This in its turn leads to the third point. To give full weight to the fact that Christ is present here and now in the Spirit should make Churches more hopeful and expectant about realizing their unity. As we have already tried to show, where Churches fail to see the right relation between Christ and the Spirit, they inevitably see their theological task as primarily defensive. They think they know Christ only in their tradition and therefore they cherish that tradition above all things as their way of cherishing Christ. To see that the Christ who is in the tradition meets them now in the Spirit and assures them that they can only keep company with Him by venturing forward into the unknown should liberate them from their defensiveness. It will, for instance, enable them to give more significance to the discovery of their possession of real functional unity with those whose history may differ from theirs in important respects. If they forget themselves in obedience to the Spirit sufficiently to discover that they are in fact able to walk forward together, they will be able to consider traditional causes of disagreement between their denominations with less reverence than is customary among theologians. They can face the possibility that the Holy Spirit, which is the bond of peace, may be exercising its reconciling work amongst them.

It need hardly be said that this does not mean that long-standing theological differences between Churches can be ignored when churchmen happen to discover that they have a great deal in common in a particular situation. Theological differences can never be safely ignored, but they need constantly to be looked at in a fresh light, and should not be considered out of relation to changes on other levels of the Churches' experience. There is a covert rationalism hidden in a good deal of theological discussion, even when it uses language very different from that of rationalism, which implies that the considerations to which the sociology of knowledge calls attention could not possibly apply to it. To put the point more positively, a clearer recognition on their part that the reconciling Spirit is at work in the Church should make theologians more alert to the possibility that long-standing differences can be removed or else be given a different significance in a new situation from that which they were once believed to possess. The presence or the absence of the "filioque" clause from the Nicene Creed has been a source of division between Christians for many long centuries and the issues connected with it remain unresolved. Has nothing happened in those centuries, and is nothing happening between the Churches now, which should prompt them to a re-examination of the whole context in which that dispute exists? Similarly, a controversy over the baptism of infants has divided Protestantism for a very long time. Has the Holy Spirit, the reconciler, nothing to say which is healing and constructive about this matter? Much is rightly heard in ecumenical circles of the need for theological repentance, but the fruits of that repentance are not yet strikingly visible. A more diligent attempt to understand the dealings with the Church of that Spirit who convicts of sin and leads to righteousness may hasten the appearance of such fruits.

The Spirit, however, does not only embolden the Church to make innovations but also provides the means by which those innovations which are made can be criticized. All the works which His people are able to do in the Spirit are made possible because Christ has gone to the Father and reigns eternally at His right hand and acts as our sole intercessor. The Spirit can lead the Church to nothing which deflects attention from that sole intercessory work, for it is that work which makes available the Spirit to the Church. Whatever can be said of the modern Mariology of the Roman Church, it is hard to see how it can be reconciled with this fundamental conception of the relation of the Spirit to the Son.

New vitality has been given to Christological study by the ecumenical conversation concerning the relation between

Christ and the Church. That conversation is still in its early stages. It can only fulfil the promise which it holds of re-defining old disagreements and pointing the way to new agreements if it takes account, in ways like those of which we have spoken, of the relation of the work of Christ to that of the Holy Spirit in the Church.

I I

THE CHRISTIAN LIFE

by R. S. WALLACE

Minister of St. Kentigern's Parish Church, Lanark

THE CHRISTIAN LIFE

by

R. S. WALLACE

1. *Jesus Christ is the source and norm of the Christian Life*

The Christian life is a life in Christ [wrote F. W. Camfield]. To let Christ be not simply the author, but the finisher of our faith; not simply the initial stimulation, and not merely the perpetual stirrer up of faith, but the one object of faith, so that faith hangs on nothing and on nobody but on Him alone—this is the Christian life, and the Christian solution to the problem of life.[1]

IN our thinking about the Christian life Christ Himself must have the central place and indeed the only place. God has blessed us with *all* spiritual blessings in Jesus Christ and has made all fullness to dwell in Him. The Christian thinker and the ordinary Christian man to-day no less than the Apostle Peter is bound to cry out "Lord to whom shall we go?"[2] in dismayed recoil against even the suggestion that there might be apart from Jesus Christ Himself some other source of wisdom and life, and some other principle, by which to order daily living.

Our Christian life must be thought of as included in the atonement. It is the life which Jesus Christ has already lived *for* us. Jesus Christ has taken our place and acted in our stead not only in suffering and dying to make atonement for the sin of mankind, but also in living out for us the Christian life. He has offered in our place and in our flesh obedience and faith and true holiness before God. Moreover, He still lives before God for us in His glorified humanity. The Christian life can be thought of, therefore, both as the life of humiliation which Jesus Christ lived for us in our human nature on earth when He was born of the Virgin Mary and suffered under Pontius Pilate, and

---

[1] *Scottish Journal of Theology*, I, 3, pp. 286–7.   [2] John 6: 68.

as the glorified life which He now lives in our human nature
for ever before God.

But this Christian life was lived out by Jesus Christ not only
in order to be substituted before God for us, but also to be imparted to us. We live our Christian life because we receive our
Christian life (indeed we receive this *one* Christian life) from
Jesus Christ and from Him alone. Anyone who reads Calvin's
preaching will not fail to be impressed by the way he reminds
his hearers time and again that all the virtue and the infinite
spiritual wealth which Christ had in His human nature He
possessed not for Himself, for He had need of nothing, but in
order that He might impart it all to His people. Christ sanctified Himself not for His own sake, but in order that His whole
Church in every generation might be sanctified through the
truth. He was not only made poor in order to save us, but He
was also set apart and made rich in order to save us, for God
ordained that all the virtue that the world needs should reside
in His human nature, and that He should be the sole channel
through which life and virtue are to flow to mankind. Therefore for our Christian life we must turn to Him and to Him
alone.[1]

We receive our Christian life through receiving Jesus Christ.
Jesus Christ imparts to us our Christian life in imparting *Himself* to us, and He does not give it apart from Himself. In receiving our Christian life from Jesus Christ, therefore, we receive
it not as a vague spiritual power that is going to inspire us to
work out for ourselves on a new basis some highly individual
spiritual achievement in virtuous living, but as a fully prepared
and finished life in which everything that is to be ours is already
completely and perfectly fulfilled in Him whom we receive.
This point is excellently brought out by Marshall in his work
on Sanctification:

> One great mystery is, that the holy frame or disposition, whereby
> our souls are furnished for immediate practice of the law, must be
> obtained "by receiving it out of Christ's fullness" as a thing
> already prepared and brought into existence for us in Christ, and
> treasured up in Him; and that, as we are justified by a righteous-

[1] cf., e.g., *Calv. Op.*, 46: 596, 736, 455-7; 47: 388; 45: 319; 52: 48; *Inst.* II,
xvii, 6.

ness wrought out in Christ, and imputed to us, so we are sanctified
by such an holy frame and qualifications as are first wrought out
and completed in Christ for us, and then imparted to us. And as
our natural corruption was produced originally in the first Adam,
and propagated from him to us, so our new nature and holiness
is first produced in Christ, and derived from Him to us, or, as it
were, propagated. So that we are not to work together with
Christ in making or producing that holy frame, but only to take
to ourselves, and use it. . . . Thus we have fellowship with Christ
by receiving that holy frame of spirit that was originally in Him.[1]

It is faith that unites us to Jesus Christ. Through faith we are
so placed in relation to Jesus Christ that everything that is His
becomes ours. We are so placed that His righteousness can be
wholly imputed to us, and His life can be wholly imparted to
us. We receive *Him* by faith, and thus we receive everything
that is His. Therefore it is impossible to think of ourselves as
being justified apart from also being sanctified by Jesus Christ.
In the event of our becoming united to Christ by faith we
receive not only our justification but also our sanctification, we
receive not only the forgiveness of sins and the possibility of a
new start in life, not only freedom from bondage to the powers
of evil, not only light in our darkness, but also really and
actually, there and then, our Christian life. Christ is "made
unto us wisdom and righteousness, and sanctification and redemption",[2] says Paul, summing it all up. It is true that justification and sanctification are quite distinct "saving graces". It
would be a poor theology that did not clearly distinguish between the one and the other, and that could not hold the one
apart from the other in thought. But though they must be distinguished they cannot be separated. There can be no justification without sanctification. When we receive the one we receive
the other in the act of receiving the one. Both are included as
two aspects of the one gift that is Jesus Christ Himself.[3]

[1] *Sanctification*; abridged edition edited by Andrew Murray, pp. 10–11.
[2] 1 Cor. 1: 30.
[3] *Inst.* III, xi, 6: "To be justified is something else than to be made new
creatures"; and again: "As Christ cannot be divided in parts, so the two things,
justification and sanctification which we perceive to be united in Him are inseparable." cf. *Calv. Op.* 49: 144, 50: 438; 37: 351; also W. Kolfhaus, *Christus-
gemeinschaft bei Johannes Calvin* (pp. 60–1). F. Hildebrandt, *From Luther to Wesley*
(pp. 166–7), has an excellent discussion on this point. "He, not a part of Him or
gift from Him, is our righteousness" (p. 121 n.). cf. p. 85, where he quotes Luther's
"Wo Vergebung der Sünden ist, da ist auch Leben und Seligkeit."

In imparting to us the righteousness that He has prepared for us, Christ seeks to break the continuity of our self-centred life by substituting for it a life centred on Himself. The Christian life is thus, in one of its main aspects, what Christ substitutes within us for our sin. He has taken upon Himself our sinfulness, bearing it in His body on the Cross in order that He might give us in its stead His righteousness. The Reformers speak of "wondrous exchange" whereby Christ takes upon Himself our poverty and wretchedness and disease and death in order to give us His wealth and happiness and health and life. This, however, must be thought of not only as a transaction that took place once for all when Christ, bearing our sin, died on Calvary, but also as a transaction that can take place here and now in the hearts of those who come to be in Him. It is true to say to-day that we can lay our sin upon Him, the spotless Lamb of God, making it His, and we can take in its place His holiness. The Christian life thus flows to us from the Cross where it is given in exchange for yielding up to Him the evil of our lives. It flows to us from the Cross because it has been perfected in the human nature that is crucified there.

It is through the power of the Holy Spirit that what Jesus Christ had becomes ours in such a way as to enable us to live our Christian life. It is by virtue of the Holy Spirit that the exchange is made by which our sins are crucified in Him and His resurrection life becomes ours. The Christian life is thus life in the Spirit. It is born within us by the entry of the Spirit into our hearts. It is increased within us by the growing inward influence of the Spirit. But the Holy Spirit can bring into our life nothing but what was first worked out and perfected in the human nature of Jesus Christ. The Spirit flows in His fullness from the exalted Christ and creates within us a participation in that life which Jesus lived when He was on earth. "The fruits of the Spirit are nothing other than the virtues of Christ."[1] To live the Christian life is therefore to walk in the Spirit and to give the Holy Spirit room to work and increase within our hearts. Progress in the Christian life can only be a "deepening of spiritual life". And yet the influence of the Spirit is never

[1] Schleiermacher, quoted by H. Wheeler Robinson, *The Christian Experience of the Holy Spirit*, p. 213.

given apart from communion with the human nature of Christ. In all efforts to deepen our spiritual lives in order that we may be better Christians we must remember that except we eat the flesh of the Son of man and drink His blood we have on life within us. A concentration on the mechanics of the working of the Spirit that is divorced in any way from concentration on the historical life and death of Jesus Christ is dangerous to true Christian living. "Deepening of the spiritual life" comes best as the partly unsought accompaniment of deepening understanding of the meaning and relevance of the person and work of Jesus Christ.

Since the source of the Christian life is the human nature of Jesus Christ, the pattern of the Christian life is a pattern of death and resurrection. Indeed in the life portrayed in the Gospels it is suggested that Jesus has worked out in His earthly life the pattern of a new kind of righteousness which will fulfil all righteousness. Before He was baptized in Jordan, Jesus said to John: "Suffer it to be so now, for thus it becometh us to fulfil all righteousness." Then followed His baptism, the meaning of which is unfolded in the whole subsequent life including His death and resurrection. The pattern of His life is therefore the pattern of a new righteousness which He has come to substitute for the righteousness of the law and in which the righteousness of the law is really fulfilled in a true way. But now that the righteousness of the law is *thus* fulfilled, the disciples of Jesus are called themselves to fulfil righteousness in this new kind of way and in this new kind of life of death and resurrection in which He calls them to follow Him. As W. Manson puts it:

> In the New Testament there is only one principle or standard of Christian knowledge, character and life—Jesus Christ Himself. All other norms of religious insight, belief and practice are superseded in Him, or if they continue to be valid, it is because they have been taken up into Him, amended, re-enacted and completed.[1]

In giving us participation in His own life, then, Jesus Christ not only substitutes His life for ours, but also substitutes a new pattern of life in place of all the other patterns of law and virtue by which we have hitherto sought to regulate our conduct,

[1] *Scottish Journal of Theology*, 3/1, p. 33.

form our ideals, and mark out our path to ultimate salvation. It is clear that, for the Apostle Paul, to work out our salvation with fear and trembling means not to follow some great moral ideal, whether embodied in some law or philosophic concept, but to follow Jesus Christ in the way of *His* humiliation and *His* salvation; becoming conformed to Him in the pattern of death and resurrection. Such a following of Christ in the path of the Cross and self-denial is nothing less than the offering of our bodies as a living sacrifice, holy and acceptable to God and inspired by the mercies of God. To make such an offering of ourselves in response to Jesus Christ within the body of Christ is the meaning of love. Through such a response to Jesus Christ human love begins truly to reflect the pattern of divine love, for even "love" must find the pattern to which it is to be conformed only in Jesus Christ. "Herein is love, not that we loved God, but that He loved us, and sent His Son to be the propitiation for our sins."[1] As Christ fulfilled all righteousness through offering Himself in such sacrificial love, so by such love the Christian fulfils the law. Thus both love and the law find their meaning in Jesus Christ.

2. *Our Christian life viewed as the unfolding of what is complete in Christ*

Since Jesus Christ has lived out our life for us and in our place before God, this means that in Him we too have already lived out our Christian life before God. The New Testament speaks as if in all that happened to Jesus Christ His people in every age have already been involved. The living, dying and rising again of Christ is an event which conditions the whole future and destiny of all who come to be in Him. Thus when a man comes to be in Christ he finds that Christ has constituted Himself as the past of his life in such a way that he can now renounce and disclaim his own actual historical past, no matter how dominating and threatening and complicated the consequences of that past. He can now identify his true past with the living and dying and rising again of Jesus Christ in the flesh.[2] Therefore in all that happened to Jesus Christ and all that He

---

[1] I John 4: 10.
[2] cf. R. Bultmann, *Theology of the New Testament*, pp. 296–9, 347–9.

accomplished in the flesh from His birth to His ascension to heaven, He has really and already determined the destiny of all His people. "By one offering He hath perfected for ever them that are sanctified."[1] When Christ died, we ourselves died. In His resurrection we were raised together with Him. In His ascension He has drawn us up in Himself to sit in heavenly places and we have been glorified together with Him.[2] All this has already been fulfilled in such a real and vital way that we can speak of what was accomplished in Him as having been accomplished in us.

This means that when a man comes to be in Christ old things are passed away. He is uprooted from the past history which conditioned his existence and determined his future, and is planted into the new and far more decisive historical situation created by the death and resurrection of Jesus and which henceforth determines his destiny. In this new situation nothing can happen which is not the unfolding of what has already happened in that death and resurrection.[3] He now participates in the life of a new age, the blessedness of which consists in the fact that it is dominated by the new beginning which has been made for all men in Jesus Christ, and which overlaps this present age.

This does not imply, however, that a man in Christ is not

---

[1] Heb. 10: 14.

[2] I am indebted here to the following passages from Kohlbrügge, quoted by A. de Quervain, *Die Heiligung*, pp. 105–6:

"As He was born of woman, so He bore His people (*Gemeine*) in Himself; as He suffered and died upon the Cross, His people also suffered and died with Him while He suffered and died for them; as He was raised from the dead, as He ascended towards Heaven and was crowned there with the blessing of the fullness of the Holy Ghost, His people also ascended with Him towards Heaven, were in Him set at the right hand of majesty and in Him blessed by God with all spiritual blessings in heavenly places. Those, however, who are Christ's have besides all this experienced a day in which it was said to them: 'Ye who were dead in sin and trespasses, He has made alive together with Christ'—a day when through the Holy Ghost what the Lord has made out of them is appropriated to them. . . ." (*Schriftauslegung*, Vol. 11, p. 93.)

". . . It is self-evident that the rebirth of all the elect has taken place in the death and in the resurrection of Jesus Christ, but for every single one of them there occurs also a time in which he becomes a partaker of this rebirth through the renewal of the Holy Ghost." (*Acht Predigten über Joh.* 3, 1–21, p. 12.)

[3] cf. Visser T'Hooft, *Kingship of Christ*, pp. 63–4; "The Holy Spirit and the Sacraments," F. C. Synge, in *Scottish Journal of Theology*, 6: 71.

also involved at the same time in his old history. He may be held down by his old faults, involved in all the moral compromise of living in this present evil world, held back by spiritual weakness, subject to the aches and pains of physical corruption and approaching death, tormented by "the slings and arrows of outrageous fortune", answerable at the bar of human judgment for the past from which Christ has uprooted him, and forced to bear the dreadful earthly consequences that are worked out in his life from the law that whatsoever a man soweth that shall he also reap. He dare not think of himself as divorced from the life of this age. He has to confess with shame his own part in its sinfulness and wretchedness and acknowledge in repentance his responsibility to seek to reform things as they are, that God's will may now be done and God's Kingdom may come.

Nevertheless, even though so involved in the life of this present age and confessing his shameful involvement in it, the Christian man will also confess with gladness that his true future and destiny is determined not by the various choices he himself might make in the moments of moral decision, not by the success or failure of the reformation he may achieve in this present world, not by the strength of his repaired will and the measure of the Christian character he might attain to by the strength of his faith, but rather by the great crisis which lies behind him, by the choice which Jesus Christ has made for him, by the growth of Christ for him into the fullness of perfect manhood, by the faith of Jesus Christ for him, by the perfect purity that He manifested and by the victory He accomplished over the powers of evil. His past is now the past that Christ has lived out for him and that he has lived out in Christ. The step of faith which is taken when a man comes to be in Christ is in reality a step out of the sphere determined by the law of sin and death into the life of the age where all things are determined by the law of the spirit of life in Christ. "He that heareth my word, and believeth on Him that sent me, hath everlasting life, and shall not come into condemnation; but is passed from death to life."[1]

The whole way of life of the Christian man is henceforth to

[1] John 5: 24.

be determined by this fact that in Jesus Christ he has already passed through the great crisis which determines everything. In Jesus Christ he has already risen above sin and has been freed from the power of evil. The Christian life is not a striving towards a distantly held out ideal of perfection depending for its attainment on how man toils and strives, but is rather the unfolding by the grace of God of the perfection that has been already attained for us and already treasured up for us in Jesus Christ. The Christian man lives the Christian life because he continually reckons himself as beyond the power of that which held him down, and he can reckon himself always as in this state because he is able continually and afresh to hear the verdict that God has blotted out his past for the sake of Jesus Christ.

The sacrament of Baptism should be regarded as a sign that our Christian life is the unfolding in this present world of what has already been held out for us in Christ as a completed event. In Baptism the whole of the Christian life which has yet to be lived out is already enacted as if it were now fulfilled. God does not mock us in the signs that He gives us. The fact that Baptism as a completed act stands at the beginning of the Christian life means that whatever happens to us in the future is conditioned by what has already happened to us in Christ, what happens within us is the unfolding of what has already happened for us and outside of us. Baptism proclaims that we are not merely washed but that we are already translated in body and soul into the new age which lies alongside this present world, and that we have already crossed the line that separates darkness from light, the realm of death from the realm of life, this present age from the age to come, this world from the Kingdom of God.

3. *The Christian Life viewed as the re-enactment within us of what is complete in Christ*

Our participation in Jesus Christ in living the Christian life may be thought of not only as a crisis in our past history which now determines our destiny, but also as a process in which there is a continuous inward participation in Christ. It must be thought of in terms of "Christ in us" as well as in terms of "us in Christ". Professor W. Manson points out that in the teaching of St. Paul "all the acts and episodes in the cosmic manifestation of Christ have their instant counterpart in the human experience of redemption".[1] The New Testament speaks not only of the work of Christ in His birth, growth to manhood, passion, death, resurrection and ascension in its cosmic and objective aspect, it speaks also of the birth and growth of Christ in the human heart in such terms that what happens in the one sphere is implied in what happens in the other sphere, and in the realm of human experience. It speaks of men as dying and rising in Christ in the inward experience of redemption. The New Testament therefore never divorces what happened once for all in Jesus Christ in the concrete field of human history from what happens within the field of the inner experience of the Church in every age. What happened in Christ in the flesh is continually reflected in what He effects within the hearts of His people.

In Jesus Christ we have the mystery of God with us in the flesh of human life taking up human nature to Himself for ever through the birth and growth and passion and victory of Jesus Christ. This mystery of God with us which became event once for all in Jesus Christ becomes event again and again in the preaching of the Word and the celebration of the Sacraments. But this mystery must find its counterpart in the immediately related mystery of Christ within His people, formed within them and growing within them from birth to manhood, conforming them to His death and resurrection—a process which will be consummated in physical death and resurrection. The whole series of acts whereby we are saved and justified must therefore be spiritually re-enacted[2] in the members of Christ till all attain the measure of the fullness of the perfect man. The Christian life has to be regarded as this process which strains towards this final consummation.

Here again we are helped in our understanding by the form in which we are given the sacraments. Baptism itself is a sign not only of a once-for-all crisis which lies behind us, but of a daily process which must determine our way of living. It is a

---

[1] *The Epistle to the Hebrews*, p. 154.
[2] A re-enactment not involving repetition.

sign of our "initiation into a life of growing participation in the death and resurrection of Christ".[1] Luther described the Christian life as a "daily Baptism".[2] Moreover, to Baptism there is added the Lord's Supper as a sign that though the crisis that once for all determines our destiny lies behind us in the death and resurrection of Christ, nevertheless we have continuous day-to-day participation in that event—that Jesus not only lived once upon a time in Galilee but also lives now in the heart of His Church, that we not only died unto sin once in Him, but die daily. In the incident of the feet washing, Jesus speaks not only of a total bath once effective for all time without which no man can have part in Him, but also of a daily cleansing necessary to supplement that total bathing. All this is placed in such a context as indicates a reference to the two sacraments of Baptism and the Lord's Supper.

4. *The twofold nature of the Christian life*

We have been forced to think of our Christian life in terms both of the life which Jesus Christ lived for us and lives for us, and of the life which we live in Him. It must be thought of also as the life which we now live through Him in the concrete historical situation in which we are placed to fulfil the duties of our station and where we make our choice of the good way or the evil way amidst the varied possibilities which lie open before us. It is in the midst of this present world of compromise and contradiction, change and decay, that Christ is born within us and seeks to shape our outward and inward life in conformity with Himself.

Our Christian life is therefore seen by us as twofold, and it can be looked at from two apparently very different aspects. We can think of it as the life which is *hidden* with Christ in God[3] —the life which we possess and live in Christ and which Christ has lived for us. But we can also think of it as the life which we now live *in the flesh* by the faith of Jesus Christ[4]—the life of struggle and growth and incompleteness and contradiction, in which nevertheless in spite of all our failure and disappointment, Jesus Christ reigns supreme and gives signs of His final

[1] John Heron, "The Theology of Baptism," in *Scottish Journal of Theology*, 8: 43.
[2] In his *Greater Catechism*.   [3] Col. 3: 3.   [4] Gal. 2: 20.

victory. When Paul reiterates that the life of Jesus has to be made manifest "in our body", and "in our mortal flesh",[1] he is undoubtedly referring to the Christian life.

Both aspects of the Christian life are equally stressed in the New Testament, and are placed together side by side as if they were simultaneously experienced. At times spatial terms are used rather than temporal terms to describe the eschatological nature of the Christian life. We are regarded as not only participating simultaneously in the life of two ages which overlap, but as living simultaneously in two distinct spheres or kingdoms. Jesus described Himself as the Door separating two realms between which the Christian man goes "in and out".[2] We are regarded as partaking of the life both of a realm that is "above" and of the life of this earth, as living now both in heaven where Christ is ascended, and in this world to which He continually descends in His grace.[3]

The apostolic exhortation to put off or crucify the old man and to put on the new man reminds us of another aspect of the twofold nature of our Christian life. It is to be thought of as the new life created within us by the seed of the Word of God whose taking root and growth produces a new creature, born out of the old man and yet indeed a new creation. The new man thus shares in the perfection and glory of the hidden life of Christ. But the old man remains; and the Christian man instead of being psychologically a unified and harmoniously integrated personality is rather a man with two natures within him in constant warfare.[4] The problem of living the Christian life involves as its main problem the question of the discipline and restraint of the old man, the bringing of the old man under the law of Jesus Christ and the reshaping of the life *in the flesh*. It is therefore in the present life which we now live in the flesh that the faith by which we live the Christian life has to be exercised in the midst of all the perplexities and contradictions of experience, and that the shaping of our outward life in conformity to Jesus Christ takes place. To live and die with Christ and to

---

[1] 2 Cor. 4: 10 and 11; Rom. 8: 11.   [2] John 10: 9.   [3] Col. 3: 1–5; Phil. 3: 20.

[4] cf. L. Newbigin, *Household of God* (p. 119). "The two ages, so to speak, overlap, lie alongside one another, and fight with one another in the world and in the soul of every Christian."

share in His death and resurrection is not a mere inward mystical experience that has no outward reflection in the concrete circumstances that form the background of the Christian's inner experience. There is no doubt, for example, that Paul looks on the actual physical sufferings which he endures as a real and concrete sharing in the death of Christ.[1]

It has been stressed previously that the Christian life is the life which Jesus Christ lived for us and the hidden life which we live in Him. We dare not say, however, that the life which we now live in the flesh is not also and equally our Christian life, for Christ is within us dwelling in the body of the flesh as truly and concretely as the bread and wine are partaken of in physical reality in the sacrament. Jesus Christ therefore claims the life which we now live in the flesh as the sphere of His lordship and the sphere which He will never forsake to death and destruction. Therefore in this realm of flesh and blood we have to live our Christian life holding on amidst all contradiction to the hope of the resurrection of the body.

There can be no divorce between these two apparently different realms and apparently different lives. They are not two lives in reality but only one simple life in Christ. We are not two men but one man in Christ. Here there is no separation and no fusion. Therefore, though the Christian life can be viewed now from one side which shows it as perfect in all its hidden glory, and again from another side which shows it as struggling and growing towards what seems a very distant consummation, there are not two Christian lives but only one Christian life.

5. *Participation in the Death of Christ for all men*

In the life which we now live in the flesh, the aspect of our participation in Christ and of our conformity to Christ which is most vividly present in our experience and most visibly manifest in the world around us is participation in the death of Christ and conformity to the death of Christ.[2] So prominent is

[1] cf. A. Schweitzer, *The Mysticism of Paul the Apostle* (E.T. ch. VIII).

[2] cf. L. Newbigin, *Household of God* (p. 116): "The Christian life is first of all a dying, of which the source is the dying of the Son of God, One for all and once for all."

R

this aspect of our participation in Christ that the process of sanctification can be described as a process of mortification.

The life which Jesus Christ lived on earth in the flesh was outwardly a process of dying. He Himself described His career as shaped by constant constraint towards the baptism of blood on the Cross which would fulfil the career outlined for Him in His baptism by John in Jordan. His life was a straining towards His passion and death, and it finds its completion in His death because it had always that orientation. To live the Christian life according to the Gospels is to follow Jesus Christ in this way of the Cross. Professor W. Manson has pointed out that the words, "If any one will come after me, let him deny himself and take up his cross and follow me," are set in a context relative to the death of Christ and to the calling of the disciples which suggests that the early Church regarded them as a definitely laid down rule for all His followers.[1] It was a sound understanding of how the Gospels were to be interpreted that led Calvin to make his account of the Christian life in the *Institutes* an exposition of the meaning of these words of Jesus, and to sum up the whole Christian life under the one heading of self-denial.[2]

For Calvin there was an outward conformity to Christ in His death[3] in which the Christian participated by being made to suffer various earthly afflictions or persecutions whether or not directly suffered for the sake of Christ. If a man yields his body to the will of God, following Christ in the outward circumstances of his life, God will shape the whole circumstances of his life into the form of a cross adequate to subdue him and humiliate him and assimilate him to the Cross of Christ. To yield himself up to God's providential ordering of his life in these sufferings is therefore to yield to a process that will more and more conform him to Jesus Christ. Persecutions for

---

[1] *Scottish Journal of Theology*, 3, pp. 37 f.

[2] *Inst.* III, vii, 1 ff.

[3] *C.O.*, 50: 55; 52: 365; 52: 119. Physical death is, of course, the final stage of this outward conformity to Christ, cf. *Comm. on Phil.* 3: 10, *C.O.* 52: 50. "We must all be prepared for this—that our whole life shall represent nothing else than the image of death until it produce death itself, as the life of Christ is nothing else but a prelude of death." cf. also 55: 213. Luther's thought is similar, F. Hildebrandt, *From Luther to Wesley* (pp. 147–8), quotes him as writing in a letter to a dying friend, "Remember, dear brother, that now thy Baptism is to be fulfilled."

righteousness' sake are a specially potent and valuable form of the Cross, but it is not given to all men in the same measure to suffer directly for the sake of Christ and Calvin has no hesitation in affirming that all the various ills of life can contribute to the cross that is to conform us to the death of Christ.[1] It is only, however, for the man of faith that the sufferings of life can become the cross that sanctifies them and conforms them to Christ. The wicked do not experience a cross.[2]

Besides the outward participation in the death of Christ which Calvin calls "bearing the cross" there is an inward participation in the death of Christ which Calvin calls "self-denial". By this term Calvin means much more than is often implied in modern usage of the term. He means a real and painful inward mortification of feeling and natural reason and desire and such an annihilation of self-will as involves the most severe and continual inward conflict in which there is no rest and no final attainment of settled and unthreatened peace.[3] For Calvin the greatest human problem is that of the concupiscence of man's flesh. The flesh is the inward natural principle of man's mind and heart and will which seeks to control and pervert his whole way of life and to plunge him always into lawlessness and excess in his affections and pursuits, whether these be good or bad, and to pervert all his thinking.[4] The tendency of the flesh is always against the law of God and the order of God and the will of God, and the flesh with its concupiscence is always in continual warfare against the new man who is reborn in Christ and the new life of the Spirit.

Bearing the Cross helps to subdue this inward principle of the flesh. By sending outward affliction God humiliates the inward man and abases and disciplines the heart.[5] Calvin in this connection can use the proverb "a rough horse requires a rough

---

[1] *Inst.* III, viii, 1. It is a mistake frequently made to say that only certain kinds of suffering such as that borne in the service of Christ constitute the "Cross" which the Christian is called on to bear. This restricted view of what constitutes the "Cross" relates Jesus Christ directly to only a part of the Christian life and tends to split life into the sacred and secular in an impossible way. Calvin is wiser—see also Bultmann, *Theology of the New Testament*, p. 351.

[2] *C.O.*, 45: 482.

[3] *Inst.* III, vii, 1–2, 8. *C.O.* 49: 348; 47: 170–1; 33: 119; 26: 160.

[4] cf., e.g., *Inst.* II, i, 8–9; III, iii, 10–12; *C.O.* 55: 171; 34: 627–8.

[5] *Inst.* III, viii, 2–3.

rider".[1] But the Holy Ghost is also given, and it is mainly through the inward mortifying power of the Holy Spirit, one of whose functions is to subdue the flesh, that concupiscence is overcome and brought under control to the will of God. The Holy Spirit thus continually fights within us against nature and gives us an inward sharing of the death of Christ by which we are enabled to deny ourselves in a radical way, mortifying self-will and conforming our life to Jesus Christ.

6. *Participation in the Resurrection of Christ*

Though so much stress has to be laid on our outward and inward participation in the death of Christ in the life which we now live in the flesh, there is nevertheless also a participation in the resurrection of Christ that can be experienced here and now. Here and now the life of the Christian man is determined by the resurrection no less than by the cross.[2] The fulfilment of the rising-out-of-the-water aspect of the baptismal rite does not necessarily need to be completely postponed till the last resurrection of the dead. The new life which we live in the power of the resurrection of Christ is identical with the life which we now live on earth.[3] If there is a daily dying with Christ there is also a daily rising with Christ. If God brings the Church, and the individual within the Church, down to the depths of despair and apparent God-forsakenness in the providence which shapes their life in the form of a cross, He also hears their cry from those depths and delivers them here and now out of their toils in ways that are at times so supernatural to those who experience them that they can be described only as resurrection from the dead. This was the experience of Israel in the great deliverances from despair and captivity that marked their history and enabled them to foreshadow and participate in the death and

---

[1] *C.O.* 35: 504; cf. 26: 5; 32: 245.

[2] cf. R. Bultmann, *Theology of the New Testament*, p. 345. Also p. 299: "According to 1 Cor. 12: 13 it (Baptism) unites the baptized with Christ into one *soma*. By baptism into His death we who have faith are 'grown together' with Him (Rom. 6: 5). This is why the believer's whole life is stamped by Christ's death, but also by His resurrection. As Jesus dying continues to occur in the apostle's body, so Jesus' life also lives in it (2 Cor. 4: 7–12. cf. 1: 5). But this is by no means true for the apostle only, but for all believers, as Phil. 3: 10 f. shows."

[3] De Quervain, *Heiligung*, p. 103.

resurrection of the Messiah.[1] It was the experience of Paul, who relates his experiences of victory and triumph in the Christian life to a sharing in the resurrection life of Jesus as he relates his experiences of suffering to a sharing in the death of Jesus.[2] It is the Christian experience. The powers of the age to come can break for the Christian into this present world of death and decay in real signs that point to the presence here and now of the new age of resurrection, and in events that are characterized by the conquest of evil powers.[3]

It is as we think of the significance of our present participation in the body of Christ that we realize best the extent of our present participation in the resurrection of Christ. The participation of the Christian in the Lord's Supper is a sign that even now on earth we have union with the body of Christ that has already been glorified and taken to heaven; and that through this union there comes to us here and now not only the power of the resurrection of Jesus, but a participation in the joys and glories of the life that is from beyond.[4]

Moreover, the Holy Spirit is given to us not only to mortify us but to be even now the first fruits of our share in Christ's resurrection as well as in His death. Through His influence He vivifies us as well as mortifies us.[5] Therefore when Paul reminds the Colossians that they are "risen with Christ",[6] the phrase not only reminds them of their participation in the eschatological event in which they are already involved by faith; it also describes the inward experience of the presence and work of the risen Christ in their hearts through the Holy Spirit, and it refers to concrete signs in their outward circumstances that here and now they have shared in part in the resurrection vic-

[1] cf. R. S. Wallace, *Calvin's Doctrine of the Word & Sacrament*, pp. 43–5.

[2] cf., e.g., 2 Cor. 4: 11.

[3] cf. O. Cullmann, *Christ and Time*, p. 47.

[4] cf. A. Schweitzer, *The Mysticism of Paul the Apostle*, pp. 109–10: "Of all that must be common to Jesus and the Elect, in order that they might be united together in the glory of the Messianic Kingdom, this stands for Paul in the foreground, namely, that they have together the resurrection mode of existence before the resurrection has begun for the remainder of the dead. The essential point in their predestined relation of solidarity is that they share a corporeity which is in a peculiar measure open to, and receptive of, the influence of the powers of the resurrection."

[5] Rom. 8: 10–12.

[6] Col. 3: 1.

tory of Jesus. The "power of His resurrection" which Paul so strains to apprehend is no more distant and vague an entity than the "fellowship of His sufferings" which he will know in its final fullness only in his own physical death.[1] Therefore it is surely right to preach in a context that emphasizes at the same time all the darker aspects of the Christian life, an inner experience of new life now which makes all things—even the old things—new, and gives the promise of constant victory and triumph over all spiritual evil, and offers the possibility that God in His grace may give us signs and tokens that even now in the outward life we share in the powers of the new age.

Such a sharing in the resurrection of Christ is bound to introduce an element of assurance, serenity and happiness into the life of the Christian. On this point no one has more to say than Calvin. Those who are thus united to the victorious and risen Lord are bound to rejoice in that nothing can separate them from His love. Moreover, since God's love is free and spontaneous, the response to Christ that is called from those who participate in Him must be one of free and spontaneous gratitude. Only such a response can give a true reflection of the initiative taken by Christ in our redemption. Therefore the Christian life is a life in which everything is dedicated to God through the willing sacrifice of the heart.[2] It is true that there must be order —we need the Word of God and His commandments. It is true also that obedience and fear are also elements in the response of man to Christ. But no matter how virtuous and perfectly ordered our life may be, it is all in vain unless the sacrifice of the heart is made along with the sacrifice of outward obedience, and unless the sacrifice of the heart is given with real spontaneous gladness and love to Him to whom it is offered.[3]

7. Paradox and contradiction in the Christian life

Since participation in the death of Christ is so inseparably connected with participation in the resurrection of Christ, our Christian experience is marked by paradox and contradiction. It reflects in varying degrees both the experience of the disciples on Good Friday and their experience on Easter Sunday. Calvin, who insists strongly that "God supplies His people in this

[1] Phil. 3: 10.   [2] cf. *C.O.* 31: 170, 26: 609, 26: 266–9.   [3] *C.O.* 31: 447.

world with everything that is necessary to a happy and joyful life",[1] admits in the same sentence that this is a "paradox strongly at variance with the feelings of the flesh". He never forgets that at the height of the triumphant description of the Christian life in Rom. 8 we have the verse about "for thy sake we are killed all the day long, we are accounted as sheep for the slaughter". Nor does he forget Paul's description of his state as "dying and behold we live . . . as sorrowful yet always rejoicing".[2] Therefore it is in the midst of humiliation that we experience our victories in Christ. It is in the midst of a process of dying with Christ that we live through Him. If we have victory, it is over a continually present principle of sin within us in the presence of which we can never take our rest. If we enjoy rest and peace, it is in the midst of conflict—a peace held by the struggle of faith against the temptation to despair. "Our present condition is very short of the glory of God's children", Calvin can say, "for as to our body we are dust, the shadow of death is alway before our eyes; we are also subject to a thousand miseries; the soul is exposed to innumerable evils so that we find always a hell within us."[3]

Our participation in the resurrection of Christ is a more *hidden* aspect of our Christian life than our participation in His death. To become conformable to Christ in His death means to share the shame and obscurity which were such a prominent part of His agony. His word: "Henceforth the world seeth me no more"[4] has its application to the Christian man as well as to Himself. "It doth not yet appear what we shall be."[5] Therefore to outward appearance there is no "halo" around the head of the Christian as he walks through life. Nor is there necessarily any manifest heavenly influence flowing from his person, the impact of which can be convincingly felt by the bystander. "For our good is hidden", says Luther, "and that so deeply that it is hidden under its contrary. Thus our life is hidden under death, our joy under hatred, glory under shame, salvation under perdition, heaven under hell, wisdom under foolishness, righteousness under sin, strength under infirmity."[6]

---

[1] *C.O.* 52: 300. cf. 32: 327, 45: 546, 55: 48, 31: 134, 154, 32: 234.
[2] 2 Cor. 6: 9–10.   [3] *C.O.* 55: 330.   [4] John 14: 19.   [5] 1 John 3: 2.
[6] *W.A.* 56: 392: 28. Quoted by Gordon Rupp, *The Righteousness of God*, p. 190. See also pp. 193, 208.

Therefore the Christian life is a constant struggle of faith to hold on to the promises of God about ourselves and His Church and about the world. For under present conditions appearances strongly contradict what we know is promised us, and what we see when we look away from ourselves and our circumstances in Jesus Christ. "The things about us are all adverse to the promises of God. He promises us immortality but we are clothed with mortality and corruption. He pronounces that He holds us as righteous, but we are covered with sins. He testifies that He is merciful and benevolent towards us, but all the outward signs threaten His wrath,"[1] says Calvin. "We hear that we are happy but we are as yet in the midst of many miseries; and abundance of good is promised us but we shall often hunger and thirst; God proclaims that He will hear us quickly but He seems deaf when we cry to Him."[2]

It is true that there are visible and sometimes spectacular changes in the way men live their lives when they come to be in Christ. There are signs witnessing at times even to the outsider that a great work of grace has taken place here and there. It is true that miracles can take place even to-day in answer to prayer as signs that Christ is risen and the Kingdom of God is at hand. New and strongly felt affections can stir within the Christian man. In the words of the Scots Confession: "He begins to hate what he previously loved and to love what he previously hated." But nevertheless such signs are never unambiguous to those who would walk by sight rather than by faith, and they are never sufficient to make moral or physical miracle a programme in the Church, or to make us too confident in trying to witness through radiant lives. "We recognize immediately that man in becoming a Christian and entering the service of God has not thereby become an angel."[3]

8. *The Christian Life as Life within the Church*

The individual participates in the life of Jesus Christ, and thus in His death and resurrection, by participating in the life

---

[1] *C.O.* 49: 84. [2] *C.O.* 55: 143–4.

[3] cf. Barth, *The Knowledge of God and the Service of God*, p. 117. Also pp. 94–5: "Jesus Christ is this change in man's life . . . and to seek this change even for a moment elsewhere than in Him, and hence to desire to see the change instead of believing it, is to confound two things and to deceive oneself."

of the Church. The members of Christ "are what they are because the Church is what it is".[1] It is the Church which is His body that Jesus Christ makes the dwelling place of His fullness. It is within and through the Church which is His body that the many receive what was bestowed upon the One, and that what the One did once for all is made effective for the many through Word and Sacraments. It is within the Church where the Spirit is operative that gifts are bestowed upon the members that will enable the whole body and each member to be nourished and grow into the fullness of His life, each member ministering to the other and each suffering for the other so that the relationship of Jesus Christ to the whole Church is reflected in the relationship of one to another within the body. It is over the Church that God exercises His providential care in such a way that the historical pattern of the life of the whole body, and of the members within the body, is shaped in conformity to the death and resurrection of Jesus Christ.

In the life of the Church, then, Christ is present in the world in a concrete and real way so that men can eat of His flesh and drink of His blood and have life. Therefore to be in Christ involves being in the Church, and to be in the Church in a real sense enables us to be in Christ.[2] It is not so much the individual who enriches and nourishes the Church. It is rather the individual who is enriched and nourished by being enabled to participate in the mutual edification of member to member within the common life of the Church. The Church has its origin and life in Christ. It is to be thought of as there in Christ in all its wealth and fullness apart from what any individual member can contribute.[3] Yet within the Church Jesus Christ seeks the individual and deals with the individual. The word in which the Church acknowledges that it hears the voice of its true Lord, is often a word in which the one single sheep finds himself guided and comforted by the Good Shepherd with quite particular and individual emphasis. The Lord's Supper is a

[1] Barth, *Dogmatik*, I/2, §16, 1.
[2] cf. Visser T'Hooft, *Kingship of Christ*, pp. 64–7: "The Church is the concrete and visible manifestation of the crucified and risen Christ in the world. The Church is that aspect or part of Jesus Christ which is tangibly present in the world" (p. 64).
[3] cf. R. Bultmann, *Theology of the New Testament*, pp. 310–11.

sacrament peculiarly for each as well as for all. Baptism, possible only with true meaning within the Church, is nevertheless administered to men one by one. Death in which Baptism finds its physical fulfilment is an entirely solitary act. The decision to enter the Kingdom of God which takes place within the life of the Church is equally solitary—how else could it be decision?

9. *Order and Purpose in the Christian Life*

Jesus Christ came to restore true order in man's life, and in doing so to be Himself the perfect example of what true order should be. The Christian Life will find its expression in a truly ordered life. If lawlessness and excess tend to mark the life of the man who is ruled by concupiscence and self-will, then orderliness will tend to mark the life of the man who has been incorporated into Christ to walk after the Spirit. The appearance of this new orderliness in behaviour in a Christian man will be a sign—though it can be no more than a sign—that a decision has been made that has uprooted the hidden life of this man from its corrupt source and has implanted it into Jesus Christ and given it new direction and tendency.

The new order in Jesus Christ will be reflected in the love which each must show for all men. If Jesus Christ died for all, then in Him we are each involved in responsibility towards all our fellow men. If He has borne our burdens we ought to bear one another's burdens. If He who was rich became poor for our sakes, we must abound in the same grace also. Such love will be recognized as the natural and human response of man to the situation in which he is placed by the grace of God. To love in this way will be regarded as part of the natural order of things[1] which Jesus Christ has come to restore. Not to love in this way is inhumanity.

The Christian man's relation to this present world will also be determined by the order seen and established in Jesus Christ. This world is a world in which Jesus Christ was born and grew up from childhood to manhood, living within it thankfully an ordered life in fulfilment of the law. It is a world which Jesus Christ has claimed as being within the sphere of His redemptive purpose and in which He has given signs of His triumph over

[1] K. Barth, *The Knowledge of God and the Service of God*, pp. 133-4.

the powers of evil. Therefore the Christian will use this world and live in thankful enjoyment of what God has made good. He will seek to overcome what is evil within the life of the world and to share here and now in the triumph of Jesus Christ. But Jesus Christ in His triumph over this world has condemned the world. Moreover, in His ascension He has risen above it to draw the hearts of all His people upwards to Himself. The tension and distance between Jesus Christ and this world is bound to create an attitude of detachment in the relation of the Christian man towards the pleasures and usages of this earth. Not merely for the sake of following some puritanical or legalistic other-worldly ideal, but for the sake of Jesus Christ, the Christian is bound to give heed to the apostolic appeal to "abhor that which is evil" and to "seek those things which are above". Calvin insisted that such detachment from this world and its life and such "meditation on the future life" was the only truly natural attitude of man towards this created world, since Adam was originally created to use this life as a preparation, and this world as a ladder, by which to ascend to a fuller and higher future life.

The Christian life finds not only its order but also its purpose in Jesus Christ. In Jesus Christ, the Christian finds his true future revealed and perfected in such a way that in grasping and possessing Jesus Christ by faith, he already grasps and possesses that which is yet to become his in fulfilled reality in the life which is to come. He already is what he will become. In encounter with Jesus Christ he finds that his true and inevitable future has already come to meet him. Yet he has to go to meet his future. The future that meets him in the present moment remains really his future. He has yet to become what he really is. It is this fact that gives the peculiar "double character"[1] to salvation—the character of something both future and yet already present—and that forces us to speak of such gifts as "righteousness" and "adoption" at one time as if already wholly ours in all perfection, and at another time as if they were yet to be perfected or even acquired.[2] It is this fact, too, that gives the Christian life its "double quality"[3] of satis-

---

[1] cf. R. Bultmann, *The Theology of the New Testament*, p. 279.
[2] *ibid.*, pp. 276–9, 319.   [3] L. Newbigin, *Household of God*, pp. 116 ff.

faction in the fact that it is what it is not, and yet restless longing to become what it already is, and that makes the Christian life a tension between rest and ceaseless striving, between possession and hope.

Thus desire and purpose mark the Christian life. What is already ours is a foretaste that makes us long for what is to become ours.[1] What we have seen as ours in Christ is to be continually reckoned as ours in the struggle of faith against unbelief, and such reckoning becomes a potent factor in our Christian growth. Moreover, all this takes place in a context which includes not only our individual salvation but the redemption of the whole creation. It is not only our individual future that has come to meet us in Jesus Christ, but the Kingdom of God, and all things made new. In Him the end of this world is at hand and all its evil has been judged. In Him the new age has dawned here and now in all its glory upon the darkness of this world. Not only so, but He is shaping even the history of this present world towards the climax of His manifestation. If Jesus Christ has a plan—even a hidden plan—in the sphere of human history, then we too must take a hand in shaping human history. If the future of this world is so certain in Him, then our labour—even in the social and international arena—is not in vain in the Lord.

[1] L. Newbigin, *op. cit.*, pp. 113–14.

12

PHILOSOPHY AND CHRISTOLOGY

by D. M. MACKINNON

Regius Professor of Moral Philosophy, University of Aberdeen

PHILOSOPHY AND CHRISTOLOGY

by

D. M. MACKINNON

This rehabilitation of the Christology is, however, not merely a piece of New Testament exegesis which challenges the adequacy of the ruling reconstruction of the development of primitive Christianity, and sets St. Paul and the author of the Fourth Gospel far nearer to the Jesus of History than is normally allowed; it has implications for Christian Theology and for philosophy which vitally affect the doctrine of the Incarnation. The New Testament scholar, who is also a Christian, cannot patiently permit the dogmatist or the philosopher to expound the doctrine of the Incarnation on the basis of an analysis of Human nature illustrated by the humanity of Jesus. He was unique; and this particularly rivets the Christian doctrine of the Incarnation to the Christology and to the soteriology involved in the Christology, and presents an awkward material to the philosopher who is operating with a rigid doctrine of evolution. There are metaphysical implications in the Christology; and the New Testament scholar, who is compelled to adopt a rather crude conception of revelation, precisely because he is a historian and has to interpret documents recording a movement of God to man and not of man to God, has nevertheless the right to demand that the Christian dogmatist should start from this particular revelation, and that the philosopher should at some point or other in his philosophy make sense of it by some other means than by obscuring the particularity of the Old Testament and by refusing to recognize that in the end the particularity of the Old Testament is only intelligible in the light of its narrowed fulfilment in Jesus, the Messiah, and of its expanded fulfilment in the Church.[1]

WITH these words the late Sir Edwyn Hoskyns, at the conclusion of an essay which was, in the main, a piece of New Testament scholarship, indicated certain wider issues concerning the nature of theology which had

[1] *Mysterium Christi*, ed. Deissmann and Bell, 1930.

been raised for him by his work on the New Testament. What he seems to be saying amounts to something like this. There are three distinguishable intellectual enterprises, named severally philosophy, Christian theology and Christology; they are distinguishable formally by the degree of abstractness and generality which they display, and it is Hoskyns' contention that, ordered as they have been in the first part of this sentence, they form a series constituted by a movement from the absolutely general to the rigorously particular. Further, it is his intention to assert without equivocation that, for the Christian, the Christology of which he speaks is sovereign both over philosophy and over Christian theology. It is with the grounds of that claim, and with the consequences that follow from admitting it, that this essay is concerned.

Much has been written concerning the relationship of faith and reason, even concerning the relationship of philosophy and theology; but there is much less material on the more crucial and more searching issues raised by the relationship of the Christological heart of the Christian mystery to philosophical analysis. To introduce this topic it may be worth while to look for a moment at one of the more shocking implications of the passage quoted from Hoskyns. Some readers of his words may have been startled by the fact that he seems to contrast something which he calls Christology with something else which he calls Christian theology; surely it may be asked: "Is not Christology a part of Christian theology?" Certainly the student of the history of Christian doctrine in the University of Oxford will be tempted to think of the development of the doctrine of the Incarnation as simply one chapter among others, of the narrative he has somehow to memorize. But Hoskyns is saying something of the greatest importance in insisting that the reality of the matter is not like this at all; Christology is rather the name of something that sets in motion, and keeps in restless activity, the whole work of the characteristically Christian theologian. The question that sets him going, and that indeed underlies and controls his every task, is the besetting riddle: "What think ye of Christ?"; this is not one question among many, any more than in the heyday of the classical physics the so-called "law of causality" was properly regarded as one law among many; rather, just as the "law of causality" was the form of all laws by which the workings of physical nature were thought to be set out, so the question concerning the Christ insinuates itself into every theological discussion and debate, transforming them and twisting them often in directions otherwise unthought and unforeseen.[1]

It is clearly Hoskyns' fear in this passage that the Christian theologian will resist the acknowledgment of this supremacy over his enterprise of the Christology. On this score it must be said that he wrote at a time when in Great Britain, and indeed in other countries, theologians were showing themselves unwilling to acknowledge the unique status of the thing called Christology; it was the age of such notorious *mots* as the saying of the late Archbishop William Temple that the language of the Council of Chalcedon revealed the "bankruptcy of patristic thought"; it was a time when there was very great confusion concerning the proper frontiers of philosophy, and theology, and when indeed this blurring of frontiers was continually praised as something at once intellectually valid, and apologetically and pastorally desirable. Even to-day those who are concerned with philosophical studies in British universities, and who also profess and call themselves Christians, are reproached by the *bien-pensants* if they do not present to their students an unhealthy hybrid called a "philosophy of life", something which is neither philosophy nor theology but a violation of the integrity of both disciplines, and indeed a standing menace to the spiritual health both of the man who purveys it and of those condemned to listen to him. If the present writer may be permitted a personal comment at this point, he might observe that for him to suppose that what he could offer the students in his ordinary class at nine in his lecture room could be in any sense whatever an adequate substitute for the mysteries of the Eucharist at which he may have assisted at seven-thirty the same day, would be a treason alike to his faith and to his philosophical conscience.

It should perhaps be remarked that, in the paragraph under

---

[1] cf. The impressive introductory sections of Heinrich Vogel, *Christologie*, Vol. 1, where he insists that we always remember that it is always Christ who puts this question to us.

discussion, Hoskyns had particularly in mind a person whom he called "the philosopher who is operating with a rigid doctrine of evolution". That is to say, just as he saw in the theologian a man continually tempted to escape from admitting the sovereignty of the Christology, so he saw in the philosopher someone tempted to borrow from the biologist the category of evolution, and with its help impose on all things in heaven and earth a particular image and shape; those indeed who knew something of the theological state of Cambridge at the time at which he wrote, would also realize that he had in mind some of the unhappier excursions into philosophy of the late Professor J. F. Bethune-Baker. He might indeed have defined the confusions he feared as a blurring of the proper task of philosophy itself; for the philosopher is concerned not to use categories such as evolution in order with their aid to build a speculatively satisfying picture of what is, but primarily in order to understand their force and function, what has been called their peculiar logic.

It is of course no accident that Hoskyns' unequivocal avowal of the sovereignty of Christology comes at the end of a piece of New Testament work;[1] in other places he repeatedly insisted that for the Christian there was no escape from the hard discipline imposed on him by the necessity of continual, critical study of the New Testament. Indeed, the acceptance of this discipline was part and parcel of the acknowledgment of the sovereignty of Christology; if one consequence of its acceptance was to make serious theological work a less delicately and closely woven unity than the theologian might desire, that untidiness was itself an expression of his fidelity to the underlying demands of his enterprise. To acknowledge the supremacy of the Christology is to confess that finality belongs somehow to that which is particular and contingent, to that which has definite date and place, to that which is described by statements that are not "truths of reason", or, in more modern language, "necessary propositions". Further, it is to involve the confession of faith inextricably with the deliverances of flickering human perception and observation; indeed, the paradoxical and bewildering character of this involvement is clearly recognized in the New

---

[1] e.g. in *The Riddle of the New Testament*.

Testament itself, where, for instance, in the Fourth Gospel, the reader meets highly sophisticated discussion of the relations of seeing and believing. If he is a philosopher, as perhaps some of those for whom the author intended his book may have been, he will recognize a certain familiarity in the often tense and emotionally charged dialogue; he may even find in it, not simply echoes of the Platonists, but curious anticipations of what men of profoundly sceptical and critical intellect like Kant and Hume were later to write on the limitations of human sensibility, imagination and understanding.

It was from his New Testament work that Hoskyns came to avow the sovereignty of the Christology; and this fact sharply differentiates the manner in which he avowed it from that in which it was confessed by another of the great British theologians of this century, the late P. T. Forsyth. It also enabled him to raise, both in the passage we are considering and in other places,[1] some of the consequences of thus exalting the contingent and particular over the necessary and universal, which received less overt attention in Forsyth's work. To exalt the Christology above theology and philosophy is not to dispense with the work either of the theologian or of the philosopher; nor is it in any sense whatsoever to deny the relevance of the work of the philosopher to the work of Christology, nor to escape the inevitable difficulties of their overlap and interplay. The very language of particularity and contingency is language which is part of the stock-in-trade of technical philosophy; to say that the proposition "Christ was crucified under Pontius Pilate" is not a necessary proposition, is to draw on the resources of an entire philosophy of logic; to suggest that in the writing of the fourth evangelist we find suggestions of the idiom of Kant and Hume is not to call attention to a superficial resemblance of outward style, but to suggest a similarity at the very heart of their several intellectual concerns. Moreover, the critical philosopher is inevitably aware of the special problems of historical knowledge; and he cannot throw over his sense of their difficulty when he comes to scrutinize the peculiar claim of Christ. Indeed, it is of the very nature of that claim to press

[1] In the introductory material to his great unfinished commentary on the Fourth Gospel (1940).

upon him these problems more sharply, even to the point of intellectual agony, if he takes them seriously. The admission of the sovereignty of the Christology is not, for the philosopher, any sort of escape from his own special problems; still less is it a device whereby he is able to say that theology has its own place, its statements their own special logic, and that it is enough for him to point out this uniqueness and to defend it against those who would impugn or critcize it. Of course, Christology is what it is and not something different, even as much as poetry and pure mathematics are what they are, and neither of them to be confused with everyday description, or theoretical physics. But poetry does overlap with conversation, and there is a most difficult problem sometimes in distinguishing the pure from the applied in the field of mathematics; and when we come to Christology the interplay is more devastating, the overlap is more bewildering. For when we say that *for us* Christ died and was buried, we speak of what men certainly saw and touched; at least we so engage ourselves that if they did not touch and see, then the whole enterprise comes to an end and there is nothing more to be said. And yet we do not stop simply at recording what men saw and touched; with our *pro nobis* we go beyond seeing and touching, and therefore are immediately faced with questions of validity that seem familiar, very like questions we have faced before in other places, and yet strangely and frighteningly outrunning them and bearing us we know not where.

We can make this clearer, if we retrace our steps. Readers may have noticed a certain ambiguity in the use of the word "Christology" in the preceding pages. Sometimes it has been used as the name of a set of propositions, sometimes with a more psychological nuance, for the intellectual processes involved in their formulation. It will be impossible to keep the two altogether distinct; but for the moment it may be wise to concentrate on the latter. What is it for men, what has it been for them, to be faced with the intellectual task of hammering out a Christology, of acknowledging its peculiar sovereignty over the movements of their minds? How indeed is Christology itself related to the Christologies that men have fashioned, even to such hard-won, authoritative insights as the Homo-ousion?

Certainly Christology is like nothing else; it is unique; and yet it overlaps here, there and everywhere; and where philosophy in particular is concerned, the overlap presents inescapable problems. These arise in many places; we have already noticed how the fourth evangelist displays a sense of the issues defined by the great eighteenth-century writers on the theory of knowledge. But also it cannot be too often recalled that, to get its own problems stated, Christology must borrow from the jargons of logic and ontology; we need, for instance, the category of radical contingency in order that the shock of the claim which Christ makes shall not be blunted.

Here I hope I shall be forgiven if I venture a brief piece of intellectual autobiography. After I had been reading philosophy at Oxford for five terms, in the long vacation of 1934, I began to move on from the study of the text of Kant to the writings of the British idealists of the nineteenth and early twentieth centuries. Almost suddenly, as it seemed, I found myself faced with a problem; why need God have created a world? Was there not in the notion of a *creatio de nihilo* something which violated any conceivable "principle of sufficient reason"? If the question of the why of creation were unanswerable, were we not committed to a blind irrationality at the heart, and at the foundation, of being? Of course I need not have gone further than Leibniz' famous correspondence with Clarke on Newton's views of space and time to find an earlier, classical statement of very much the same difficulty; only, in this correspondence the range of the discussion is restricted to the compatibility of a particular view of space and time (one which admittedly lay at the basis of Newtonian physics), with the "principle of sufficient reason", whereas the idealists seemed, by their use of it, to put a question mark against the opening clauses of the Nicene creed.

But even before I thus allowed the teachings of the absolute idealists to affect the fabric of my faith, I was aware that philosophically some of their most characteristic doctrines had not gone unchallenged. Green, I knew, had written much in criticism of Mill's logic; but I was dimly aware that others like the Austrian Gottlob Frege and the Englishman Bertrand Russell had shared Green's profound dissatisfaction with Mill, but had not found in Green's intellectual masters the answers they sought to such questions as the nature of arithmetic. In the winter I passed on to the study of Russell and Moore and found, in their logical pluralism, something which was at once more profoundly disturbing intellectually, and yet in certain ways oddly reassuring. It is of this ambivalence that I would like to speak.

Both Russell and Moore seemed, in different ways, conclusively to refute any sort of ontological argument; here indeed they seemed to resume the accents of the authentic Kant, the Kant of the Dialectic, and to speak his meaning with an inescapable rigour and clarity. There was no road from essence to existence, from concept to reality; no sleight of hand could make of existence a predicate or attribute. Between truths of reason and truths of fact there was a great gulf fixed; by no *a priori* reasoning was it possible to establish the nature of what is. To know whether or not something existed, appeal must be made to observation; it was impossible from attention to any description we might entertain to decide whether or not it applied in reality.

Of course there was something very disturbing about such a doctrine, and the further exploration of its consequences was not initially reassuring; it seemed as if the universe were falling apart; the acceptance of some relations at least as genuinely external to their terms seemed to take any sort of deep-level connectedness out of things. This impression was deepened by the strength of the case made out by philosophers of this school, for treating causality as a sort of "regularity of sequence", even for identifying it more simply with the possibility of establishing functional correlations in the world of experience. There seemed in the world of the atomist no pathway towards God, no means even of seeing the world as a whole as something setting a problem by its existence; the very notion of the world as a whole seemed logically suspect. Perhaps, from time to time, one looked back wistfully at the confused profundities of the idealists from which one had been emancipated.

And yet there was gain as well as loss. For one thing, Moore made it possible for me to be a realist; his laborious arguments concerning the status and nature of objects of perception made it clear that, whatever perceiving was, it was a finding rather than a fashioning. Further, truth was not to be identified with an internally coherent whole of judgments; it resided in the correspondence of proposition and fact. Thinking had a reference beyond itself; even if it was hard to speak of any sort of "sufficient reason" in things, yet things were somehow there to come to terms with. They might lack any sort of connectedness; it might even be impossible to speak of being *per se* as intelligible. Yet for the logical atomist, there *were* things with which men were coming to terms; the world was not simply an expression of their immanent rationality, but something given.

Looking back now I can see that what I welcomed was in the end some sort of rehabilitation of the notion of the transcendent. Whatever else they did, the philosophers of the Cambridge school seemed to me the settled foes of metaphysical immanentism; it was this which attracted me *religiously* towards them, even while I knew that they were, some of them at least, avowed atheists. Somehow, although this atheism challenged and unsettled me, it seemed a more honest and somehow less corrupting thing than the monistic insistence on, for instance, the rational necessity of evil to the articulation of the good.[1]

If I may comment on this fragment of autobiography, I must say three things. Presumably there is something here which can fall under the rubric *fides quaerens intellectum*; I came to philosophy as one already committed to Catholic Christianity, and I suppose that in philosophy I sought at once confirmation of my beliefs, and an apologetic instrument whereby I might make those beliefs more congenial to other minds. But I found neither of these; rather, first, the demands of rationality in the sense of the absolute idealists seemed to impugn the first article of the creed, seemed to make irrational the very notion of a creator God; then the rigorous criticism of their doctrines seemed to push me further away from any sort of ease in respect of the language of faith, even while at the same time it did become a little less impossible to admit the transcendent as something sheerly given, although the manner of its givenness seemed utterly obscure. Thus the quest of faith for understanding seemed to end, if not in a cul-de-sac, at least in a maze.

[1] I am referring to evil both in the sense of *Übel* and of *Böse*.

Yet faith survived; or rather I suppose that I should say it did not let me go; and the study of the New Testament gradually awoke in me the realization of something which I later found expressed in the passage from Hoskyns quoted at the outset of this essay. There was something called Christology which was unique, a kind of human intellectual response to the overwhelming fact of the ministry, crucifixion and resurrection of Jesus. The four books of theological history, which we call the Gospels, were examples of this sort of response; they were compact of factual record and interpretation, and the effort to disentangle the two moments seemed sometimes hardly worth making. But even if the facts to which they were a response seemed to elude articulation in detail, the Gospels remained a vital testament to something altogether incommensurable with ordinary human experience, yet at the same time organically one with the particularities of an individual stretch of human history. And to this the Church's Liturgy also bore witness in the effectual remembrancing of the Christ.

But if faith was autonomous, its autonomy was not the bare independence of something which could exist altogether unaffected by the questionings of philosophy. Thus it could be said that the logical atomists had restored a clear perception of the irreducible difference between existential and attributive propositions; to say that tame tigers existed was to assert a fact of a wholly different logical order from that conveyed by the statement that tame tigers growled. Essence certainly did not entail existence; the principle of the ontological argument was logically invalid. Looked at from one point of view this movement of thought could be regarded as a preamble of faith, a sort of catharsis of the mind whereby it was made ready to admit that the sheerly particular could be "the place where it is demanded of men that they should believe". But, of course, neither Moore nor Russell saw their logical work like that; and the believer who finds their arguments seem to make the way of faith more accessible to him, must remember and take seriously the context to which those arguments belong. They are not offered in any sense as a preamble of faith; they belong to philosophical thinking which frankly is atheistic in bias, and the believer who finds them enlightening must acknowledge the setting in which they occur and treat it with a proper seriousness.

It may be that this seriousness will take the form of saying that, in the last resort, atheism may be less hardly reconcilable with faith than certain sorts of idealism, even that atheism is a dialectical moment, for some at least, in the argument of faith. That is a bold step of which more will be said later in this essay; but now it must be clearly insisted that if the Christian believer flirts with atheism, he is transforming, by his very flirtation, the object of his attention. There is something opaque to him in the atheist's position, as the atheist himself accepts it, whether the atheist be a logical pluralist or a Marxist. This may be, of course, because the Christian has moved on to a place, or towards a place, where the atheist's repudiation of God has become almost trivial in comparison with his own sense of the sheer Godlessness of being; it may be because he has a little approached, as the saints have undoubtedly done, towards the place and the hour wherein Christ cried: "My God, my God, why hast Thou forsaken me?" Or it may be because he is intellectually slothful, and prefers to cheat. But the fact remains that faith cannot somehow swallow up the philosopher's atheism; the latter has to be acknowledged as something which has its own laws, even its own dignity; and if the believer is at the same time technically competent in philosophy, he will be conscious of himself as arguing about the issues this atheism raises in two ways at the same time. He will certainly see the thing *sub specie aeterni*, even *sub specie crucis*, which is perhaps the same perspective; and yet he will also know that for instance the arguments of the logical atomist raise questions which must be faced at their own level. Thus it is by no means clear that the treatment of inference by Russell and Wittgenstein[1] altogether dispenses with the need of invoking some sort of "synthetic *a priori*" truth. But this is a technical question which can be discussed only by those who are professionally competent to undertake its discussion.

So the movement between Christology and philosophy seems, if our illustrations are in any way representative, not to con-

---

[1] In the latter's *Tractatus Logico-Philosophicon*, and in the former's lectures on The Philosophy of Logical Atomism, published in *The Monist*.

form to any pre-conceived pattern; certainly the two enterprises have a genuine autonomy. And yet at the same time the
gulf between them is crossed, now in one way, now in another.
The man of faith will be aware of his faith as something which
may work as an unconscious, even an unacknowledged, motive
in his intellectual picking and choosing; he will even have to be
on guard against a certain sort of intellectual masochism,
whereby he shows himself ready to assent to arguments simply
because they seem to make faith harder for him. But all the
time, if he is a philosopher, he will see a kind of intellectual
attraction and repulsion at work between the concepts and
categories whereby he secures to himself Christ's very grasp
upon him, and those by which he shows forth to himself the
stuff of the world about him in all its familiarity and diverse
richness.

Yet it will be remembered that in the passage with which
this essay began Hoskyns asserted the sovereignty of Christology
not only over philosophy, but over theology. He was writing in
1930; and since then, in the growing fullness of Karl Barth's
dogmatic exposition, we have a working out of the consequences of such an acknowledgment of the sovereignty of
Christology by a theologian which is truly classical alike in
comprehensive range and detailed thoroughness. For Barth
there are no problems in theology which are not in the end
Christocentric; whether it be the relation of time to eternity,
the predestination of men to heaven or to hell, the besetting
facts of sin and evil, the flickering impulses of love of an un-
attainable, unimaginable beauty in the human heart, the political obligations of men in organized society—all must be seen
in terms of Christ, who in His very concreteness is God's dealing with men. His method can be illustrated in every sort of
way; but perhaps a reference to a part of His attack on the
problem of the evil will throw into clear light its utter concreteness. In the end, for Barth, the problem of the evil will *is* the
problem of Judas Iscariot; the theologian must not speculate
in the sense of asking how evil can be somehow the occasion of
good. He must allow his thinking on this subject to be riveted
to what he knows of God's actual engagement with the issue,
an engagement of which in a sense the whole Bible speaks, but

which reaches its sharpest point in the upper room, when Jesus bids Judas go forth into the night to do what he has purposed to do, and when in the garden His receiving of the kiss of betrayal precipitates the traitor upon the road which leads him to "his own place". This concentration on Iscariot is in no sense an illustrative device; it is justified because he is the place where the problem is raised with archetypal and definitive seriousness. Every detail of the relations of Christ with Judas demands the closest possible scrutiny, and no hermeneutic effort can be spared to lay bare the very depth of their controversy; for *there* is the problem of evil, seen not apart from, but in terms of, the betrayal and rejection of Christ.

In the end the traditional distinction between particular and universal disappears; we cannot speak of the crucifixion of Jesus, and the events which led up to and achieved it, as an instance of human evil-doing. In one sense, of course, it most certainly is that; the language of Caiaphas, for instance, is that of "ecclesiastical statesmen" all down the ages; we can catch the hints of a similar accent in Archbishop Geoffrey Fisher's hesitancy to give full support in unequivocal terms to men like Father Trevor Huddleston in their struggle against the morally and theologically intolerable policies and actions of the South African nationalists *vis-à-vis* the Bantu. But because Jesus is who He is, His rejection and crucifixion can only be—evil itself.

Jesus is sheerly concrete, sheerly particular; He is "man for man" only through having a place in history, through belonging to a particular time, and through being exposed to its peculiar needs and tensions. But the self-giving which makes Him thus "man for man" and "man for God" belongs to eternity; this life, so ordinary in so many ways, so cribbed and cabined, so pitifully incomplete, has its ultimate ground and setting in the love of God, which indeed it makes concrete in the depth of human history. We could dare to say, we would be justified in saying, that the ministry of Jesus is not an instance or an example of the love of God, but rather its very substance; a point of which in the New Testament itself the epistle to the Ephesians offered a classical exposition.

There is in Barth's thought a note of positivism. He is always the champion of the concrete against, for instance, the abstract

or merely possible. In his discussion of the meaning of predestination, he will have nothing to do with any theorizing
which averts attention from Christ. The mysteries of election
can only be approached across, through, and in the One whom
God has chosen, in whom His choice of men is concrete. If we
are to speak of "double predestination", we should perhaps
begin by recalling the Lucan dialogue between the thieves
crucified with Jesus, and even in our beginning remember that,
in those three hours, the very sense of hell itself is being transformed by the One who had entered the darkness of human
condemnation. Abstract theorizing and preaching concerning
the final destiny of man which averts from the manner in
which the very foundations of their destiny are laid, namely
the ministry, death and resurrection of Jesus, is worse than
sterile.

There is certainly a note of positivism here, something
analogous to that sounded by Bertrand Russell when he said,
suggesting the application of the methods of mathematical
logic to the solution of classical philosophical problems: "Whenever possible, let us substitute logical constructions out of the
observable for inferred, unobserved entities." There is in Barth
something analogous to this recommended logical economy.
We must, he insists, substitute for abstract, general statements
concerning the being and purposes of God, and of men, statements that show them in terms of, or set them in relation to,
Jesus Christ. We cannot speak of something called the "Christian doctrine of man" without mention of the prayer of Jesus
in the wilderness, on the hillside, and in the garden, of His
compassion for leper and for blind, for tax-gatherer and for
prostitute. His inexorable sternness towards scribe and pharisee
(the self-righteous heart turned in upon itself); we certainly
cannot write of that doctrine without, as it were, setting at the
head of our page the laconic, cynical *double-entendre* of Pilate;
"*Ecce Homo.*" The impossibility here is a logical impossibility;
its disregard is sheer self-contradiction.

Barth's standpoint, then, has a positivist quality; and it is
also strongly ontological. If his quarrel with the *analogia entis* of
Erich Pryzwara and other Catholic theologians is a decisive,
even a fundamental moment in his thought, we did not need to

wait for the publication of his pamphlet on Rudolf Bultmann[1]
to see that his thinking throughout the *Dogmatik* is ruled by a
sense of the primacy of what is over our thought of it. Thinking
for him does not "make it so"; it can only, if it is valid, achieve
for the thinker some sort of correspondence between his thinking and what is, a being which at its very foundatior, i.e. its
relation to God, is pivoted upon Jesus Christ, true man and true
God. In a way Barth's very quarrel with the *analogia entis* is
rooted in his conviction that it seems to assign to an abstract,
or at best to an analogically participated transcendental, the
role that belongs to Christ alone.

His thought is positivistic *and* ontological; and as von Balthasar has pointed out so clearly,[2] he displays a remarkable
kinship with some of the great masters of the spiritual life in the
Catholic tradition. For if in Catholic theology the "five ways"
are often presented as a kind of rational "preamble of faith",
Catholic ascetic theologians have never forgotten (with all their
quite proper regards for the rights of human reason), that
Christ is *the* way to God, and that men by baptism are set upon
that way, and none other; the way which leads from Galilee to
Jerusalem, from life to death; the way which reaches its term,
and receives its definition, in the creative and inclusive mystery
of the Paschal night, of whose abysses it would seem that those
who wrote, for instance, of the "dark night of the soul" were
also speaking.[3] Barth's Christocentrism is passionately evangelical; but it is also something which enables those who are
rooted in the great traditions of Catholic spirituality to understand anew the inwardness of their inheritance. In his theology
there is no element of philistinism, only the intellectual
achievement of a profound Christocentric self-discipline.

To a large extent the same was true of Forsyth; even if his
writings were not given, by reason of their circumstances, the
sort of direction and unity which Barth has achieved for his.
But with Forsyth too there is the same patient, yet inexorable,

---

[1] *Rudolf Bultmann; Ein Versuch zu ihn verstehen* (1953).

[2] In his *Karl Barth: Darstellung und Deutung seiner Theologie* (1951). In this most
valuable book the cruciality of Barth's study of Anselm for his development is
stressed.

[3] cf. here Père Yves Congar, O.P., on *Le Purgatoire* in the volume *Le Mystère de
la Mort et sa célébration chrétienne* (1951).

insistence that the centre of the Christian mystery shall not be obscured by any speculative dialectic; such concepts as reconciliation, and the overcoming of evil by good, are to be interpreted in terms of the *opus operatum* of the ministry of Jesus, and not vice versa. Forsyth had read widely in philosophy, and he shared with Sören Kierkegaard the sense that the Hegelian outlook trivialized the tragic depth of human existence, making even of Gethsemane itself a charade. For those who are concerned with the interplay of philosophy and theology, it is always interesting to remark how Forsyth invoked against the Hegelians the Kantian doctrine of the primacy of the practical reason. He found Kant's metaphysical agnosticism congenial, and like him, used it as a means of bringing out the supreme importance of the moral order, even the unscaled and unplumbed heights and depths of the world of freedom. He was on edge in the presence of ontological divinity, coining the word "Chalcedonism" to express his (certainly unfair) impatience with all its forms. Although he does not use the concept of "myth", nor show any sense of its logical complexity, there is no doubt that he would have claimed for the "mythological", properly understood, a place near the heart of any human understanding of the *mysterium Christi*, or at least of any understanding of that understanding; for he made a use of the notions of *Kenosis* and *Plerosis* to give a defence of that mystery from the unskilled and irreverent probing of the undisciplined intellect, almost classic in its profundity, and in these notions there is certainly (in their fusion of the metaphysical and the factually descriptive), an element of the "mythical". But of this Forsyth was unafraid, only insisting that if we were serious in finding our way to the Father in the Son's glorification of Him upon earth, and in the Father's glorification of the Son in the raising Him from the dead, we must be content to let our representations of the Absolute experience the full weight of a Christocentric transformation.

Perhaps enough has now been said to bring out something of what a subordination of theology to Christology must involve; and, as the examples of both Barth and Forsyth have illustrated, this subordination does not involve any indifference to philosophy. Rather it was possible to remark in Barth's case a certain analogy between his procedure and that recommended by Lord Russell in his well-known "method of logical constructions"; even to speak of his method as positivist is to say something about it which it would be, perhaps, possible only for a philosopher to say. Further, in Forsyth's case, we have noticed his appeal to Kant; there is no doubt that he called Kant his philosophical master and that he accepted this allegiance partly because such a philosophical method as Kant's seemed to him to secure the proper autonomy of the Gospel, the possibility of being engaged by the self-revelation of God on its own terms. It is almost certainly no accident that the philosophical names mentioned in this paragraph are both of them names of men whose work has a dignity of its own as philosophical work. They were neither of them apologists of Christianity; indeed, Lord Russell's avowed atheism has only recently been tempered by a gentler, agnostic note. But they were considerable philosophers with whose philosophical work any serious student of the subject must engage at their own level; Russell's "method of logical constructions", Kant's "synthetic a priori"—these are the names of serious opposing options in respect of some of the most perplexing and continuing problems of the subject. Neither Kant nor Russell will be of much service to the man who wants to prostitute his faith and his intellectual integrity alike to the caprice of something called a "Christian philosophy of life"; but for the man of faith who is also a philosopher their work will continue to raise most serious and most searching questions, questions that clearly touch the things of faith, yet without finally overthrowing their interior castle.

The world of philosophy is one world; the world of faith is another; and yet in the mind of the individual these worlds continually interpenetrate, and it would be illusion to deny the reality of their conflict. Here of course there is nothing unique in the case of philosophy, which is, after all, only one human activity among others, although one with a very great and a most serious dignity. There is nothing to commend one piece of philosophizing against another in the fact that the former lends itself more easily to the role of *ancilla theologiae*; the philosopher who is a Christian knows that sometimes he will have to sacrifice his own image of what the faith is to the claims of the discipline he professes. He will owe much in such moments to the mystery of the communion of saints in which he lives,[1] much also to the extent to which he can come to see his own experience in relation to the substance of the Christocentric ascesis. It is a terrible and a testing experience; yet there is nothing *altogether* unique in it; others have known it on the plane of actual human conduct and choice. One thinks of the inspiring example of those Spanish Catholics of whom Mr. Albert Camus wrote at the end of his *L'Homme Révolté*.[2]

The choice these men made was a terrible and a bitter one; but their place *sub specie aeterni* in the history of the mystical body of Christ is sure, and their protest against the willingness of ecclesiastical authority to enforce its claim upon men, by reliance on lawless armed force, on murder and on tyranny (as the Spanish Church has certainly done since 1936), is a thing maybe of deeper eschatological significance than the often quoted examples of the resistance of high-placed Church dignitaries to Communism in eastern Europe, and in China.

In Christ's name, a man may have to choose that which seems not of Christ; and in the cause of the knowledge of God, a man may have to turn his back on more than the silly respectabilities of so-called religious philosophy.

No one, however, who has come even to the frontiers of the conflict between faith and philosophy can lightly esteem its *Angst*. To-day, of course, it usually takes the shape of a sense of deep powerlessness to attach meaning or intelligible use to theological and religious expressions, or to set out the sort of ground on which they can be treated as valid.

Now this impotence does not have its source in a wilful refusal to recognize the sort of tasks religious language actually performs. We are not dealing with an intellectually undisciplined anthropomorphism, or with a philistine unwillingness to acknowledge the claims of poetry as well as of prose; we are not face to face with Bentham *redivivus*, repeating parrot-like the cry: "poetry is misrepresentation". Of course no one supposes the *pro nobis* of the phrase "crucifixus *pro nobis*" to have the

---

[1] cf. H. U. von Balthasar, *Elisabeth von Dijon*.   [2] Paris, 1951; pp. 375 f.

same sense as the words "for us" in the sentence, "Uncle John kindly settled the hotel bill for us", or even the same as "for his friend" in the sentence (referring to a shipwreck), "if ever a man gave a life for his friend, Hector did by surrendering his place in the boat". Yet it is insisted by those who believe the creed that there is *some* resemblance between the uses, that *pro nobis* in "crucifixus *pro nobis*" is not a mere ejaculation, or (more seriously) that the language of the creed has something in common with the language in which we describe, and communicate about, fact as well as with that of, e.g. Shelley's *Ode to the West Wind*, or even of the *Aeneid* or *Iliad*.

Certainly it may be pointed out as the discussion develops that the fundamental language of religion is prayer, perhaps a statement in the formal syntactical mode of speech of the familiar thesis, Religion is adoration. Others may point out how important in religion is the language of address, of "I" and "Thou", of the sermon addressed to individuals and calling them to decision;[1] others may point to such phenomena as the "prophetic actions" of the prophets,[2] and indeed of Jesus Himself in cursing the fig tree,[3] bidding us further extend our view to the sacraments. Thus in a Catholic devotional near-classic, Father W. Roche, S.J., speaks of the *"hic est calix sanguinis mei"* as a "deed rather than a word";[4] and even those who do not share Roche's understanding of the sacrifice of the mass may well allow that he brings out something of the special linguistic character of the "words of consecration". We may, we must, work further, more exhaustively and more minutely, and lay bare for instance the precise character of the language of the Gospels; for the Gospels are certainly unique in the matter of their literary form, equally certainly have "their own sort of logic". But is it a "logic of illusion", a logical *Unding*? Is the enterprise of representation which they attempt something inherently incapable of attainment? Is there a logical lie here, a kind of cheating through failure to acknowledge the authority of the necessary forms of human thought, and description? For

[1] cf. Prof. H. H. Farmer, *The Servant of the Word* (1942).
[2] These actions were minutely studied by the late Principal H. Wheeler-Robinson.
[3] cf. Prof. C. H. Dodd in his essay in the volume *Mysterium Christi*.
[4] In his *Mysteries of the Mass in Reasoned Prayer*.

T

however complex, diverse and rich the world of Christian language, that language in the end draws its point from the belief that some things are the case; but if the content of this belief is something to which no sense can be given, and in respect of which we can specify in words no conceivable test (the word is not used in a restricted laboratory sense) for deciding whether it is true or false, the axe is laid to the root of the tree. This, of course, is supremely true when the theological belief in question stresses concrete factuality in the way of one which insists on the primacy of the Christology. If we speak of the "fact of Christ", what sort of fact is this?

These difficulties, it must be insisted, do not disappear when, for instance, with Dr. Friedrich Waismann, we reject a rigid Kantian paradigm of the limitations of the human intellect.[1] The question of fact cannot be by-passed; the "factuality" of God in Christ sets us an inescapable problem, and it is simply not fair for the Christian *bien-pensant* to accuse those who experience its bitter pressure of, e.g. being in bondage to a mistaken view of theoretical physics as the paragon and canon of human knowledge. Christian believers who are serious philosophers, and not the purveyors of dubious apologetic wares for the edification of Church congresses and ecumenical gatherings, have to face them in their own terms, and know on their pulses the virtual estrangement from this substance of their being which that facing brings.

Something too of the same sort of virtual estrangement from the substance of himself may be known by a man who is compelled, by his psychological condition, to submit to the ordeal of deep Freudian analysis. For such a one, as for the philosopher, and even for the one who rebels against the sickening cruelties of the clerical spirit, in the name of human mercy and pity, the temptations are grave indeed. He may take the ordeal (for it is an ordeal), too lightly; or he may take himself as he undergoes it too seriously. He may treat as of little importance the challenge to his faith, and fail that way; or he may allow himself to forget that, by baptism, he is unchangeably set upon a way, upon that way which is Christ Himself, movement from

---

[1] cf. his paper on Verifiability, Ar. Soc. Proc. Suppl. Vol. 1945; reprinted in *Logic and Language* (1st series), edited by Prof. A. G. N. Flew, 1950.

God to man, movement back from man to God; upon that way which is also the communion of saints.

Here are analogies, perhaps, for the predicaments of the philosopher who is also a Christian. But the essay cannot end here; for if it did so, the author might suggest the illusion of a happy, or a satisfactory ending; and that would be to deny the rule acknowledged in its course that thought must follow being. We will end where we began, with the problem of contingency; but first we must pay attention to some aspects of it of which so far we have not said enough.

No theology whose axiom is the sovereignty of Christology can escape the problems of *history*. For such a theology it is not, for instance, a light thing that e.g. Codex Vaticanus omits from its text of St. Luke's Gospel the so-called "first word" from the Cross. For such a theology, the establishment of principles for the proper interpretation of the Fourth Gospel is a matter of very great significance; it cannot, for one moment, treat the obscurity of the features of the earthly Jesus as a matter of little importance. A theology in which the Christ-ology is sovereign is one which cannot escape the question of historical reality by such familiar escape-routes as that offered by an idealist philosophy of religion, or by the ideas of early twentieth-century "Catholic modernism". Its underlying temper of realism, its sense of the primacy of the deed done by Christ in flesh and blood, must deny it the use of such expedients.

It is of course, again, the issue of *fact*; overlapping with, but of course distinguishable from, that raised a few paragraphs back in connection with the philosopher. Did these things happen? It is crucially illustrated, of course, by reference to the old-fashioned "problem of miracle". Certainly the evangelists themselves distinguish carefully between the various events and actions we now bracket together as miracles; they have no general concept of miracle in our sense. They saw what they recorded; and the unity which they bestowed on the diverse occurrences we tend to group together as miraculous was one of their setting in the ministry of Jesus, and His movement from life to death. But that movement has undoubtedly assumed its status as the structural framework in which these events have

T*

been set by the synoptists, because "the Father raised Jesus from the dead". Of course this "raising" was something that none could see, none could perceive; it is not an event in time like the burial of Jesus or the visits of mourners to His tomb. But (to speak very crudely) the emptying of the tomb is in some sense such an event, or group of events, as those; that is to say, if the tomb was empty, there must have been a moment in time when the body of Jesus was in the tomb, and a moment afterwards when it was not. And if we say this (and it is the present writer's view that we must), we are in some sense putting ourselves in bondage to the settlement of questions which are questions of historical fact.

The question: "What is an historical fact?" is, of course, in a real sense a philosophical question; but it is one that cannot possibly be tackled by philosophers without attention to the actual practice of historians, any more than, for instance, a logician can determine the criteria of a good physical hypothesis without attention to the practice of theoretical physicists. But the philosopher has important work to do in disentangling confusions and illusions, which may have their source in the imposition of a restricted and inflexible paradigm of what it is to be a fact, upon the domain of the historians concerned. Yet although there are different sorts of fact, they are different sorts of—*fact*, of *actuals*. Of course actuals do not form a class, or a species, or a genus, like the entrants to a college in a given year, or cats or mammals. But all the same we are fudging if we allow ourselves to suppose that we do not recognize a distinction between the actual and the non-actual, between the eruption of Vesuvius and the murder of Caesar on the one side, and the birth of Venus from the foam, and the exploits of St. George with his dragon, on the other; and it is a matter of crucial importance for Christian belief that the resurrection of Jesus belongs with the former, and not with the latter.[1] This does not imply that the word "Resurrection" is the name of what men could have seen, felt, touched, even smelled; but it does imply that between the ultimate mystery of the raising of

---

[1] See G. E. Moore's excellent discussions of the meaning of the word "real" in *Some Main Problems of Philosophy* (1954), pp. 216 ff. ; cf. also Lord Russell's *Philosophical Essays*.

Christ by the Father from the dead, and a certain perceptible event or set of events (the emptying of the tomb) there is a necessary relationship.

It should be clear from the foregoing that there is a very important work of ascetical discrimination to be done in respect of the status of the sort of experience of radical doubt which we have been describing as likely to be, to-day, the lot of the Christian who is a philosopher. Inevitably one asks how that experience is related to the sort of thing described by those far advanced on the way of the knowledge of God, who have spoken of, e.g. *dépouillement*, dereliction, the destruction of the images, and the rest. Clearly the two are not the same; it may be that the former only approaches the latter asymptotically so as never to reach it, but so as still to have some sort of relation to it. Or, more profoundly and more exactly, we may describe the former as some sort of analogue of the latter, itself, of course, only called dereliction because of its remote likeness to, in utter dependence on, the fontally creative stripping and dereliction of Christ.

What is true of the case of philosophy is true also of the possibly sharper and more taxing tension between historical knowledge and faith which remains even when a proper self-consciousness concerning e.g. the actual logic of historical descriptions and explanations has been achieved. The fourth evangelist said much relevant to this problem in his profound theological discussion of the relation of seeing and believing; for him the former could no more pass into the latter than, e.g. for Kant, the discursive intellect could pass into the intuitive. Yet faith was nothing apart from relationship to the visible, tangible flesh of Jesus, which is (in Hoskyns' phrase), "the place where it is demanded of men that they should believe". It would be a serious mistake, of course, to treat the problem of the relation of faith and historical knowledge, as it has been raised for men after the advent of New Testament criticism, as if it were on all fours with the theological problem of which the evangelist is speaking. Again, there is perhaps a kind of asymptotic relation, and analogical correspondence between the two; the spiritual combat of faith with unbelief of which the evangelist speaks perhaps belongs to the same universe of discourse as the writings of saints and mystics on the inwardness of *dépouillement* and the rest.

Moreover, the historical critic is perfectly justified in asking whether, as a matter of fact, the author of the Fourth Gospel was justified in seeing this theological problem as raised by the ministry of Jesus. No doubt it is an important fact that this problem, and not another, was raised and faced by St. John, just as it is important that the special framework of a journey from Galilee to Jerusalem for passover was adopted by Luke, and used by him in the way it was. But this importance is the importance for a man attempting a piece of historical reconstruction, simply of an item of historical evidence. If it is also more, if for the man who believes it tells him much of the very arcana of the way of believing, this is not by itself something that absolves him from the tension of engaging with the historical problem at its own level, even if it shows him the context in a Christ-centred spiritual life, to which that engaging, as all other things, belongs. But to treat something as the index of an all-inclusive setting, and to treat it as historical evidence for something else, is to treat it in two ways which, even though they must crucially overlap, are and must be logically distinguishable.

The involvement of faith with history is close-knit indeed, and historical uncertainty can sap the very foundations of faith, especially when the theological primacy of the Christology is demanded and accepted. Yet faith is most certainly not another name for historical certainty, nor does the achievement of a greater measure of such certainty make faith itself less a problem and a mystery. Faith is something which goes before historical reconstruction, and is something which even conditions its most radical exercise, relating it to its own intense and searching discipline.

Here, certainly, we are again conscious of the communion of saints, of the membership enjoyed by Christians one of another, in faith, in hope and above all in charity. The ultimate ground of this communion is, of course, the *ultimately* mysterious *perichoresis*, the *circumincessio* of the three Persons within the abysses of the Trinity.

There is certainly some sort of correspondence between the

experience of the saint, and the dry intellectual struggle of the man who is battling in his study with the historical problems of Christian origins; there is, *mutatis omnibus mutandis*, an analogy between his efforts, as a historian, to achieve a *relative* security concerning the temporal beginnings of Christianity, and the patience with which men of faith have awaited the "revelation of the mystery". It is clear that, according to the Catholic tradition, there is in that latter patience something reflecting, *per speculum in aenigmate*, because participating in, the fontal and creative patience of the Son who acknowledged, and accepted, that the secret of the last hour was the Father's only, learning here as always obedience by the things that He suffered.

The perplexities of the historian, like those of the philosopher, are certainly not out of relation to the central mystery; and yet they do not lead directly towards it. For that mystery involves and encompasses them. The Kenosis of the Incarnation, the self-emptying of the Son, His conformity to the limitations of human particularity, all alike reveal concretely, decisively and effectually the manner of the presence of God, in His changeless love and all-powerful humility, to His creatures. As has been said above, we cannot see that love apart from the Kenosis; and it may be remarked that if we keep the two inseparably together, part at least of the contradiction between those who insist on divine impassibility as necessarily involved in God's transcendence, and those who, like the late Geoffrey Studdert-Kennedy,[1] were moved by their knowledge of the reality of human suffering to deny it, may be resolved. Kenosis is an ontological mystery; that first, but, as men like Gore, Scott-Holland and Weston realized, it is one that has a profound bearing on the way we represent, for instance, the manner of Christ's consciousness as incarnate. It enables us to take the familiar philosophical cliché, "the limitations of human knowledge", and ask what happens to it when its sense is revised against the background of, and in terms of, the obedience of the Incarnate, the circumstances and manner of His mission.

Moreover, Kenosis is, *mutatis omnibus mutandis*, a crucial category of ascetic theology; this comes out most clearly in St. Paul's second epistle to the Corinthians. Here again, of course,

---

[1] cf. his *The Hardest Part.*

if we invoke its aid we must remember that its background is ontological; what Paul speaks of is not something that he records as "the contents of his consciousness", but a sense of his mission and its significance that he has won through daring to see it in the light of the Cross. He knows that the ground of his mission, to which it belongs, is all. So there is a deep movement in his language between what is almost autobiographical description, what is theological interpretation, and what is, in effect, the expression of a deepened understanding of the mystery of the Cross through the refraction of that mystery, in the arcana of his own spiritual life and suffering. And yet, because all is under the sign of Kenosis, the final note is of a radical self-abandonment.

So indeed it is with all the saints, who provide, for those who know the kind of perplexities of which this essay has spoken, at once reminders of that encompassing perplexity into which Christ Himself entered and sure promise of succour in them. There is only analogy between the perplexities; but those who face without flinching the contradictions of which this essay has spoken, whether in Franco's gaols, or in their studies, are sometimes aware that the prayerful compassion, for instance, of the true contemplative is to them the effectual sign of that "which it has not entered the mind of man to conceive".[1]

Only there is no escape from contingency. If Barth protests against, e.g. the offering of the "argument from contingency" as a possible preamble to faith, it may be partly because he sees clearly how the coming of Christ "as the place where it is demanded of men that they believe", has radicalized and transformed the notion of the contingent. The sheer contingency of Christ provides a new sort of use for the logical ontological notion, a new standard for its employment; for in the Incarnation there is contingency so sheer and unequivocal that inevitably at all levels we shrink from it, preferring "necessary absolutes", whether abstract values, or institutions, or even spiritual experiences. As the saints have, however, known, the Church herself is involved in that contingency, and the sin of her rulers is always in the forgetting of it. Involvement in its consequences runs right through the whole life of the believer,

[1] cf. Pierre Henri Simon's remarkable novel, *Les Raisins Verts*.

almost in a kind of downward spiral, in all his relationships; but this burden is laid upon him because he is also partaker of its strange glory. For the believer knows that the supremely revealing and the supremely authoritative moment in human history (the hour which the Son received from the Father) was that in which He cried upon the Cross: "My God, my God, why hast Thou forsaken Me?" Thus it was made plain that in the Son of God's acceptance of the ultimate triviality and failure of human existence, whose deeps at that moment He *finally* plumbed, the whole language of perplexity, uncertainty, bewilderment, hopelessness and pain, even of God-forsakenness, was laid hold of and given a new sense by the very God Himself and converted into the way of His reconciling the world unto Himself.